Charles Warren Fox

ESSAYS ON MUSIC FOR CHARLES WARREN FOX

ESSAYS ON MUSIC
for
CHARLES WARREN FOX

Edited by Jerald C. Graue
Introduction by Edward G. Evans, Jr.
Foreword by Robert S. Freeman

EASTMAN SCHOOL OF MUSIC PRESS
Rochester, New York
1979

Library of Congress
Catalog Card No.: 79-54212
        Graue, Jerald C., ed.
        Essays on Music for Charles Warren Fox

        NY: Eastman School of Music Press
        7908   790713

ISBN-0-9603186-0-7

FOREWORD

In November 1972, when I succeeded Walter Hendl as director of the Eastman School of Music, the School had just celebrated its 50th anniversary. Part of those festivities had involved a series of papers by distinguished music historians from all over the western world, put forward in homage to Eastman's Charles Warren Fox, professor of musicology at the School from 1933 until the time of his recent retirement. The publication of the Fox *Festschrift* was delayed for a time by the adjustments natural to a new administration, and then further, by my own concern that any published tribute to Dr. Fox would be unthinkable without representative contributions from his students and colleagues here. Professor Jerald Graue, chairman of the Department of Musicology at the Eastman School since the fall of 1975, has ably put together the harvest of essays from 1972 with others completed more recently. They are here offered, with the original preface written in 1972 by Edward Evans, then chairman of the Department, as a tribute to one of Eastman's most beloved teachers, a man who from his usual place under the clock in the School's main corridor, continues with his generous counsel to us all.

Robert Freeman
May, 1978

TABLE OF CONTENTS

INTRODUCTION

On April 13, 1972, a large gathering of students, friends, faculty colleagues, and distinguished guests from the United States and Europe rose from their seats in Kilbourn Hall at the Eastman School of Music to applaud Charles Warren Fox. As most of us know, musicologists seldom bask in the heart-warming bravos and applause accorded conductors, composers, and performing artists. But this was a special occasion, and a special announcement had just been made.

As part of the school's Fiftieth Anniversary Year, administrators and faculty members had planned a four-day Musicology Symposium. It consisted of papers, panel discussions, formal meetings, and casual social affairs where points of view could be formulated and exchanges of ideas take place. To this end, ten scholars had been invited to participate — nine of whom were to offer papers. Six of those papers (by Professors Frank Harrison, Imogene Horsley, Frits Noske, Ruth Steiner, Denis Stevens, and Kurt von Fischer) appear in the present volume along with more recent contributions by other long-time friends, former students, and colleagues of Charles Warren Fox (Professors Truman Bullard, Michael Collins, Louise Cuyler, Jerald Graue, David Levy, Ernest Livingstone, Erich Schwandt, Robert Stevenson, Jurgen Thym, Glenn Watkins, and Craig Wright with Robert Ford). The tenth guest of the Symposium, Professor Gustave Reese of New York University, did not prepare a paper, but was accorded the honor of delivering the opening convocation talk on ''The Place of Musicology in a School of Music.''

To return to the special announcement mentioned above, I quote from my opening remarks, for these provide the *raison d'être* for the applause:

> When early plans for this Fiftieth Anniversary Festival Year first indicated that a symposium for musicologists would take place, we naturally turned to Dr. Fox for guidance and counsel. His reputation as a scholar, his stature as a teacher, and his inestimable contributions as a personality on the scene at Eastman for thirty-eight years made it clear to all concerned that he should hold center stage on this momentous occasion.
>
> We are gathered here today to pay homage to this friend, colleague, and teacher, and to acknowledge publicly the gratitude of the Eastman School of Music's faculty, students, and alumni to this kind, modest, gentle, beloved scholar-teacher who has inspired so many lives.
>
> As of June 1970, Dr. Fox officially retired, but he still haunts the halls of Eastman and Sibley Music Library, he teaches an occasional class, and, happily for us, his animated presence continues to grace us all.
>
> To a man who seems, like Dr. Fox, to have read everything, those of us who planned the symposium felt we had but one last resort in our efforts both to honor and surprise him; namely, to present him with something he could not possibly have read. To this end, the visiting musicologists assembled here agreed to contribute articles to a Charles Warren Fox *Festschrift*. This is, perhaps, the greatest tribute we can pay him: essays by

distinguished scholar-friends to be published later in the form of an anthology honoring Dr. Charles Warren Fox, Professor Emeritus of Musicology of the Eastman School of Music.

The scholars who participated, along with various administrative officers, faculty members, and staff members who had planned and organized the symposium, apparently succeeded in creating a complete surprise. The idea of a *Festschrift* had been a closely guarded secret kept from Dr. Fox. It was a splendid moment in his long career at Eastman — a public recognition of the profound influences he has exerted and of the respect he commands.

Charles Warren Fox was born in Gloversville, New York, on July 24, 1904. After graduation from Gloversville High School in 1921, he entered Cornell University as a major in psychology. Recognition of his scholarly capabilities came early, in the form of his election to Phi Beta Kappa and Phi Kappa Phi. In June, 1926, he was awarded the A.B. degree from Cornell. Later that year he enrolled for graduate work in psychology and mathematics at the University of Illinois, where he remained for almost three years. An opportunity to teach psychology at Temple University for the spring semester in 1929 led, in turn, to further graduate study, still in psychology and mathematics, at Cornell. Again a teaching opportunity arose, this time at the Eastman School of Music in Rochester, New York, where he became a part-time teacher of psychology in 1932. The following year, after receiving his Ph.D. degree from Cornell, he began a full-time career as a teacher of music history and musicology at Eastman and gradually shed his commitment as a teacher of psychology.

How is it that one trained in psychology and mathematics is offered an appointment to teach music history and musicology at a famous music school? The answer appears to lie partly in his deep attachment to the art of music from childhood on, and partly through providential contact with the almost legendary Otto Kinkeldey, who became the first Professor of Musicology in the United States with his appointment to Cornell University in 1930.

Charles Warren Fox, a graduate student in psychology, began musicological studies with Otto Kinkeldey, as Dr. Fox puts it, "for the fun of it." But a close relationship and mutual admiration quickly developed between the experienced musicologist and the young psychologist who was twenty-five years his junior. Exciting months passed. What had begun as a casual sideline exploded into a passionate pursuit of *Musikwissenschaft*. When, in the fall of 1932, Professor Kinkeldey was asked by Howard Hanson, Director of the Eastman School of Music, if he knew a first-rate musicologist who could be brought to Eastman to develop a program in that discipline, Kinkeldey, much to Dr. Hanson's surprise, advised the young Director that Eastman already had its man — a young psychologist named Fox. With Kinkeldey's recommendation, Dr. Fox embarked upon a new career.

Shortly after his full-time appointment to Eastman in 1933, Dr. Fox devoted himself to music history and musicology. During the next three decades he taught, at some time or another, every course ever offered at Eastman in those fields. Over forty students, many now holding important positions in American colleges and universities, completed their Ph.D. dissertations directly under his guidance. Many honors were to come his way during those years, for he was active as a teacher, guest lecturer, publishing scholar, editor, and as an energetic officer in scholarly organizations and societies.

The music of the late fifteenth and early sixteenth centuries has been the subject of much of his research, and it figures prominently among the more than one hundred articles and reviews he has written during the last thirty-five years for *The Musical Quarterly*, the *Saturday Review of Literature, Collier's Encyclopedia*, the *American Journal of Psychology, Notes, Modern Music*, the *U.S. Quarterly Book Review*, the *Journal of the American Musicological Society*, and other publications in this country and abroad. He was vice-president of the American Musicological Society from 1950 to 1952 after having served as editor for the MLA's quarterly, *Notes*. From 1945 to 1956 he was program annotator for the Rochester Philharmonic Orchestra. Since 1955 he has been serving as the American representative on the Editorial Board of *Documenta Musicologica*, an impressive set of facsimiles of old and valuable musical books long out of print.

In addition to the organizations already mentioned, Dr. Fox has held memberships in the Mediaeval Society of America, the Vereniging voor Nederlandse Muziekgeschie-denis, the Société Belge de Musicologie, and the American Psychological Association. Short biographical material on him may be found in *Baker's Biographical Dictionary of Musicians, Grove's Dictionary of Music and Musicians*, the *Riemann Musiklexikon, Die Musik in Geschichte und Gegenwart*, the *Algemene Muziekencyclopedie*, and the *Encyclopédie de la Musique*.

In 1971, two further honors were accorded him: he was named Professor Emeritus of Musicology, and he was given an alumni citation by the University of Rochester. Extracts from that citation appropriately conclude this introduction.

CHARLES WARREN FOX

Charles Warren Fox, sharp of wit, deep of knowledge, formidable of scholarship, you have been in Rochester since 1932. Coming from Cornell University, fresh from earning your doctorate, you first served the Eastman School of Music as instructor of psychology and then as Professor of Musicology and Head of your department.

A favorite with both undergraduate and graduate students, you have instilled in them the same dedication to learning, the lively curiosity about all things, and the appreciation of music that you have yourself — that is, after your amazed students overcame their wonder at your prodigious, encyclopedic knowledge.

For many years of professional life given to this University and to the world of music, and in recognition of your personal attainments, we honor you with an Alumni Citation to Faculty.

Edward G. Evans, Jr.

ACKNOWLEDGEMENTS

This volume owes its existence to the extraordinary efforts and good will of a dedicated collection of individuals. First among them are the authors of the articles, whose numbers have grown since the book was first conceived. They have been uniformly cooperative, patient, and supportive throughout the complicated history of this volume. The administrative officers of the Eastman School of Music have provided the financial assistance and practical counsel without which this work could not have been completed. Two secretaries of the Department of Musicology — Susan Thomson and Terry Adler — have devoted countless hours and great expertise to the physical preparation of the volume. Thomas A. Denny, a doctoral student in musicology at Eastman, helped immeasurably with the proofreading, and he expertly prepared the paste-ups of the page proofs. The firms of G. Schirmer, Inc. and Belmont Music Publishers have graciously permitted us to quote from copyrighted musical scores. The staffs of the Courier-Journal and IPS MacDonald Printing Co., Inc. of Rochester have expeditiously transferred our requests into the printed page. For all of this help, we are sincerely grateful.

The Editor

THE MASS CYCLE OF THE TRECENTO MANUSCRIPT F—Pn568(Pit)

by Kurt von Fischer

In comparison with the well known secular music, the sacred works of the Italian Trecento have received relatively little attention. The only detailed studies of a large part of the repertory are the unpublished Harvard dissertation of Bill Layton, who gives some fine analyses of the mensural pieces for the *Ordinarium missae* from 1350 to 1450 in Italy, and an article of mine.[1] Layton is right to distinguish between pieces in Italian and those in various French styles. In addition, a large and important group of Mass movements, including the Benedicamus Domino, in non-mensural or partly mensural notation must be taken into account. These pieces, now accessible in a facsimile edition,[2] are to be considered the normal and average type of liturgical music for monasteries and smaller churches of the 14th and 15th centuries, while the mensural pieces are something like the avant-garde music of the era. One of the main features of the non-mensural pieces is their old-fashioned two voice style—not even to be called an ars antiqua but ars "antiquissima:"[3] both voices move within the same ambitus; crossing of voices, sometimes combined with elements of "Stimmtausch," is very frequent; parallel fifths, octaves, unisons and even sevenths are used. In some pieces the liturgical melody starts as the upper but ends as the lower voice. The following example is taken from the Agnus of the MS I - Bc 11 (Bologna, Civico museo bibliografico musicale, Q 11), fol. 5v /6:[4]

---

[1] B.J. Layton, "Italian music for the Ordinary of the Mass 1350-1450" (Ph.D. diss., Harvard, 1960); cf. also K. Fischer, "The Sacred Polyphony of the Italian Trecento," *Proceed RMA*, C (1973/74), pp. 143-158.

[2] F. A. Gallo and G. Vecchi, *I più antichi monumenti sacri italiani* (Bologna, 1968.)

[3] Cf. K.v.Fischer, "Musica e società nel Trecento italiano," *L'ars nova italiana del trecento* (III), Centro di Studi (Certaldo, 1970), p. 13.

[4] The Sigla are quoted according to *RISM* B, IV, 3 and 4 *(Handschriften mit mehrstimmiger Musik des 14., 15. und 16. Jahrhunderts, beschrieben und inventarisiert von Kurt von Fischer,* [München, 1972]). For a facsimile of the above-mentioned piece cf. Gallo-Vecchi, *op. cit.,* Tav. XXIV; for a transcription cf. M. Lütolf, *Die mehrstimmigen Ordinarium Missae-Sätze vom ausgehenden 11. bis zur Wende des 13. zum 14. Jahrhundert* (Bern, 1970), II, No. 57. For another example cf. Gallo-Vecchi, *op. cit.,* Tav. XXII (I-Bu2886), a Benedicamus which is also known from earlier sources (c.1400): D-Bs40563 and I -Vm160. For the sources I-Bu2886 and I-Vm 160 cf. R. Strohm, "Neue Quellen zur liturgischen Mehrstimmigkeit des Mittelalters in Italien," *Rivista Italiana di Musicologia,* I (1966), pp. 86-87.

Example 1

A - gnus De - i qui tol - lis ... no - bis.

Its style corresponds to the single polyphonic example given by Johannes Affligemensis in his treatise *De arte musica* at the beginning of the twelfth century.[5]

Thus we have at least three main groups of polyphonic pieces for the Mass within the Italian sources of the Trecento: non-mensural polyphony, mensural polyphony in various French styles (composed by Italian and French composers) and, as we shall see, different types of Italian mensural music. The total number of mensural Mass movements (including the Benedicamus) in presently known Italian sources is approximately fifty if one excludes the works of Ciconia, Matteo da Perugia and Zacara. But of these pieces more than fifty per cent are only fragments.[6] Within this mensural repertory only about twenty-five percent are written in a style which shows more or less typical features of Italian Trecento music.

Among this relatively small group of pieces the Mass cycle of the famous MS F - Pn568(Pit) has special interest.[7] The five movements, Gloria, Credo, Sanctus, Agnus and Benedicamus, written by different composers, represent the only sacred pieces in the whole manuscript.[8] They are copied on the last folios (131v-138) by the same hand as the preceding Italian Ballate of the fascicle. The quality of notation is excellent. There are, with the exception of a few wrong caudae in the Benedicamus, practically no errors. After the Benedicamus (fol.138), which may be a slightly later addition,[9] there follow only two secular pieces later added on the last two folios of the manuscript (fol. 138v-

[5]Cf. Johannes Affligemensis, *De arte musica*, ed. Smits van Waesberghe, CSM 1, American Institute of Musicology (Rome, 1950), p. 160.

[6]Cf. the Italian MSS in RISM B, IV, 3 and 4. An edition of the sacred pieces of the Italian trenncento is published by K.v. Fischer and F. A. Gallo in the Oiseau-Lyre series *Polyphonic Music of the Fourteenth Century*, vol. XII (1976), vol. XIII is in preparation.

[7]Cf. G. Reaney's inventory of the MS in *Musica Disciplina*, XIV (1960), pp. 49ff. and *RISM* B, IV, 4: MSF - Pn568. The MS dates from the very early 15th century.

[8]These pieces are published in the following editions: G. de Van, *Monuments de l'ars nova*, Fasc. I (Paris, n.d.): Gloria, pp. 1ff.; Credo, pp. 5ff.; Sanctus, pp. 13ff.; Agnus, pp. 16ff.; Benedicamus, pp. 18ff. N. Pirrotta, *The Music of Fourteenth Century Italy*, CMM8, I and III, American Institute of Musicology, 1954 and 1962: Gloria, vol. I, pp. 53ff.; Credo, vol. I, pp. 1ff.; Sanctus, vol. III, pp. 1f.; Agnus, vol. I, pp. 55f. The quotations and numbers of measures are taken from the Pirrotta edition except for the Benedicamus. The musica ficta was added in square brackets (for technical reasons) by the author of this article. All these pieces are now also published in the aforementioned edition (cf. note 6) as numbers 3, 12, 15, 20 and 27.

[9]Reaney, *op. cit.*, p. 35.

140). The position of the Mass cycle within the manuscript shows that the pieces, although of various authorship, were purposely put together as a cycle, and that they represent a complementary addition to all the preceding secular pieces. All five movements are written in the same tone (at least they end all on the same tone d). The Sanctus by Lorenzo was probably transposed up a fifth by the compiler of the manuscript to fit within the cycle. This would explain the extremely high range of the two voices (g-c'').[10] This sort of cyclic arrangement of five Mass movements is unique within the Italian Trecento repertory. The only other known grouping of pieces in an Italian manuscript, forming a much less complete cycle, is the one linking of the plainsong Kyrie and an anonymous three-voice Gloria (ending on d) and Credo (ending on c) written in French style at the end of the MS GB-Lbm29987 (Lo).[11] The style is probably due to the French influences at the Visconti court to which the manuscript seems to be related.[12] A last example may be mentioned. It is not impossible that the Gloria and Sanctus by Gratiosus de Padua in the fragments I - Pu684 and I - Pu1475 (both belonging to the same MS) were originally parts of a cycle.

Before examining the style of the five pieces we ought to discuss some details of the Tuscan (Lucca?) MS I - Pn568.[13] As Ursula Günther has shown, fascicles 1-5 and 9-14 (to which the Mass cycle belongs) were most probably written about 1405, the later added fascicles 6 and 8 between 1406 and 1408.[14] The naming of four composers for the Mass cycle, Gherardello, Bartholus, Lorenzo and Paolo, shows that the pieces were put together by the compiler of the manuscript. The scribe wrote the Gloria, Credo, Sanctus and Agnus in a mixed Italian-French notation with French mensural signs. The added Benedicamus by Paolo is written in pure Italian notation with mensural letters. As has been known since Pirrotta's study on Paolo Tenorista, the Paris-MS was not only owned but most probably also ordered by the Florentine family Capponi.[15] And since the manuscript is the most important source for Paolo's works, a close relation between

[10]There are examples of transposition within the secular repertory of Trecento pieces; cf. the Madrigal "De sotto 'l verde" which appears in the Fn26 (fol. 51) a fifth lower than in the older Ms. I-Rvat215 (fol. 1). Both versions are published by Pirrotta, *op. cit.*, II, No. 9.

[11]Cf. facsimile in G. Reaney, *The Manuscript London, British Museum, Additional 29987*, MSD 13, American Institute of Musicology (1965), fol. 81v-85; cf. further Layton, *op. cit.*, pp. 367ff.

[12]Cf. K.v.Fischer, "Ein Versuch zu einer Chronologie von Landinis Werken," *Musica Disciplina* XX (1966), p. 38 and note 26.

[13]Cf. K.v.Fischer, *Studien zur italienischen Musik des Trecento und frühen Quattrocento* (Bern, 1956), p. 93 (quoted as v.Fischer, *Studien*). U. Günther, "Zur Datierung des Madrigals 'Godi Firenze' und der Handschrift Paris, B.N., fonds it.568 (Pit)," *Archiv für Musikwiss.*, XXIV (1967), pp. 111ff. (quoted as Günther, "Godi Firenze").

[14]Cf. Günther, "Godi Firenze," pp. 99ff. and esp. pp. 114. Approximately the same dates were proposed in 1956 by v.Fischer, *Studien*, pp. 93.

[15]N. Pirrotta, *Paolo Tenorista in a New Fragment of the Italian Ars Nova* (Palm Springs, 1961), pp. 25ff. For a new critical approach to the problem cf. Günther, "Godi Firenze," pp. 109ff.

Paolo and the Capponi family is to be assumed.[16] But there is another name of interest: Bartholus, the composer of the Credo, who is mentioned in Filippo Villani's chronicle together with Laurentius Masij (Lorenzo Masini, the composer of the Sanctus), Johannes de Cascia (Giovanni da Firenze) and Jacobus Bononiensis (Iacopo da Bologna).[17] As I showed some years ago, a man by the name of Antonius Bartholi was priest and rector of the church Santa Lucia dei Magnolis in Florence from at least 1413 until 1424.[18] This church was patronized by the family da Uzzano which was related to the Capponi.[19] Antonius Bartholi ordered the magnificent MS I - FI 999 which contains exclusively plain-chant pieces, except for a very short "Verbum caro" in ars antiquissima style and a two-voice Introitus by Paolo who composed a melodically and rhythmically sophisticated mensural superius over the plain-chant melody, "Gaudeamus omnes."[20] The occurrence of only one mensural piece signed with the author's name in a plain-song manuscript for liturgical use is a unique situation within the corpus of Trecento MSS. This fact alone offers substantial evidence of the close relation between the commissioner of the manuscript (Antonius Bartholi) and the composer (Paolo), even if the latter was dead at the time the manuscript was written. Paolo died in 1419, the manuscript was copied in 1423/24.[21] Now the question arises: Is it only by accident that the Credo by Bartholus appears precisely in a manuscript (F-Pn568) which is strongly related to both Paolo (the probable friend of Antonius Bartholi) and the Capponi family? Could it be that Antonius was a descendant of the composer Bartholus?[22] We shall have to come back to this question after a stylistic examination of the pieces. In any case the Capponi, Paolo, Antonius Bartholi and perhaps also Bartholus comprise a group of related names.

The compiler of the MS F,Pn568 was evidently interested in writing down not only a Credo, but a Mass cycle. Since it was not common at that time in Italy to compose polyphonic Kyries,[23] he had to look only for a Gloria, a Sanctus and an Agnus which he found among works that Gherardello and Lorenzo had composed several decades earlier. Here it may be mentioned that Gherardello probably also wrote a Credo which has not

[16]Cf. the two quoted studies in note 13 above.

[17]Cf. E. LiGotti, "Il più antico polifonista italiano del sec. XIV," *Italica,* XXIV (1947), pp. 196ff.

[18]Cf. K.v.Fischer, "Paolo da Firenze und der Squarcialupi-Kodex (I - F187)," *Quadrivium,* IX (1968), pp. 9f. (quoted as v.Fischer, "Paolo").

[19]Cf. v.Fischer, "Paolo," p. 11.

[20]Cf. v.Fischer, "Paolo," pp. 6ff; a transcription of the piece on p. 21ff.

[21]Cf. v.Fischer, "Paolo," pp. 7 and 13.

[22]Cf. v.Fischer, "Paolo," p. 19, note 55.

[23]Cf. the one-voice plainsong Kyrie in the previously-mentioned Ms.GB - Lbm29987. Within the whole Italian Mass repertory of the Trecento and early Quattrocento there is only one polyphonic Kyrie (in French style) known: I-Rvat1419,f.90v, publ. in *Polyphonic Music of the Fourteenth Century,* XII, no. 1.

come down to us.[24] That the compiler did not choose this piece but chose the Bartholus Credo may be another hint at the relations between Bartholus and the Capponi-Paolo-Bartholi group.

From this résumé of the biographical data let us now turn to a short stylistic analysis of the pieces. All five movements are written in a so-called Italian Trecento style. There is no doubt that several features of the pieces, at least of the two-voice Gloria, Credo, Sanctus and Agnus, are related to the contemporaneous secular style of the mid-century madrigals. But despite such resemblances there are very important distinctions to be made. Three features common to all five pieces as well as the Italian madrigal are:

— The many changes of mensural divisions within one piece.
— The resemblance of the last part of each piece to the ritornello part of the
madrigal:
    Gloria: "Cum Sancto Spiritu (novenaria) and "Amen" (senaria
    perfecta).
    Credo: "Amen" (novenaria).
    Sanctus: "Hosanna" (senaria perfecta).
    Agnus: third "Agnus Dei (duodenaria).
    Benedicamus: (do)-mino (quaternaria).
— The simultaneous pronunciation of syllables in all voices. Viewed from the
liturgical texts, the first four pieces for two voices merely have a greater
number of words in common than does the Benedicamus. This circumstance
makes an approach to the style of the madrigal easier. The same is true for
the typical mixture of syllabic and melismatic passages.

Another feature relating the four two-voice pieces is the appearance of something like a second rhythmic mode in the senaria imperfecta and novenaria parts. This can be related to an earlier practice sometimes found in the madrigals and caccie of the early trecento:

Example 2a
Maestro Piero, *Caccia* "Ogni diletto", measures 36/37.[25]

Che mer - ci me   soit o - re

[24]Cf. the twelfth line of the Sonnet on the death of Ser Gherardello written by Francesco de Messer Simone Peruzzi and sent to F. Sacchetti:
    "*Credo* nella fronte scolpita avia.
    L'altra *Gloria* dicendo a lei s'accolse."
Cf. J. Wolf, "Florenz in der Musikgeschichte des 14. Jahrhunderts," *SIMG*, III (1901-02), p. 611.

[25]Publ. by Pirrotta, *op. cit.*, II, No. VIII, mm. 36-37.

Is it merely by chance that this rhythm appears in a ritornello with French text?

Example 2b
Bartholus, *Credo*, measure 56.[26]

Des-cen - dit de cae -

Example 2c
Gherardello, *Agnus*, measure 19

qui tol - lis pec - ca - ta

Example 2d
Lorenzo, *Sanctus*, measure 42/43

- ne -di - ctus qui ve-nit in no -

A liturgical cantus prius factus cannot be pointed out for the four two-voice pieces.[27] Despite the appearance of some liturgical melodic formulas it is very probable that the use of a pre-existing plain-chant was not intended.

If we look at the melodic lines of the superius, there is, as in many early and mid-century madrigals, a very clear emphasis laid on descending lines. An exception is again to be made for Paolo's Benedicamus. Such descending movements are also present in some passages of the tenors of the Gherardello and Lorenzo pieces.[28] Another feature associating the four two-voice pieces with the early madrigal is the employment of cadenzas on several different tones within the same piece. The main sections of Gherardello's Gloria end on five different tones of the hexachordum naturale. The Credo by Bartholus even uses all six tones of the hexachordum molle.

So far the relationship between the four two-voice pieces and the madrigal has been stressed. But now let us turn to the differences among those four movements. In the following discussion the two Gherardello pieces (Gloria and Agnus) are considered as one because they not only are written in the same style, but also display such evident resemblances as to seem conceived as two pieces of a single cycle to which the lost Credo possibly also belonged.[29]

---

[26]For this and all the following examples cf. above note 8.

[27]There is a certain resemblance between a South German fifteenth-century Agnus and the tenor of the Gherardello piece:

    Liturg. melody: d' c'   a f g d f d c d e c d
    Gherardello: d' c' d'ba g d   c d e   f g

Cf. M. Schildbach, *Das einstimmige Agnus Dei und seine handschriftliche Überlieferung vom 10. bis zum 16. Jahrhundert* (Phil.Diss. Erlangen-Nürnberg, 1967), Melodie No. 12.

[28]Cf. the very beginning of the Gloria, Sanctus and Agnus.

[29]Cf. note 24 above.

Example 3a
Gherardello, *Gloria*, meas. 1 – 3

Et in ter-ra pax ho-mi-

Example 3b
Gherardello, *Agnus*, meas. 1 – 4.

A - - - - [gnus]

Example 4a
Gherardello, *Gloria*, measures 22–25

Gra-ti-as a - gi-mus ti - - bi

Example 4b
Gherardello, *Agnus*, measures 30 – 35

qui tol-lis pec-ca-ta mun - di

The style of the Gherardello pieces can be thought of as a more or less faithful reproduction of the technique used in his own and other contemporaneous madrigals: the ranges of both voices are about a fifth apart. Consequently there is nearly no crossing of voices. If there is any, it is restricted to one or two returning notes:

Example 5a
Gherardello, *Gloria*, measure 44

Do - mi-ne De -

Example 5b
Gherardello, *Gloria*, measures 78 – 80.

[Pa] - - - - [tris]

While in the whole Gloria there are only three such places (measures 44, 58 and 78-80) there is none at all in the Agnus.

The different ranges of the voices are also responsible for some large intervals like the twelfth at the beginning of the verses "Glorificamus te," "Domine Fili," "Qui tollis," "Quoniam," and "Amen" of the Gloria, and of the third "Agnus."

Another similarity between the earlier madrigal and the Gherardello pieces is the frequent occurrence of parallel fifths and sometimes also parallel octaves. Other parallel motions of perfect consonances are only slightly hidden:

Example 6
Gherardello, *Gloria*, measures 31 – 33.

- ne De - us, Rex cae - le - stis.

Such parallelism, as well as the aforementioned melodic structure of the tenor, indicates that the superius may be considered as the main voice and the tenor a sort of accompanimental part, as in the early and mid-century madrigals.[30]

The settings of Bartholus' Credo and Lorenzo's Sanctus differ in several respects from the Gherardello pieces. The ranges of both voices are the same—Bartholus, Superius c-g', tenor c-e'; Lorenzo, Superius a-b', Tenor g-c'. Hence there are many voice crossings and only a few direct parallel perfect consonances. It is even possible that the only direct parallel fifth on the word "Deus" in Lorenzo's Sanctus is a symbol for the perfection of God. On the other hand, there are, especially in the Lorenzo piece, many hidden parallel unisons. Although the following example from Bartholus' Credo is the only one of this sort in the whole piece, the similarity to Lorenzo, where such examples are frequent, is striking:

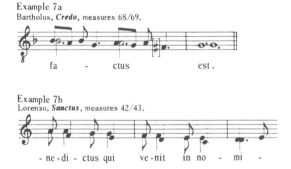

Example 7a
Bartholus, *Credo*, measures 68/69.

fa - ctus est .

Example 7b
Lorenzo, *Sanctus*, measures 42/43.

- ne - di - ctus qui ve -nit in no - mi -

[30]Cf. K.v.Fischer, "On the Technique, Origin and Evolution of the Italian Trecento Music," *Musical Quarterly*, XLVII (1961), pp. 47ff.; M.L. Martinez, *Die Musik des frühen Trecento* (München, 1963), pp. 27ff.

On the other hand, the equal range of both voices leads the composer to the not infrequent use of "Stimmtausch," a very old technique in medieval polyphony. This is especially true for Bartholus:

Example 8
Bartholus, *Credo*, measures 74/75

measures 82/83

The next example shows a free combination of imitation and "Stimmtausch:"

Example 9
ibid., measures 44/45.

In the shorter piece of Lorenzo there is only one such passage:

Example 10
Lorenzo, *Sanctus*, measures 20 – 23.

The following measures may help us to discover the origin of such stylistic elements:

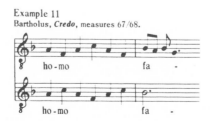

Example 11
Bartholus, *Credo*, measures 67/68.

This passage corresponds to the beginning of the organal Agnus of the above-mentioned (example No. 1) Bologna Ms.Q 11 (I - Bc11) written about 1300. Without denying certain organal influences like parallelisms of voices and "Stimmtausch" in the early madrigals,[31] one can see that the technique of the Mass settings by Bartholus and Lorenzo bears a much closer relation to the liturgical polyphony of the "ars antiquissima," especially regarding the range of voices and the voice crossings. Thus, while the pieces by Gherardello represent faithful copies of the madrigal style, the Credo and the Sanctus are a combination of the old organal and Cantus binatim style with some ornamental features of the madrigal.[32]

Up to this point the two pieces by Bartholus and Lorenzo have been considered as a certain stylistic unity. But this is not the full truth. For while the Credo has separate melodic lines for each voice (the passage quoted in Example 7a is an exception), the Sanctus by Lorenzo is crowded with parallel unisons hidden in a very refined and sophisticated manner (the passage quoted in Example 10 is an exception). Many passages look like heterophony:

Example 12a
Lorenzo, *Sanctus*, measures 1 – 4.

San

Example 12b
ibid., measures 56 – 58.

[Ho]

This technique can be understood as another and very special way of improving upon the old organal style. In addition to stylistic elements mentioned earlier, the Bartholus Credo shows another interesting feature: there are short textless one-voice passages[33]

[31]Cf. the Ritornello of the madrigal "Lavandose le mane," publ. Pirrotta, *op. cit.*, II, p. 19.

[32]For the term "Cantus binatim" cf. F.A. Gallo, " 'Cantus planus binatim', Polifonia primitiva in fonti tardive," *Quadrivium*, VII (1966), pp. 79ff.

[33]The only two-voice passage is to be found between the words "omnia saecula" and "Deum de Deo."

which form a bridge from one verse to the next:

Example 13
Bartholus, *Credo*, measures 34 – 37.

ve - ro,   ge - ni - tum

The similarity of such a procedure with those used in the Gloria and Credo of the Tournai Mass and the Machaut Mass is striking. But the same technique is also employed by Iacopo da Bologna, Lorenzo and others to connect the single lines of a madrigal stanza. In view of the Credo by Bartholus, another remark by Filippo Villani assumes particular interest. In his chronicle he says that Bartholus was the first to replace the old fashioned Credo, performed in alternation by men's choir and organ, with "living voices" ("Vivis vocibus").[34] Pirrotta feels that this description well suits with the Credo of the Ms. F - Pn568.[35] Would it be possible to consider the connecting textless passages as reminders of the older alternatim practice? The whole question, including the problem of these passages in fourteenth-century French Masses, deserves further research.

Villani provides another important piece of information regarding the composers. At the beginning of the passage concerning the Florentine musicians he mentions not only Bartholus but also, in the same breath, Lorenzo: "But there were only a few who in this science (= music) produced something. Among them Bartholus and Ser Lorenzo made better and more artistic music in comparison with the others."[36] When one considers the style of both composers one does not necessarily need to assume, as do LiGotti and Pirrotta, that Bartholus was older than Lorenzo.[37] For although the technique is not the same there are many common features. Lorenzo died, according to F.A. Gallo, in 1372 or 1373.[38] If so, and if Bartholus was a contemporary of Lorenzo, then the hypothesis that the aforementioned Antonius Bartholi, who ordered the Ms. I-Fl999, was the son of Bartholus becomes more probable. It would then not even be impossible that in his

[34]E. LiGotti, *op. cit.*, p. 198, note 7, quotation according to the MS Barb.2610.

[35]*Op. cit.*, I, p. I.

[36]"Sed qui in ea scientia aliquid ediderunt pauci extant inter quos Bartholus et ser Laurentius Masij pre ceteris prestantius et artificios(i)us cecinerunt."

[37]Cf. LiGotti, *op. cit.*, and Pirrotta, *op. cit.*, I, p. I.

[38]F.A. Gallo, "Lorenzo Masini e Francesco degli Organi in S. Lorenzo", *Studi musicali*, IV (1975), pp. 57-63. According to F.D'Accone Gherardello died 1362-63 (cf. F.D'Accone, "Music and Musicians at the Florentine Monastery of Santa Trinità, 1330-1363," *Memorie e contributi alla musica . . . offerti a F. Ghisi . . .* [Bologna, 1971], I, pp. 131-152).

youth Paolo met the old Bartholus, the father of his friend Antonius, still another explanation for the inclusion in the same manuscript and in the same Mass cycle of a piece by Paolo and one, much older, of the famous Credo by Bartholus.

Only a short word on Paolo's Benedicamus. The composer's name was erased in the manuscript but was not cancelled in the original index.[39] Paolo's Benedicamus is the only three-voice piece of the cycle. Like the "Gaudeamus omnes" from the Ms.I - F1999 discussed earlier, the composition is based on a non-mensural plain-chant melody.[40] The two upper voices, which never go below the tenor, move in considerably shorter note values than the tenor and within the same range. More striking even than the several direct parallel fifths and fourths are the many parallel seconds and even sevenths:[41]

Example 14a
Paolo, *Benedicamus*, measures 21,22

Example 14b
ibid., measures 31 – 34.

The whole setting is written in the style of a motet but with the same text in all three voices. The simultaneous progression of syllables is clearly indicated in the manuscript. The whole piece, like the two-voice Introitus "Gaudeamus," gives the impression of a very interesting and sophisticated combination of cantus firmus technique with elements taken from the Italian Madrigal style as well as from the old organal style of the pieces in the Ms.I-Bc 11.

[39]Cf. Günther, "Die 'anonymen' Kompositionen des Manuskriptes Paris, B.N., fonds it.568 (Pit)," *Archiv f. Musikwiss.*, XXIII (1966), p. 85-86.

[40]Benedicamus In Festis Solemnibus. In primis Vesperis (*LU*, p. 124).

[41]This piece has been recorded by the Dutch ensemble "Syntagma musicum" (conductor: Kees Otten). The excellent performance shows that such parallels must not necessarily create shocking effects.

Paolo, the abbot, reveals in his two preserved pieces of sacred music a creative consciousness of a new liturgical style. But he had no successors. The great evolution of the liturgical music in Italy started from the northern Italian courts where Ciconia, Matteo de Perugia and Antonio Zacara da Teramo composed their works and where, for sociological reasons, the French style exerted an important influence on Italian music.[42]

Liturgical polyphony in Florence either remained in the style of the monastic "ars antiquissima," or else composers tried to combine sacred and secular elements on different levels and in different manners. Such a combination is due to a great extent to the social origins of the composers who were either laymen, priests or friars. Notwithstanding Villani's references to a performance of a Credo by Bartholus "in our church . . . with a great gathering of people"[43] such music as appears in the Florentine Mass cycle was hardly suited for large churches. Its compilation and codification within a private family manuscript and its more or less direct connection with such specific personalities as Bartholus, Paolo and Antonius Bartholi indicates that these pieces were most probably intended to be performed in a liturgical service of the family Capponi in the early fifteenth century.

[42]Cf. the article mentioned in note 3 above, pp.12ff.

[43]"in nostra majori ecclesia . . . magno concursu populi;" cf. LiGotti, *op. cit.*, p. 198.

OTELLO: DRAMA THROUGH STRUCTURE

by Frits Noske

Since the beginning of the nineteenth century, opera in Italy has often been called *melodramma,* the term simply meaning that the drama in question is realized through music. Nevertheless, a connection with the concept of melodrama in its more popular sense should not be excluded, even in cases where the libretto is based on spoken tragedy.[1] Certainly no Italian operagoer would call Verdi's *Giovanna d'Arco, Luisa Miller, I Masnadieri,* or *Macbeth* tragedies.[2] Even *Otello,* which is claimed to follow its model more closely than any other work of Verdi, is basically different from Shakespeare's work. In the latter, characters develop in the course of the play, often expressing themselves in an ambiguous way, and leaving room for more than one interpretation. In contrast to this, Verdi's characters show little development and may seem flat. Their words and actions are unequivocal, if not to each other, certainly to the audience.

Do these qualities identify *Otello* as a melodrama? This is difficult to accept. As a dramatic genre, melodrama has a bad name because of the excesses generally associated with it, but even if this low reputation is disregarded, one must admit that next to Jago (the "perfect" villain) and Desdemona (the "perfect" angel), Otello himself is difficult to place. He is surely not the hero in the traditional melodramatic sense. We may accept him as a hero because the idea is presented to us at the beginning, but we invariably *see* him in actions which contribute to his downfall. Lodovico, the envoy from Venice, expresses our feelings:

"Quest'è dunque l'eroe? Quest'è il guerriero dai sublimi ardimenti?"[3]

In the opera everything concerning Otello's glory is conveyed to the audience solely through his memories; but in his own mind those memories gradually lose their value. This may be seen as early as the second act, where he complains:

---

[1] In order to avoid misunderstandings about the English term "melodrama" it should be observed that in the present article the word has exclusively the meaning of "a dramatic genre characterized by heavy use of suspense, sensational episodes, [and] romantic sentiment." *(The American Heritage Dictionary of the English Language* [Boston etc., 1969] entry "melodrama.") See also Eric Bentley, *The Life of the Drama,* (New York, 1967), Chapter 6.

[2] Verdi's librettists, however, sometimes did. The librettos of *Alzira, La Battaglia di Legnano* and *I due Foscari* designate them as "tragedia lirica."

[3] "So this is the hero? This is the warrior of sublime courage?" (Act III, sc. 7).

14

Ora e per sempre addio sante memorie,
addio sublimi incanti del pensier!
Addio schiere fulgenti, addio vittorie,
dardi volanti e volanti corsier!
Addio vessilo trionfale e pio!
E diane squillanti in sul mattin!
Clamori e canti di battaglia, addio!
Della gloria d'Otello è questo il fin.[4]

Herein lies a basic difference between the opera and the play. In the first act (omitted by Boito and Verdi) of the latter, we witness Othello's great moral courage in defending himself before the Venetian Duke and Senators against Brabantio's accusations. There we see the whole man on the stage, and this enables us to *share* his memories in later moments of despair (e.g., III, sc. 3, v. 351-63). In the opera, however, these memories merely refer to information that has been given in quite a different context, principally in the last scene of the first act. The information is more or less abstract and therefore cannot arouse our pity (an essential element of tragedy) to the same degree as the scene witnessed in Shakespeare's play.

Another important difference concerns the dramatic approach. Since the characters in the opera are simple, unequivocal, and, compared to those of Shakespeare, basically not very interesting, the stress lies instead on situations. These are realized in a way which might be expected from an operatic composer, namely with emphasis on purely musical expression of mood. In opera, lyricism and dramatic action do not exclude each other: "outer" or "inner" action (or both) proceed during scenes dominated by the expression of feelings. The second-act quartet, for example, is a piece of strong emotional intensity (Desdemona's melodic line prevails over the other parts), but it contains a good deal of action; similarly, the singing of the Willow Song is a human act, indispensable for the fulfillment of the drama. As will be shown below, even such items as the mandolin chorus (II, sc. 3), which seems to be no more than a set piece, are fully integrated in the drama's development.

If in *Otello* we watch the actors with fascination, it is for what they do, rather than for what they are. And because nearly every action stems from Jago, it is he who may appear to determine the structure of the drama. Before we assign the work to a particular dramatic category, we should investigate its general structure, as well as the role of Jago and of the other principals. Are not the theoretical observations which might lead one to label *Otello* a melodrama contradicted by our experience in the theater? Who would, at the final curtain, still speak of flat characters?

---

[4] Now and forever farewell, sacred memories,
farewell, sublime enchantments of the mind!
Farewell, shining legions, farewell victories,
swift spears and flying steeds!
Farewell, standards triumphant and holy
and reveilles ringing in the morn!
Clamours and songs of battle, farewell!
This is the end of Otello's glory.
(Act II, sc. 5)

15

General Structural Features

Otello is known as a continuous opera. This, however, does not alter the fact that quite a number of "pieces" may be discerned: the tempest scene, the fire chorus, the drinking song, and the love duet of Act I; Jago's *Credo*, the mandolin chorus, the quartet, and the vengeance duet of Act II; the Otello-Desdemona duet, the terzetto, and the great septet with chorus of Act III; the Willow Song and the *Ave Maria* of Act IV. It is conspicuous that most of these items are choruses and ensembles; the few solo pieces are written either in a recitative or arioso-like style, or have the characteristics of songs. Actually *Otello* is an opera without true arias. Furthermore, it may be noticed that many ensembles and choruses are linked with operatic tradition: *temporale,* drinking song, chorus of vassals, vengeance duet and *preghiera* are all old acquaintances from early nineteenth- or even eighteenth-century opera.[5] But they differ from their models in being fully integrated in the drama. Consider, for example, what is generally held to be the most "separate" piece of the opera, the mandolin chorus in the second act. Its function is clear; the homage of the Cypriots to Desdemona serves to illuminate her angelic character. The offering of the lily (a traditionally pure and sacred flower), the allusion to the Blessed Virgin, and the comparison to "a holy image" are particularly significant. Toward the end of the chorus, Desdemona repeats its final melody on the words:

> Splende il cielo, danza l'aura, olezza il fior . . .
> Gioa, amor, speranza cantan nel mio cor.[6]

while watching her, Otello utters, "sweetly moved":

> Quel canto mi conquide.[7]

Not only the text, but also the music expresses Otello's appeasement and confirms the strong bonds of love between man and wife. His melody is merely a simplified version of Desdemona's (ex. 1).[8]

---

[5]Significantly one Verdian stock item is missing: the *battaglia*. In *Otello* everything concerning battles and glory on the battlefield refers to the past and is only revealed through memories.

[6]"The heavens shine, the breeze dances, the flowers smell sweet . . . Joy, love and hope sing in my heart."

[7]"This song quite overcomes me."

[8]Musical examples are quoted from the newly revised edition of the full score (FS) published at Milan in 1954 by Ricordi. For practical reasons I also refer to the vocal score (VS), edited by Mario Parenti, and published by Ricordi in 1964. Since the measures in both scores lack numbering, only page numbers are given.

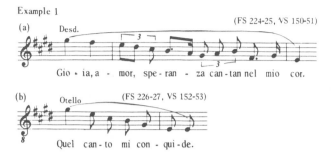

Example 1

(a) Desd.   (FS 224-25, VS 150-51)

Gio - ia, a - mor, spe - ran - za can - tan nel mio cor.

(b) Otello   (FS 226-27, VS 152-53)

Quel can - to mi con - qui - de.

Thus the mandolin chorus does not function only as an indirect characterization of Desdemona, it also paradoxically maintains the tension by tipping the scale in favor of her conjugal fidelity. From a dramatic point of view the chorus works as a *recul pour mieux sauter;* when in the next scene Desdemona makes her unfortunate plea for Cassio, Otello will be upset once more. Finally, the insertion of the homage chorus serves the aesthetic needs of both drama and music (which indeed cannot be separated even in analysis). The work abounds in dialogues or duets (Jago-Roderigo, Jago-Otello, Jago-Cassio, Otello-Desdemona, Desdemona-Emilia); although logical in terms of the plot, this structural feature contains the danger of monotony, and therefore the insertion of contrasting ensembles was necessary.

Other ensembles are integrated in an analogous way. They are subtly related to foregoing or following materials, in this way simultaneously establishing musical and dramatic links. The choruses of the first act are especially striking in this respect. Although there is little demonstrable connection between the storm scene and the fire chorus, these pieces have an affinity of atmosphere, due to the extremely brilliant orchestration. Moreover, a small motif (chordal arpeggios in contrary motion) occurring at the breathing spaces of Otello's first sentence (ex. 2a) reappears in the bonfire scene, similarly as an orchestral interruption of speech (ex. 2b). A variant of this formula (ex. 2c) persists into the following scene of Jago, Cassio and Roderigo (ex. 2d); another variant (ex. 2e) forms a link with the introduction of the drinking song (ex. 2f). Finally a rhythmically changed version (ex. 2g) not only recurs in the same introduction, but dominates the accompaniment of the brawl scene which follows the drinking song (ex. 2h).

However unimportant these connections may seem, they clearly testify to Verdi's conception of the major part of Act I as a whole, the parts of which are unified in spite of their inner contrasts.[9] The fact that *Scena I* of the first act is excessively long cannot be explained by a mere formal reason (i.e., the Cypriots remaining on the stage). It has a deeper meaning; from the beginning the plot must be clear and simple, and no separate scenes must divert our attention. Besides, the scene's length contributes to making

---

[9]*Scena I* runs to 88 pages of the vocal score, i.e., more than four-fifths of the first act and nearly one fourth of the whole opera. In the full score, indication of scenes is omitted.

Example 2

(a) (FS 36, VS 22)

(b) (FS 61, VS 37-38)

(c) (FS 60, VS 36)

(d) (FS 82-84, VS 55-56)

(e) (FS 61, VS 38)

(f) (FS 88, VS 59)

(g) (FS 74-75, VS 49)

(h) (FS 123ff, VS 81ff)

Otello's reappearance and his first fatal step (the degradation of Cassio) dramatically effective.

The score contains numerous instances of relationship between consecutive items. In some cases the melodic material of a piece is anticipated in previous sections. An example of this device is provided by the vengeance duet at the end of Act II. Its melodic kernel, a descending fourth (ex. 3a), dominates the whole piece, including the astonishing series of parallel triads in the orchestral postlude (ex. 3b). During the preceding section (a short monologue by Otello ending with the "Sangue!" exclamation) this descending fourth is already announced in the triplets of the orchestral accompaniment (ex. 3c). The last-quoted example also anticipates another detail of the vengeance melody, the emphatic minor sixth resolving in the dominant (cf. ex. 7 below).

The opposite device, the "reverberation" of material into the following section, may be illustrated by an example from the *Credo*. The pentatonic interruptions of Jago's speech (ex. 4a) dissolve into a series of three-note rhythmic motifs (ex. 4b), which are maintained during the beginning of the next scene (Jago watching Cassio and Desdemona, ex. 4c), and reappear in its final measure (ex. 4d).

18

Example 3

The autograph manuscript of *Otello* shows that originally the last variant of the motif (octave leaps of the first horn: A-a-A) persisted even into the following scene (dialogue Jago-Otello), during which it interrupted Jago's words, "Cassio? no . . . quei si scosse come un reo nel vedervi." Verdi noted the motif twice, first to be played by a horn and a bassoon (FS 194, m. 5; VS 124, m.9), and then by a horn alone (FS194, m.7; VS 125, m.2). Later he tried to erase the motif in both measures; nevertheless the first version is still legible, giving an insight into his original intention: to connect three consecutive items (the *Credo*, the watching scene, and the dialogue) by means of a single motif.[10] That the rhythmic formula refers to Jago's machinations is proved by its previous occurrence, namely, in the first act. There it dominates the scene in which Jago induces Cassio to drink (FS 82-84, VS 55-56).

[10]The author is indebted to Signore Luciana Pestalozza Abbado and Signor Fausto Broussard for their kind permission to examine the autograph score of *Otello* in the Ricordi archives at Milan.

Example 4

The tight and logical building of the drama by Boito and Verdi has always been admired. Its construction reminds us that in Latin countries romantic trends have never destroyed classical tradition. Each of the first three acts represents a phase of Jago's machinations and Otello's decline. In Act I the ensign induces the general to degrade Cassio; in Act II he successfully upsets his master's peace of mind; in Act III Otello accuses Desdemona, Jago plays his last trump, showing the handkerchief in Cassio's possession, and finally Otello's mental disintegration is shown in front of all his subordinates as well as the Venetian envoy. This leaves Act IV as a structural problem.

During the first three acts we have seen Jago almost continuously on the stage.[11] Now that his work is completed he disappears, and our attention is drawn to Desdemona. Verdi must have felt the danger of a break in the unity of the work, especially with regard to the first half of the last act, which from a dramatic as well as from a musical point of view (the two solo songs) seems essentially different from what we have seen and heard before. Probably for this reason he establishes musical links with the previous acts. The first and most important of these is his special use of the English horn. This in-

---

[11] Jago is absent only during the two Otello-Desdemona duets (Act I, sc. 3; Act III, sc. 2).

strument appears at only four places in the score: the love duet (Act I, sc. 3), the Willow Song (Act IV, sc. 1), Otello watching the sleeping Desdemona (*ibid.*, sc. 3) and finally, after he has stabbed himself, as he stands by her corpse (*ibid.*, sc. 4). In the love duet the instrument plays but a subordinate part; in the prelude of Act IV and the Willow Song, however, its dark timbre determines the atmosphere. Furthermore, in both scenes 3 and 4, the English horn melody precedes the famous *bacio* theme. The instrument therefore functions psychologically and dramatically as a denominator of these four scenes, expressing the double concept of love and death.

In this respect, Otello's words in the love scene are significant:

> Venga la morte! e mi colga
> nell'estasi di quest'amplesso
> il momento supremo![12]

The text of the Willow Song is equally revealing,

> Egli era nato per la sua gloria, io per amarlo e per morir.[13]

whereas the two scenes later in Act IV speak for themselves. In three of these instances the use of the English horn is closely tied to the kiss theme. Its specific function, however, is that it integrates the Willow Song in the totality of the drama.

Other connections between the Willow Song and foregoing scenes are of a melodic nature. The entire song is governed by *descending* minor thirds, either as a leap (ex. 5a and b), or filled with an intervening note (ex. 5c). A second melodic characteristic is the use of the leading note as a *cambiata*, leaping downwards to the fifth (ex. 5d). Both of these features have already appeared in the great third-act ensemble. The following examples, all from Desdemona's part, hardly need any commentary (ex. 5e, f and g).

Finally, it should be noted that in the *preghiera* immediately following the Willow Song, the dominating interval is the *ascending* minor third (C—E-flat), which we hear immediately at the beginning, and which is repeated several times in the course of the piece. In other respects, too, the *Ave Maria* forms a dramatically efficient contrast to the Willow Song. Both songs have a short "refrain" which is thrice repeated: the one is sung on unaccompanied dissonant notes ("salce!"); the other, of purely instrumental origin, is harmonized by simple subdominant and tonic triads. There is in addition a striking difference in orchestration. The prelude to the fourth act is written exclusively for woodwinds and one horn; during the song itself the same instruments dominate the accompaniment as well as the interludes. The *Ave Maria*, on the other hand, is scored entirely for strings.

[12]"Let death come! And may the supreme moment take me in the ecstasy of this embrace."

[13]"He was born for his glory
And I to love him and to die."

Example 5

Desdemona's prayer is not without affinity to other scenes of the drama. In both of her duets with Otello (I, sc. 3; III, sc. 2), she refers to her religious feelings and thoughts:

Desd.: Disperda il ciel gli affani
       e amor non muti col mutar degli anni.
Ot. : A questa tua preghiera
       Amen risponda la celeste schiera.
Desd.: *Amen* risponda . . .

                  (I, sc. 3)[14]

---

[14]Desd.: "May heaven drive away care, and love not change with the changing years."
  Ot. : "To this your prayer let the celestial host answer *Amen*."
  Desd.: "May it answer *Amen*."

Desdemona's exclamations during the third-act duet ("Iddio m'aiuti!" and "No . . . no . . . pel battesmo della fede cristiana . . .")[15] should therefore be taken in their literal sense. Like many Verdian heroines, she is a deeply religious woman.

As love and religion are closely related in this opera, it is not surprising to find in the *Ave Maria* not only a textual reference but also a musical quotation of the first-act love scene (ex. 6a). Its words referring to Otello are significant: "e pel possente, misero anch'esso, tua pietà dimostra."[16] The motif first occurred in the violoncello quartet which leads to the duet (ex. 6b). But we have heard it in several other scenes, too, such as the love duet itself (ex. 6c), Jago's first direct "attack" (II, sc. 3), where it twice underlines the last moments of Otello's peace of mind (ex. 6d), the end of the second Otello-Desdemona duet (ex. 6e), bitterly illustrating the words "quella vil cortigiana ch'è la sposa d'Otello,"[17] and finally the last scene of the drama when Otello, after the truth has been revealed to him, looks at the lifeless Desdemona (ex. 6f).

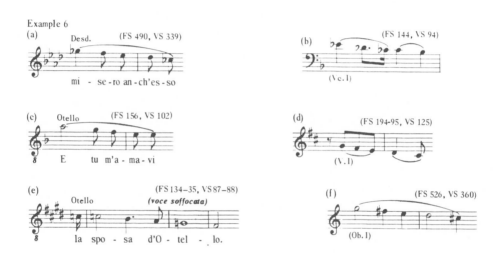

Love, religion and death, these interrelated concepts, constitute a spiritual atmosphere to which Jago has no access.

Two other motifs found repeatedly in the score draw our attention. Students of Verdi's operas will be familiar with both of them, since they occur in most of his works. The first, the emphatic minor sixth, has already been mentioned in connection with the vengeance duet (see ex. 3a and c above). This is the common use of the motif, known from such famous examples as the B-double-flat of Lady Macbeth's sleepwalking scene and the Fate melody in *La Forza del Destino*. In *Otello*, however, the motif is used also in a more specific way, as a *repeated* "appoggiatura," as is shown in example 7.

[15]"God send me aid" and "No . . . no, by the baptism of Christian faith . . ."

[16]". . . and to the mighty, wretched also, show thy pity."

[17]". . . that vile whore who is Otello's wife."

Example 7

24

Strictly speaking not all of these examples are appoggiaturas; nevertheless they are closely interrelated. This holds especially for examples 7(a) and (b), taken respectively from the introduction of the drinking song and the end of the brawl (Act I, sc. 1); here we have one more proof of Verdi's striving for unity. Example (c), occurring in Jago's *Credo*,[18] obviously comments on the preceding words "vile son nato,"[19] the melody of which consists of the same notes (A-flat—G—F). The next three examples refer to various stages of Otello's fury and despair: (d) "M'hai legato alla croce! Ahimè! . . . ."[20] (II, sc.4); (e) "Le parole non odo . . . Lasso! e udir le vorrei! Dove son giunto!"[21] (III, sc. 5 during which Otello, hidden behind a pillar, watches Cassio and Jago); (f) "E quello! è quello! Ruina e morte!")[22] (the same scene after Otello has seen the handkerchief). Example (g) is from the final measures of Act III; it seals the complete breakdown of the Moor and is in bitter contradiction to the off-stage cheers of the Cypriots ("Viva! Viva! Viva Otello!"). The last two examples are seemingly of a gentler tone, but the dramatic situations in which they occur are no less moving than the foregoing. Example (h) comments on Desdemona's request to be buried in her bridal garment (IV, sc. 1), and example (i) is the melody of Otello's entrance into his wife's bedroom, where he watches her as she sleeps (IV, sc. 3). The common element in the frequent use of this motif is the high degree of emotional tension. Although the motif itself has no specific meaning, it functions structurally within the frame of the drama.

On the other hand the second motif, which can be traced in nearly all of Verdi's operas, does possess a special connotation.[23] It refers to death, and occurs in two versions, one played by wind instruments, the other by a kettledrum (ex. 8).

Example 8
(a)   (b)

As in previous operas, Verdi employs the death motif in *Otello* in an implicit and prospective way. Since it is connected with "fatal" rather than with "natural" death (which includes death on the battlefield), the occurrence of the motif (a) in connection

---

[18]In the vocal score the reading is inaccurate.

[19]"Base am I born."

[20]"You have bound me to the cross . . . Alas!"

[21]"I can't catch the words . . . O misery! I would hear them! To what have I come!"

[22]"That's it! That's it! Death and damnation!"

[23]To mention only a few examples: *La Battaglia di Legnano* (IV, sc. 2); *Luisa Miller* (poison scene and final scene); *Il Trovatore* (IV, sc. 1); *La Traviata* (III, Finale); *Les Vêpres Siciliennes* (*passim*); *Aroldo* (II, sc.2); *Un Ballo in Maschera* (III, Quartet); *Macbeth*, 2nd version (III, Gran scena delle apparizione); *La Forza del Destino*, 2nd version (IV, sc. 9); *Aida* (II, duet Aida-Amneris; IV, duet Amneris-Radamès; trial scene); *Simon Boccanegra*, 2nd version (Prologo; II, poison scene; III, duet Doge-Fiesco). See also Verdi's *Requiem* ("Dies irae" and "Libera me").

with Otello's war memories in the love duet (I, sc. 3; FS 147-50; omitted in VS) and with his monologue quoted at the beginning of this paper (II, sc. 5; FS 257-259) may seem ambiguous. In both scenes it does not refer to the battlefield, however, but to the ultimate fate of Otello. The same anapaestic motif, softly played by brass and bassoons, accompanies Desdemona's words in the third-act duet:

> Esterrefatta fisso lo sguardo tuo tremendo;
> in te parla una Furia, la sento e non l'intendo.[24]

Here, too, the motif is used in a prospective way; Otello's fury will ultimately lead to Desdemona's destruction.

In order to illustrate actual death, Verdi uses the second version. It occurs in the scene where Otello speaks to Desdemona's corpse:

> Fredda come la casta tua vita, e in cielo assorta.[25]

These words are accompanied by plucked strings which alternate with the drum playing motif (b).[26]

Most of the structural material thus far discussed consists of short motifs. Themes, defined here as periodic musical sentences, never function as reminiscent or associative melodies. Even the best known orchestral melody of the opera, the *bacio* theme, is not a complete phrase, since it starts with an appoggiatura on a six-four chord. There are indeed very few "regular" themes in *Otello*. They occur in choruses like the drinking song (I, sc. 1), the homage of the Cypriots to Desdemona (II, sc. 3), and in other "ceremonial" scenes, such as the vengeance duet (II, sc. 5), the beginning of the second Otello-Desdemona duet (III, sc. 2), and the two fourth-act songs. But the great majority of scenes are written in a free melodic style, full of exclamations, unfinished phrases, and interruptions, which almost extinguish the differences between aria, arioso and recitative. It is in this respect that the opera varies most widely from its predecessor, composed sixteen years before. *Aida* was not only commissioned for a ceremonial occasion, but also is in itself a ceremonial opera. Since ceremony depends essentially on control, the actors express themselves in regular phrases, however strong their emotion may be. The structural materials of *Aida,* i.e., the themes of the titular heroine, of Amneris, of the priests, and the melody of rivalry, all of which recur several times in the course of the drama, never deny their original periodic structure, even in those cases where they are only partially quoted. If we compare the death scenes of *Aida* and *Otello*, the difference becomes perfectly clear. Aida and Radamès sing in regular phrases, supported by simple harmonies. Their death is not only the consequence of a ceremony (the trial) but also forms part of it. The death scenes of Desdemona and Otello, on the other hand, are for the most part depicted by musical disintegration. There is no

---

[24] "Terrified, I fix your terrible look. A fury speaks in you; I feel it, but understand it not." (III, sc. 2.)

[25] "Cold as your chaste life, and gathered to the skies."

[26] In the vocal score the drum motif has been omitted.

question of themes, only of exclamations and bits of phrases, supported by tremolos or a paratactic sequence of chords (see for instance FS 510-11, 525; VS 352-53, 360). It may be argued that Aida dies of her own free will, whereas Desdemona does not. But this is only true in terms of the plot; from a dramatic point of view they are both victims of Fate.

The underlying reason for the structural differences between the two operas is that in contrast to the ceremonial character of *Aida*, the essential dramatic quality of *Otello* is the dissolution of ceremony. Apart from the crucial moment in the third act, when, in the presence of the Venetian envoy, Otello strikes out at Desdemona and throws her down, we have already witnessed disorder in previous scenes. The drinking song (in itself a sort of ritual) degenerates into a brawl, and at the end of the second duet with Desdemona, Otello is unable to maintain even a sarcastically courteous tone; his voice is suffocated (FS 342, VS 225). *Otello* is the drama of a human passion that proves stronger than social order and convention.

*　　*　　*

The Working of the Poison

Verdi's Jago: a born villain with not half the motivation of his Shakespearean namesake. Jago professes villany as a gratuitous occupation, as the natural consequence of his existence. In themselves, pure villains, like pure saints, hardly provide interesting human material for the dramatist; on the stage, both soon become boring. Verdi's achievement seems to contradict this rule, however. His insistence on the continual reworking of the *Credo* proves that from the beginning it was this kind of Jago he had in mind. And he certainly succeeded in bringing him to life. The question is, therefore, how did he do it?

Jago sets himself a task: the destruction of Otello. He holds no personal grudge against Desdemona, nor even against Cassio. In view of his self-revelation in the *Credo*, one might even question his genuine hatred for the Moor; to be disappointed in military advancement seems hardly sufficient explanation for his perfidious conduct. However this may be, Verdi has clearly marked the beginning and the end of Jago's path. It is done by a melody which we first hear as an aside to Roderigo during the storm scene ("May the frantic belly of the sea be her tomb"),[27] and then at the moment of his triumph ("Who can now prevent me from pressing this forehead beneath my heel?") (ex. 9).

Jago has several musical attributes which already appear in his first dialogue with Roderigo: the downward leap of an octave with short appogiatura, the vocal or orchestral trill, the *unisono* accompaniment, and the descending chromatic scale. All of these are shown in the following fragment (ex. 10).

[27]The words refer to Otello's ship.

Example 9
(a)

(FS 50, VS 17)

(L'al-vo fre - ne - ti - co   del mar   sia la   sua tom - ba!)

(b)

(FS 460-61, VS 322)

Chi può vie - tar   che   que - sta fron - te   pre - ma col mia   tal - lo - ne?

The octave leap which seems to have the connotation of sneering occurs twice in the Jago-Roderigo dialogue, both times in the orchestra. It also closes the introduction to the drinking song (FS 89, VS 59), while during the song the motif is taken up by Jago himself, characteristically in a changed $\frac{2}{4}$ meter which interrupts the flow of $\frac{6}{8}$ measures (FS 90, 100; VS 60, 65). In the *Credo,*, the four leaping bassoons sneer at the "honest man" whose tears, kisses, and sacrifices are said to be no more than lies (FS 183, VS 117). The octave leap appears again in the fifth scene of Act III, which shows another instance of Jago's manipulation of Cassio and is therefore dramatically related to the drinking song. Here, too, the orchestral interruption leaves the impression of a sneering aside.

The trill which occurs more frequently in connection with Jago's part often leaves the impression of a jeer but also pictures gentle persuasion. In the drinking song and in the third-act terzetto it may have the ambiguous meaning of both playfulness and devilry. Other scenes in which the vocal or orchestral trill appears are the *Credo* (*passim*), the *idra* fragment (FS 203, VS 131) and its elaboration as introduction to the third act (FS 305, VS 204), the dialogue preceding Jago's relation of the faked dream (FS 270, VS 184), and his final exclamation with a gesture of horrendous triumph: "Ecco il Leone!" (III, sc. 9; FS 461-62, VS 322).

The arioso-like passages accompanied in unison are not numerous, but they express Jago's most pregnant words. Apart from the fragment quoted in example 10 below, all of them are addressed to Otello (II, sc. 3: FS 203, 206; VS 131, 133; and III, sc. 9: FS 459, 460-61; VS 321, 322). The descending chromatic scales are similarly connected with Jago's most perfidious manipulations, especially in those cases where they are assigned to the voice. A striking example is found in the dream fragment, where a chromatic passage of parallel sixth chords proceeds in the no man's land between two keys, underlining the fictitious words put in Cassio's mouth (ex. 11a). The melisma on "beva" in the drinking song shows another instance of this device (see below, ex. 12). Moreover, at the moment when Otello hurls himself against the crowd (III, sc. 9), Jago's hypocritical words ("A malady which deprives him of all sense now assails him") are rendered by a chromatic melody (ex. 11b). The use of descending chromaticism in the orchestra only may be interpreted as an indirect picture of his perfidy (see ex. 10 above, and also passages from the brawl scene, i.e., the asides addressed to Roderigo, from the introduction to Act II, and from Jago's strophe of the vengeance duet; ex. 11 c, d and e).

Example 10

ed io ri - man - go di sua Mo - re - sca Si - gno - ria___ l'al -

fie - re! Ma, com' è ver___ che tu Ro - dri - go

sei, co - sì è pur ve - ro che se il Mo - ro io fes - si, ve -

der - mi non vor - rei d'at - tor - no un Ja - go.

29

Example 11

30

Finally it should be noted that melodies and motifs in triple time or in triplets form an important musical feature of Jago's language, especially in his dealings with Otello and Cassio. During the first act this is apparent only in the drinking song in which Jago plays a leading part, but from the second act onward the triplets or ternary meters dominate nearly all of his dialogues with the two men he wants to destroy. The first measures of Act II are characteristic in this respect: the triplets played *forte* by four bassoons and the violoncellos picture Jago in all his ferocity, but later they underline his gentle persuasion of Cassio. The motif persists into the *Credo* which, in spite of being written in common time, is full of triplets. Key-points of the drama, like the *idra*-arioso (FS 203, VS 131; see also the prelude of Act III), the dream fragment (FS 272ff., VS 186ff.), the vengeance duet (FS 283ff., VS 193ff.), and the third-act terzetto (FS 363, VS 236) are all written in simple or compound triple meters. Generally Jago addresses Otello or Cassio in common time only in recitative-like passages.

Jago keeps some of his musical attributes for himself (the octave leap, the trill, and the unison accompaniment); other characteristics, however, creep into the parts of Otello, Cassio and the Cypriots. This is done by what I consider the most important structural feature of the opera: the working of the poison. Twice in the course of the work Jago pronounces: "il mio velen lavora,"[28] first after the second-act quartet, later at the moment of Otello's complete collapse (end of Act III). The poison works indeed, not only in the text and in the visible action on the stage, but also and even more subtly in the music.

A characteristic example of this device is found in the drinking scene of Act I. Verdi conceived the song in the traditional *bar* form, consisting of two strophes and an *abgesang*, which are unified by a common refrain. Moreover, the song is preceded by an orchestral introduction, and its three sections are separated by short interludes (asides of Jago and Roderigo). This form-type particularly suited his dramatic purpose: what begins as an orderly situation (the two strophes) deteriorates into disorder (the *abgesang* in which Cassio is mocked at, followed by the brawl). But at the same time Verdi stays within operatic tradition; the refrain guarantees the unity of the song as a musical entity. It is in this refrain that the poison works. Jago exposes his melody, which contains the descending chromatic scales that are so typical of his musical language (ex. 12).

Subsequently the melody of the refrain is taken up by the chorus, characteristically without the chromatic passages. These are sung by Jago who is shortly afterwards joined by Roderigo, his spineless tool (ex. 13).[29]

[28] "My poison works."

[29] Only the last four notes of the longest chromatic scale are doubled by the male voices of the chorus.

Example 13

In the second strophe this procedure is repeated with the sole difference that all the actors sing *con voce soffocata*, obviously as a result of intoxication. Not until the refrain of the *abgesang* section does Jago succeed in bringing the people over to his side; the whole chromatic scale descending a ninth (from f' to e) is doubled by the tenors and basses of the chorus. It is clear that in this instance chromaticism has worked as a poison, inducing the people in the tavern to mock Cassio and to provoke him.

Many instances of the contaminating force of Jago's chromatic melodies occur in Otello's part. During his initial private encounter with the ensign (II, sc. 3) his words, ". . . nei chiostro dell'anima recetti qualche terribil mostro,"[30] are sung on a melody which seems to be borrowed from Jago's spiritual atmosphere (ex. 14a). Otello's exclamation, "la prova io voglio,"[31] is supported by a similar melody (ex. 14b); in this instance the example is the more conclusive since the melody is played by a bassoon and low strings, instruments that are often encountered in connection with Jago. Other examples are found at the end of the monologue, "Ora e per sempre addio" (ex. 14c), in the second Otello-Desdemona duet (III, sc. 3) and its postlude (ex. 14d), in the unison passages of the following scene (ex. 14e), and at the moment of his breakdown (a chain of parallel sixth chords, chromatically descending from a'' to d'; ex. 14f).

Examples of descending chromaticism appear also in the parts of Desdemona and Lodovico; these have a plaintive character and are far removed from Jago's realm. Nor does Cassio undergo Jago's influence, but the latter's chromatic scales are heard when the degraded captain tells him about the *fazzoletto* (FS 370-71, VS 240-41).

Equally efficient is the working of the poison by means of orchestral triplets. Derived from a phrase of the *Credo* (ex. 15a), they first appear in Otello's rhetorical monologue, "Ora e per sempre addio" (ex. 15b); covered by the dull *pizzicato* of the divided double basses,[32] they are hardly perceptible. But in the following section (FS 260ff., VS 176ff.), which ends with his assault on Jago, these triplets dominate the orchestral accompaniment. They reappear after Jago's recounting of the dream and, as has already been shown, provide not only the material of the vengeance duet (another rhetorical piece), but also its pathetic introduction written on the text, "Jago, ho il cor di gelo" (see above, ex. 3a and c).

[30]"In the cloister of your mind you house some fearful monster."

[31]"I want proof!" (II, sc. 5)

[32]Verdi may have borrowed this orchestral device from Berlioz (*Symphonie fantastique*, 4th movement, "Marche au supplice").

Example 14

(a) Otello   (FS 198, VS 128)
nel chio - stro del - l'a - ni - ma ri - cet - ti___ qual - che ter - ri - bil mo - stro.

(b)   (FS 268, VS 182-83)
(Fag. I, Vc., Cb.)

(c) Otello   (FS 259, VS 176)
Del - la glo - ria d'O - tel - - lo è que - sto il fin.

(d)   (FS 345, VS 225-26)

(e)   (FS 346, VS 226)
pp   pppp

(f)   (FS 458-59, VS 320)
dim.   etc.

Example 15

(a)   (FS 181, VS 116)
Cre - do con fer - mo cuor, sic - co - me cre - de la ve - do - vel - la al tem - pio,

(b)   (FS 255, VS 174)
(Vla.)
(Vc.)

33

Thus the triplets entirely dominate the last part of Act II. The complete text of the melody from which they are derived is significant:

> Credo con fermo cuor, sicome credo
>   la vedovella al tempio,
> che il mal ch'io penso e che da me procede,
>   per mio destino adempio. [33]

Another motif of the *Credo* (the sixteenth-note triplet) reappears in Otello's A-flat minor monologue "Dio! mi potevi scagliar tutti mali della miseria, della vergogna" (III, sc. 3; FS 346ff., VS 226ff.).[34] Finally the *unisono* orchestral accompaniment to Otello's discovery of the handkerchief in Cassio's possession ("È quello!")[35] is clearly reminiscent of the *Credo* (FS 377, VS 244).

A third means by which the poison infects Otello is a special four-note formula that may be called Jago's designing motif. It appears in different forms but invariably retains the shape of three stepwise ascending notes followed by a descending interval. The latter may vary from a minor second to a double octave plus a major third. Sometimes it is a dissonant interval (diminished fifth, minor or diminished seventh); when it is consonant the motif is often repeated with emphasis (ex. 16).[36]

However numerous, these examples are far from complete. The orchestral beginning of the *Credo* (F—G-flat—B-flat) and several vocal phrases of this piece (". . . e che nell'ira io nomo,"[37] "Credo che il giusto è un istrion beffardo . . .,"[38] "E credo l'uom gioco d'iniqua sorte . . ."[39]) are certainly related to the motif of designing.

The motif is first used to characterize Jago and his manipulation of Cassio (ex. 16 a-e). From the moment the ensign speaks the fatal words, "ciò m'accora . . .,"[40] the motif begins to serve its main purpose: the destruction of Otello's peace of mind (ex. 16 f-j). During the third and fourth acts the motif functions as a reminder. When Desdemona asks why she is the innocent cause of Otello's grief, the four notes significantly interrupt her speech (ex. 16k); in the terzetto the motif underlines Otello's despair (ex. 16l) and

---

[33]"I believe with a firm heart, as ever did widow in church, that the evil which I conceive and which from me proceeds, I will achieve by my destiny."

[34]"Oh God! Thou mightest have heaped upon me all the ills of misery, of shame."

[35]"That's it!" (III, sc. 5)

[36]Repeat signs indicate reiteration of the motif (at least twice).

[37]". . . and whom, in hate, I name."

[38]"I believe that the honest man is a jeering buffoon . . ."

[39]"And I believe man to be the sport of a malign fate."

[40]"I like not that" (cf. *Othello* III, sc. 3, v. 35). In the opera the words are found in II, sc. 3 (FS 193, VS 124).

Example 16

35

Ex. 16 *cont'd.*

Jago's ambivalent words, "Questa è una ragna dove il tuo cor casca, si lagna, s'impiglia e muor"[41] (ex. 16m). The last two examples (ex. 16n and o), occurring just before and immediately after the strangling of Desdemona, remind us once more of the man who is the source of the catastrophe.

Thus the poison works in a threefold manner; by means of descending chromatic scales, by triplets, and by the use of a special motif. The importance of this structural device is clear: our whole attention is drawn to what is really happening, not on the level of the fable, but on that of the drama. It may be that the device was not new. One thinks of other operas in which the spell of one person over another is shown by musical means (for instance, the relationship Fiordiligi - Ferrando in *Così fan tutte*, where the influence is particularly evident, although unconscious from the two characters' point of view). But I wonder if, before or after Verdi, a composer ever used the device in such a penetrating way, making it the structural essence of his work.

*   *   *

Desdemona

Desdemona is Jago's antipode, not only as a person, but also as to her role in the plot. Her passivity is set off in sharp opposition to his machinations. Desdemona's sole active contribution to the development of the plot is her repeated plea for Cassio; but even this can hardly be considered a free act, since it is both the result of Jago's intrigue and the compelling consequence of her innate goodness. Without the contrasting villain, a personality like hers would certainly bore us. The viability of her role rests on the interdependence of the leading characters, which is so essential to the structure of this opera. Still, the Desdemona-Jago relationship reveals a curious paradox, in a drama

[41]"This is a web wherein your heart stumbles, cries out, entangles itself and dies."

which is virtually enacted by no more than three persons, two of them never really speak to each other.[42] Strange as this may seem, on second thought it becomes perfectly logical. Only by keeping Desdemona apart from Jago does Verdi succeed in making her purity acceptable. While it is true that by means of their contrasting characters the drama opposes good to evil, nevertheless a *direct* confrontation of these embodied concepts is almost systematically avoided.

As might be expected, Desdemona's musical physiognomy is also the complete opposite of Jago's. In contrast to the latter's slithery ariosos written in triple meter, she sings her quiet, expressive melodies in common time. Only the second-act quartet and the middle section of her third-act duet with Otello are exceptions to this rule; in the former ensemble, however, her part contains a characteristic descending scale in duplets (ex. 17).

Example 17

The same example shows another feature contrasting with Jago's musical language: the descending *diatonic* scale.[43] In Act III, shortly after the arrival of the Venetian ambassadors, Desdemona sings the following words, indirectly addressed to Otello (ex. 18).[44]

Example 18

---

[42]In Act III, sc. 7, Desdemona's words referring to Cassio's return to grace ("Jago, I hope so; you know I feel true affection for Cassio") do not form part of a dialogue but rather of a conversation in which several persons are involved (Lodovico, Jago, Desdemona). Actually the words are addressed to Otello, who is reading the Doge's letter but listening at the same time.

[43]When, under the pressure of her deep sorrow, Desdemona exceptionally sings a chromatically descending melody, the expressive accompaniment with its accelerating harmonic rhythm is completely alien to Jago's style (see III, sc. 8, FS 417-18, VS 272-73).

[44]"I think he will return to grace."

A few moments later this melody is taken over literally by Jago who only substitutes the word "forse" for "credo."[45] Here, by changing his habitual chromatic scale to a diatonic one, the ensign slyly adapts himself to Desdemona. The opposite would be impossible, since Otello's wife is virtually incapable of imitating the true Jago. Besides having no idea of the kind of man he really is, she forms part of a world of unassailable values, and is therefore immune from the poison.[46]

Generally the accompaniment to Desdemona's singing underlines her mental equilibrium with steadily repeated chords in slow harmonic rhythm. The following phrase from the love duet is a characteristic example (ex. 19).

Example 19

Similar instances are found in Act II, sc. 4 (Desdemona's first plea for Cassio, FS 228ff, VS 99ff), Act III, sc. 2 (her complaint in the middle of the second duet with Otello, FS 329ff, VS 218ff), and the great ensemble in Act III, sc. 8 (FS 416, 422, VS 272, 277). The harmonies, which especially in the two great duets show a certain French influence, are very expressive and compensate for the lack of rhythmic variety.

Nowhere in the opera has Verdi shown more clearly Desdemona's curiously distinctive function than in the second-act quartet. The piece in question is a typical specimen of operatic ensemble in which each of the characters involved simultaneously expresses his or her own feelings. Like its famous forerunners (e.g., the quartets from *Idomeneo, Fidelio,* and *Rigoletto*), it forms a dramatic climax in the work, realized by a device of which verbal drama is incapable. This is the situation: Jago urges Emilia to give him Desdemona's handkerchief. Emilia does not understand why he wants it. Although she has no idea of her husband's machinations, she suspects him of evil intentions and refuses; finally Jago wrenches the handkerchief from her. At the same time Desdemona addresses Otello in the following terms:

---

[45]"Perhaps"

[46]One could hardly be as sure of Shakespeare's Desdemona.

La tua fanciulla io sono
umile e mansueta;
ma il labbro tuo sospira,
hai l'occhio fiso al suol.
Guardami in volto e mira
come favella amor.
Vien ch'io t'allieti il core,
ch'io ti lenisca il duol. [47]

But Otello does not listen; instead he soliloquizes:

Forse perchè gl'inganni
d'arguto amor non tendo,
forse perchè discendo
nella valle degli anni,
forse perchè ho sul viso
quest'atro tenebror,
ella è perduta e irriso
io sono e il core m'infrango
e ruinar nel fango
vedo il mio sogno d'or. [48]

The structural problems of this ensemble could have been solved in various ways. A division into two simultaneous duets would seem logical, since the "lower" couple is dealing with a specific matter which is far removed from Otello's and Desdemona's preoccupations. Even more acceptable would have been a division into two plus one plus one, since only Jago and Emilia are having a real dialogue; Otello's soliloquizing sets both him and Desdemona apart. Verdi, however, chose a solution which, although

[47] I am your handmaiden
humble and submissive;
but your lips sigh,
your eyes are bent on the ground.
Look me in the face and see
how love does speak.
Come, let me cheer your heart,
let me assuage your pain.

[48] Perchance because I do not understand
the subtle deceits of love,
perchance because I have passed
the heyday of my years,
perchance because I have upon my face
this sombre hue,
she is lost and I am mocked
and my heart is broken
and ruined in the mire
I see my golden dream.

contradicting the "superficial" dramatic situation, actually underlines an essential element of the drama: Jago's hold on Otello. Naturally the parts of Jago and Emilia are closely connected, but they are also rhythmically and melodically linked with Otello's soliloquy. A motif of Jago (ex. 20a) reappears in Otello's part, is again taken up by Jago (ex. 20b), and is finally quoted in the third-act ensemble (ex. 20c).[49]

Over and against this "terzetto" stands Desdemona's beseeching melody which, compared with the rhythm of the other parts, is written in approximately doubled note values.[50] She is the one person who has not the slightest idea of what is going on, not only because of her innocence, but also because she is incapable of understanding anything evil. The fact that she sings in large melodic curves, dominating the other actors' parts and consequently the whole piece, is particularly significant. Unknowing and passive, she is nevertheless the main figure on the stage.

Another famous Verdian ensemble, the first-act terzetto of *Aida*, seems to me to have served as a structural model for this quartet. The situation is somewhat analogous. Aida is completely ignorant of the tension between Amneris and Radamès; she has her own emotional problem, the conflicting love for her native country and its main enemy. Her part, too, is written in double note values and therefore widely differs from the other two.[51] In *Otello*, however, this structural device has a deeper meaning. One might say of the quartet that while its text furthers the development of the plot, its music truly serves the drama.

---

[49]The motif also serves to connect the quartet with the next scene. It provides the musical material for the transition, appearing first in 16th, then in 32nd notes, finally as triple appogiaturas (slides) of the initial chords of *scena* 5 (see FS247-50, VS 169-71).

[50]The respective numbers of sixteenth notes (practically the shortest note value in the quartet) are significant: Jago (103), Emilia (61), Otello (71), Desdemona (2).

[51]The respective numbers of eighth notes (the shortest value) are: Amneris (54), Radamès (61), Aida(1).

The old question of whether Otello—either Shakespeare's or Verdi's—is a jealous man cannot be answered unless there is agreement about the concept of jealousy. Unfortunately this consensus is lacking. "Jealousy" may have different meanings varying from "envious attitude" to "watchfulness,"[52] but Otello is certainly not jealous in either sense. Envy which deprives a man of his dignity could perhaps serve as theme for a comedy, but surely not for Shakespeare's tragedy or Verdi's opera. On the other hand, to call Otello merely "watchful" would be equally unconvincing. Jago's cunning advice to beware of *gelosia* certainly does not refer to "watchfulness." Whatever the meaning of "jealousy" may be in the drama, one thing is certain: it is a human passion. And being "watchful" is not exactly a passionate state of mind. In order to understand the real nature of Otello's attitude, it is necessary to analyze the text of his part; the monologues and soliloquies prove particularly revealing.

In his first line Otello already speaks about "pride and glory." Since these words refer to the victory over the Mussulman there is nothing exceptional in them. Still, in the course of the drama the term "glory" acquires a specific and personal meaning. Otello's glory is not just the renown of a brave soldier; it is the fruit of a lifelong struggle against handicaps. Two of these are referred to in the love duet, "the life of exile" and "the chains and grief of the slave." But Otello is much more explicit in his soliloquy during the second-act quartet, the text of which has already been quoted above. First, he is a black man; secondly, he is incapable of understanding fashionable and subtle frivolities in love; and finally, he marries the youthful Desdemona at middle age. The relationship of all these drawbacks with the concept of glory and its loss is emphasized repeatedly in the course of the drama. In the love duet Otello recalls the time of courting, when he told his beloved of his previous sufferings:

> Ingentilia di lagrime la storia
> il tuo bel viso e il labro di sospir;
> scendean sulle mie tenebre la gloria,
> il paradiso e gli astri a benedir.[53]

Desdemona takes up this thought:

> Ed io vedea fra le tue tempie oscure
> splender del genio l'eternea beltà.[54]

"The subtle deceits of love" (see Otello's text in the quartet, quoted above) seem to refer to Cassio, who is a fashionable Florentine bachelor of nobel birth (Jago sneeringly

---

[52]See the *American Heritage Dictionary of the English Language*, entry "jealousy."

[53]"Your lovely face ennobled the story with tears, and your lips with sighs; on my darkness glory, paradise and the stars descended with a blessing."

[54]"And from your dusky temples I saw the eternal beauty of your spirit shine forth."

characterizes him as "dressed up"; see FS 57, VS 34). Like Jago and Roderigo he is considerably younger than Otello; the latter is incapable of understanding Cassio's frivolities, not only because of his age but also because of his totally different background and the sufferings of his youth. This may explain the naiveté through which he is ensnared by Jago; Otello is unaware of the fact that the seemingly frivolous Cassio is his own and Desdemona's most loyal friend. Conspicuously, a musical phrase of Cassio sung in the course of the third-act terzetto is very much akin to the melodic language of the Cypriots in the homage chorus of Act II and thus underlines his innocence and loyalty (ex. 21).

Example 21

The explicit proof of Cassio's love and esteem for his general is his cry "Ah ferma!"[55] at the moment that Otello stabs himself, while Lodovico and Montano only exclaim "Sciagurato!"[56] In spite of all that has happened, the captain still wants Otello's life to be saved.

But the Moor's fate is sealed. He believes his *gloria*, of which the marriage with Desdemona is not only an integral part but the very crowning, has been destroyed. And since in the course of his life "glory" has become the basis of his existence, Desdemona's supposed unfaithfulness destroys the past as well as the present. Hence the monologue "Ora e per sempre addio," quoted at the beginning of this paper. Life becomes vacuous to Otello: "L'alma mia nissun più smuova."[57]

Musically the Moor's sufferings are pictured by an alternation of "disintegrating" and "rhetorical" monologues. His outburst following Jago's first move (FS 197-99, VS 127-29) already contains the characteristics of his later breakdown: irregular phraseology and tonal instability. After the quartet, Otello's despair cries out in stronger terms. Especially at the end of this section, in which he expresses the torments of doubt and

[55]"Oh! Stop!"

[56]"Wretched man!"

[57]"Nothing can touch my soul any more" (FS 377-78, VS 244-45).

42

suspicion, a chain of dissonant chords reveals his unstable state of mind. This is followed rather suddenly by the rhetorical monologue "Ora e per sempre addio" which, in spite of the soft triplets in tremolo reminding us of Jago's poison (see ex. 15b above), is firmly supported by consonant chords. At the end of the second act Otello expresses himself in a similar way by means of two contrasting sections. After Jago's mention of the handkerchief seen in Cassio's hands, the Moor is very close to a breakdown ("Jago, ho il cor di gelo," ending with the triple exclamation of "sangue!" FS 280-82, VS 191-93). This is followed by the rhetorical first strophe of the vengeance duet, a mode of expression which is cunningly adopted by Jago in the second.

In the third act, "disintegration" gets the upper hand from "control." After the great E major duet, which begins and ends in a bitterly sarcastic ceremonial style, Otello's true state of mind is pictured by a short but violent orchestral interlude. This is followed by a monologue in A-flat minor in *bar* form, which still maintains the character of a "controlled" piece of music. Each of its three sections is preceded by a solemn chromatic scale in double-dotted rhythm, descending from the dominant to the tonic (see above, ex. 14e). But Otello is no longer capable of controlling his voice; "con voce soffocata" he sings a complaint which is perhaps the most moving piece of the whole opera.

After the septet there is no longer any trace of rhetorical style in Otello's language. He has become unable to utter anything but separate bits of phrases and single words referring to previous scenes: "Sangue!" "ciò m'accora!"[58] "il fazzoletto!"—the breakdown is complete.

Otello's steadily growing despair and loss of control do not imply the disintegration of his relationship with Desdemona. The bond between man and wife remains insoluble throughout the drama and even transcends death. The kisses (I, sc. 3; IV, sc. 3 and 4) are the visible symbols of this union; perhaps not by chance the accompanying theme is the best-known melody of the opera. Apart from this, another structural element underlines the unbreakable ties between Otello and Desdemona: two special keys, or rather chords.[59]

As has been pointed out, Otello's marriage with Desdemona forms an integral part of his "glory." This is the reason why the two concepts of "union" and "glory" are constantly interwoven. Verdi symbolizes them by the major triads of C and E, appearing at crucial points of the drama. Though it seems at first that the chord of E major serves to stress exclusively Otello's military exploits and renown, it soon appears that both triads are coupled or used individually to emphasize Otello's past as well as his relationship with Desdemona. It should be observed, however, that these chords are by no means Otello's or Desdemona's "property;" Jago's tale of the dream is in C, the fire chorus in E.

The cry "È salvo!" (FS 30-31, VS 18) and the exclamation "Vittoria!" (e.g., FS 44-45, VS 26), both on an E chord, refer to Otello's exploits prior to the drama. More pregnant is the use of both chords in the love duet. The fragments preceding the *bacio*

---

[58]Jago's "first" words (II, sc. 3, FS193, VS 124).

[59]I am deeply obligated to my friend and colleague Pierluigi Petrobelli for drawing my attention to this structural aspect, as well as for his interest shown in various matters dealt with in this paper.

theme ("Disperda il ciel gli affanni," and "Ah! la gioia m'innonda si fieramente;" FS 158-61, VS 104-105) are both in C, while the theme itself is in E with a turn to C in the seventh measure. In Act II, the choice of E major for the homage chorus is anything but fortuitous, since it stresses the meaning of Desdemona's words ("Splende il cielo," etc.) as well as Otello's appeasement ("Quel canto mi conquide;" see above, ex. 1). The final measures of Otello's monologue, "Ora e per sempre addio," seem to turn to E major (actually it concerns the Neapolitan chord of the key of E-flat); the text of this passage is particularly revealing:

> Clamori e canto di battaglia, addio!
> Della gloria d'Otello è questo il fin.[60]

Bitter ironic use of the key of E major is emphasized by Verdi in the third-act duet. At its end, the initial section is repeated in a shortened version, as if nothing has happened between. Desdemona, however, now remains silent, and Otello's true state of mind is indicated by the stage direction "mutando d'un tratto l'ira nella più terribile calma dell'ironica."[61] In the course of the third act the irony is reinforced in various ways. The fanfares announcing the arrival of the Venetian ambassadors are in C (FS 387ff., VS 23ff.); the cries of the Cypriots "Evviva il Leone di San Marco!" end in the same key (FS 398, VS 259). Towards the end of the act the ironic bitterness reaches its climax. While the offstage Cypriots exclaim "Evviva Otello! Gloria al Leon di Venezia!" (mostly in unison on the note C), Jago triumphantly points to the inert Moor, "Ecco il Leone!" The final measures underline this image: the third act concludes with the chords of E and C (ex. 22).

Example 22

(FS 463, VS 323)

During the last act the two chords are mostly coupled. Otello's entrance into the bedchamber is accompanied by a motif built on the notes of the E major triad with a characteristic appogiatura on the sixth. A few moments later the motif reappears in the key of A (FS 493, VS 341), introducing the *bacio* theme. This is played a fourth higher than in Act I but, at the moment of the third kiss, the melody turns again to E, the

[60]See footnote 4.

[61]"Changing suddenly from anger to the even more terrible ironic calm."

chord of which is followed by the six-four chord of C (as in the love duet).[62] Yet the expected cadence in the key of E fails to appear; instead Desdemona's awakening is accompanied by a sudden modulation to F minor, the key that announces her fate.[63]

Any remaining doubt about the dramatic and psychological meaning of the two chords is removed when we hear the accompaniment to Otello's words while he is standing by Desdemona's corpse, "Ecco la fine del mio cammin . . . Oh! Gloria! Otello fu" (ex. 23).[64]

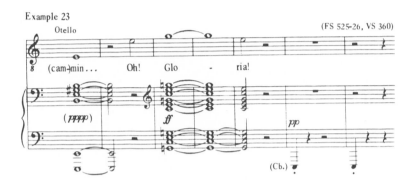

The final reprise of the *bacio* theme, virtually identical with its appearance in the first-act love scene,[65] hardly needs any comment. The fact that the opera ends in the key of E major is significant. Jago may have driven Otello and Desdemona into death, but he has failed to destroy their union.

<hr />

[62]It should be noted that in Otello's vocal part Verdi has scrupulously indicated the exact moments and duration of the three kisses.

[63]This "silent" scene has been brilliantly analyzed by Joseph Kerman in his *Opera as Drama* (New York, 1956), p. 9ff, especially with regard to the possibilities and impossibilities of musical and verbal drama.

[64]"This is my journey's end . . . Oh glory! Otello's day is done."

[65]I, sc. 3.

Melodrama or Tragedy?

In his invaluable study entitled *The Life of the Drama*, Eric Bentley discusses a number of the elements present in tragedy: reality, pain, guilt, anxiety, awe, compassion, and death.[66] If we test Otello's character, actions, and experiences against the first of these criteria, it is immediately apparent that his situation, struggle, failure, and ultimate crisis are *real* beyond any doubt. They are not at all products of an artificial world of daydreaming, but belong to this world and could be the lot of the man behind some *faits divers* recounted in today's newspaper. With some changes, of course, but essentially of the same type. The racial problem comes to mind first, but Otello's experience could in fact be that of any person who because of something in his background is only partially accepted by society, and therefore is destined to occupy an unstable position.

Once we have recognized Otello's reality, we understand and even feel his pain, his guilt and his anxiety.[67] Of course, our feelings cannot be identical with his. Otello's guilt, for example, stems from his social inferiority; hence his staking of his whole existence on a single chance (the ''glory''), hence his hidden insecurity, his susceptibility to Jago's fomentations, and his lack of faith in Desdemona and Cassio. Our own guilt, on the other hand, is less easy to determine. If we do not identify entirely with Otello, we at least have some empathy with him and perhaps to varying degrees feel somehow responsible for his suffering, so that we cannot ignore him or his fate. Nor can we disregard death, which Otello desires. (In the first-act love scene, he even calls it the supreme moment). We may not share his death wish, but since death is something which constantly confronts each of us, when it is presented on the stage in a framework of reality we cannot but be moved by it.

In melodrama, on the contrary, the emotions and experiences of the heroes and heroines are basically *unreal*, so that we cannot participate in them. We may fool ourselves briefly by imagining that we share their feelings, because we want a vicarious thrill. But neither the villain's guilt and death, nor the hero's virtues and final happiness can arouse anything but superficial emotions; and these will vanish as soon as we leave the theater.

These considerations lead to the inescapable conclusion that Otello is a tragic hero. But what of Jago, is he a melodramatic villain? And if so, which of the two is the real protagonist and determines the nature of the drama? In the case of Jago, categorization is particularly dangerous; he seems to possess all the characteristics of the typical scoundrel of melodrama. Unlike Otello he has neither past nor future, and this condition is significant. Verdi and Boito let him go unpunished, as did Shakespeare. Jago just vanishes, and we in the audience do not care, because our attention is focused on Otello.[68]

---

[66]E. Bentley, *The Life of the Drama* (New York, 1967), pp. 257ff.

[67]''Reality gives pain . . . Reality makes us feel guilty, and so arouses anxiety.'' (Bentley, *op.cit.*, p. 258.)

[68]It may be argued that, since he dies, Otello has no future either. But this is paradoxically the very reason why he ''lives on'' after the final curtain. It is through death that his existence is transcended.

Nevertheless, one can hardly deny that on the stage Jago has at least the outward appearance of reality and thus seems to contradict the melodramatic nature of his role. During his performance Jago strikes us as a very real human being, however monstrous his machinations may be. The explanation lies in the fact that he represents iniquity *in* a tragedy, and since in principle tragedy does not deal with villainy, it follows that Jago is not the protagonist, despite his almost continuous presence on the stage during the first three acts. He merely functions as a melodramatic agent for the fulfillment of the drama. This explains his absence in the fourth act, during which it becomes apparent that we are watching (and taking part in) a tragedy. Jago's dramatic significance is that he dominates the *plot*. Otello, however, dominates the *drama* and by being a tragic hero identifies the drama as tragedy.

The question remains as to why Verdi needed melodramatic means to create a musical tragedy. The answer is that he had no intention of breaking with tradition. The relationship of *melodramma* to melodrama is rooted not only in his own work from *Oberto* to *Aida*, but in all Italian opera of the *risorgimento*.[69] Emotions are transferred with a ''melodramatic'' immediacy of which only music is capable, while ambiguity, an important feature of higher dramatic forms, is rejected. This does not mean that *melodramma* is identical or even analogous to melodrama. Study of Verdi's earlier operas may similarly reveal their character as tragedies realized through melodramatic devices. But only with *Otello* did he raise the genre to a level which, up to the present, appears unrivaled.

[69]See Luigi Dallapiccola, *Words and Music in XIXth Century Italian Opera* (Dublin, 1964.)

THE 'ENGLISH CADENCE' IN EIGHTEENTH-CENTURY FRANCE:
A PROBLEM IN THOROUGHBASS

by Erich Schwandt

With his cantata *La Fortune*[1]—the first cantata of his first book—Michel Pignolet de Montéclair challenged the imagination of the 18th-century thoroughbass player by presenting him with several thorny problems to solve. More than 250 years later the problems are still there: the success or failure of *La Fortune* as a piece of music still depends, to a large extent, upon the musical ingenuity of the accompanist. Indeed, his power of invention is put to the test with the very first note of the cantata, where collaboration between performer and composer must begin in earnest. The cantata, for soprano and continuo, opens with a dazzling "Prelude for the Goddess Fortune." Montéclair calls upon the accompanist to improvise both melody and harmony for the prelude, a 36-measure unfigured bass which is twice interrupted by brief snatches of unaccompanied *récitatif*. The composer has not provided any guides to help the accompanist realize this important and substantial part of the cantata.

Another problem confronts the accompanist of *La Fortune*. Certain passages in the cantata, although they are fully figured, seem to call for harmonies that are richer, and sometimes even different from the harmonies that the composer has indicated in his figures. For example, in the air "O Fortune puissante" quite a few ninths and sevenths, as well as other dissonances, could be introduced by the accompanist to enhance the pleading and doleful affect of the air. Should they be introduced? It is the thoroughbass player who must take the responsibility for making such decisions about the harmony—decisions that are not always easy to make.

Perhaps the most puzzling problem that Montéclair set for the accompanist in *La Fortune* appears in "La douce esperance"—the first air of the cantata—where a motive sung by the soprano alone is immediately repeated in the continuo alone. Unfortunately, the rather full figuring of the bass ceases for the passage in question, which is shown in Ex. 1.

Example 1 "La douce esperance," mm. 30-33.

Basse-continue

[1]Ed. Erich Schwandt (Victoria, 1976); from *Cantates à voix seule, et avec simfonie*, Livre I (Paris, *ca.* 1709), pp. 1-8.

The problem here lies not so much in deciding what harmonies will best express the composer's intention as in deciding what the harmonies *are*. The first c^1 of the bass can be harmonized with a plain triad; after this the choice of chords is frustrating. The next note is troublesome. A triad will not work. A major triad will be contradicted immediately by the b flat in the bass, and a minor triad will be awkward in light of the progression of the bass in the next measure. Other chords seem equally inappropriate. Every other note of the bass in this passage is problematic as well.

Several options are open to the accompanist, not all of which are satisfactory solutions of the problem. The accompanist can, of course, avoid the problem by playing "tasto solo." This is no real solution, for Montéclair is careful to mark such directions into his music when he desires such a technique. The accompanist can choose to provide a single voice—a melodic accompaniment which will more or less follow the bass at the sixth above. If, however, he rises to meet the challenge of providing an accompaniment in two or three voices, he will immediately be in difficulty, for as we have seen, almost every note of the passage presents some problem.

No French thoroughbass treatise of the time gives any passage even faintly resembling this one, nor does any French theorist offer a solution to the problem posed by Montéclair. The only writer who seems to shed any light on the question is an Englishman, Dr. John Blow; and although his treatise is somewhat early for our purposes and comes from the wrong country, the pertinent section of his "Rules for playing of a Through Bass"[2] is worth quoting in full, because it may open a way that will lead to a clarification of Montéclair's intent.

RULES FOR PLAYING OF A THROUGH BASS UPON ORGAN & HARPSICON . . . .
The half Cadence divided by 4 Crochets, ♭6, 5th, [4th], & 3 : *

Example 2

* [Arnold's footnote]: this beautiful form of cadence—which Dr. Burney would doubtless have condemned along with the two following Exx. (see Burney, "Specimens of Dr. Blow's Deformities or Crudities" [Brit. Mus. Add. 11586, fols. 46-48]; and "Specimens of Dr. Jno Blow's Bestialities" [Brit. Mus. Add. 11587, fols. 36, 96, 147, 167, 213])—was commonly used by Byrd and other sixteenth-century composers.

[2]British Museum Add. Ms. 34072, fols. 1-5. The entire treatise is printed in F. T. Arnold, *The Art of Accompaniment from a Thorough-Bass* (London, 1931), pp. 163-172. The section reproduced here, from p. 170, includes Arnold's commentary.

The common Cadence divided by 4 Crochets, 3, 9th, & 8th, & 7th:

The common Cadence divided by moving from the ♭ 9th & 3d to yᵉ 3d: **

**[Arnold's footnote]: i.e. from $\frac{6}{3}$ ⁹ on b flat to $\frac{5}{3}$ on g. The expression "♭ 9th" (for "9 on a flattened Bass") is simply a slip on Blow's part. His figuring would be quite incomprehensible if the upper parts were not given. The figuring required is

The $\frac{5}{4}$ *under* the bass is simply a reminder that the whole progression is a sophisticated form of $\frac{5}{43}$ on g.

What Dr. Blow proposes to the accompanist is a species of cadential ornamentation—a "division"—to be improvised extempore. This kind of ornamentation is akin to one which was widely used in England and on the Continent in the 16th century and in the early years of the 17th century, especially by composers of keyboard music.[3] The phenomenon, a cadence which involves a cross-relation, is so closely associated with

[3]See Erich Schwandt, "The Ornamented *Clausula Diminuta* in the Fitzwilliam Virginal Book" (Ph.D. diss., Stanford University, 1967), especially pp. 59-73.

English music that it has been termed "English cadence" or "English seventh" by various modern authorities. The effect of the cadence comes from breaking the notes of one of the cadential voices "in division." Because the seventh degree is made to function in two different capacities—as a leading-tone (the raised seventh) and as the turning point in a modal melodic inflection (the flat seventh)—a cross-relation is present at the cadence. It is the melodic content of the cross-relation that gives the "English cadence" its characteristic sound. In 16th-century pieces, both instrumental and vocal, the cross-relation is written out and forms a cadential embellishment which is part of the fabric of the piece. Blow's instructions are for a purpose somewhat different from this: he is encouraging not the soloist or ensemble player, but rather the *accompanist* to improvise cadential ornamentation of a curious sort. Blow, it seems to me, is not trying to describe a 16th-century practice, nor is he attempting to revive a practice of the past; he is documenting a usage of his own time. It is not really clear to what situations Blow meant his "divided Cadences" to apply, nor how frequently he meant them to be used; there is no way of telling whether he is advocating their use in accompanying solo pieces, ensemble works, choral music, music of the past, contemporary music (including his own), or foreign music.

Aside from Dr. Blow's rules, the only other theoretical discussion of the "English cadence" is by Morley.[4] The famous passage has been quoted in full several times in recent years and does not need to be quoted again. Morley's description of the workings of the "English cadence" agrees with Blow's to some extent, but it should be noted that Morley condemned this sort of cadence on theoretical grounds. Blow seems quite at ease with the cross-relation.

Certain questions immediately arise. (1) What authority might a 17th-century English source have for solving an 18th-century French problem? (2) Can Montéclair's passage (see Ex. 1) be considered as resulting from the same compositionsal or improvisational procedures as Blow's "common Cadence divided" (see Ex. 4)? (3) Even if the two passages are analogues, is Blow's solution a viable one for Montéclair? Answers to these questions are necessary before the discussion can proceed, and since the French treatises provide no answers, we must turn to French music contemporary with *La Fortune*.

From the late 17th century until about 1725, progressions like that shown in Ex. 5 were extremely popular in France.

Example 5   "L'Autre jour une Bergère," mm. 3-5. From *Brunetes*, I (Paris, 1703):122.

[4]Thomas Morley, *A Plaine and Easie Introduction to Practicall Musicke* (London, 1597), pp. 153-54 and 162-64.

This melodic-harmonic cliché appeared dozens of times in music of all kinds by such French composers as Couperin, Hotteterre, Michel de La Barre, Campra, L'Affilard, Dandrieu, etc. It will be noticed that this progression has features in common with Dr. Blow's "half Cadence divided" (see Ex. 2) but employs only the "division" and the bass. As it stands, it is an incomplete half cadence, for one essential voice — the voice with the leading tone — has been suppressed. French pieces that contain the progression shown in Ex. 5 normally use it to arrive at a cadence, the leading tone must be supplied on the penultimate beat by the accompanist, who will also supply at lease one additional part. There are several different ways of managing the harmony, as is evidence by the figures provided by composers over the bass, but in almost all cases the accompanist is called upon to introduce a cross-relation — the leading tone. Some of the two-voiced versions of this cliché also exist in full-voiced settings.[5] There can be no doubt about harmonies (including cross-relations) when they are written out fully in notes.[6] The figures of the progression commonly indicate chords of the sixth (see Ex. 6), but occasionally the penultimate beat is figured 7 #6. The composer can also employ a more elaborate melody (see Ex. 7) or a more elaborate bass (see Ex. 8). In addition, there are numerous two-voiced settings which, like Ex. 5, are entirely unfigured.

Example 6 "Marche en rondeau," m. 6. From Michel L'Affilard, *Principes très-faciles*, 5th ed. (Paris, 1705), p.127

Example 7 Sarabande "l'Aînée," mm. 3-4. From Michel de La Barre, *Pièces pour la flûte traversière*, 2nd ed. (Paris, 1710), *Suite II*.

sur la Trompette" (the second coupler of the Kyrie of the *Messe pour les "couvents"*), the fugue subje

[5]There are a great many examples of the cliché in André Campra, *Les Festes Venitiennes* (Paris, 1710), ed. Max Lütolf (Paris, 1972). For a very clear instance compare p. 226 (the two-voiced progression) with pp. 229-30 (the restatement by full orchestra and chorus).

[6]See François Couperin, *Pièces d'orgue*(Paris, 1690), ed. Paul Brunold (Monaco, 1949), p. 62. In the "Fugue sur la Trompette" (the second couplet of the Kyrie of the *Messe pour les "couvents"*), the fugue subject, which has both a raised and a lowered seventh, is harmonized with a cross-relation at measure 23.

Example 8 "Le charme," mm. 3-4. From François Couperin, *Les Goûts réunis* (Paris, 1724), Concert IX.

Basse-continue

We are now ready to return to the series of questions which was posed earlier. It is not likely that an English practice would suddenly have been taken up in France late in the 17th century, and I think that the notion of one-sided influence, whether English-French or French-English, must be set aside for lack of documentation. On the other hand, it is quite possible that the two nations achieved the same effect in slightly different ways, and that both French and English usages of the "English cadence" stem from an international 16th-century practice, one which has become exclusively associated with English music only in modern times. In 17th-century England, the "English cadence" continued in use, and this keyboard device became the basis for the "divisions" that Blow's accompanist was to supply at certain cadences. From the 18th century on, the "English cadence" was cultivated as a deliberate archaism, especially in Cathedral Music(ke). In 17th-century France, the "English cadence" likewise continued in use. It abounds in the organ music of Titelouze; it occurs in harpsichord pieces by Louis Couperin and Etienne Richard; Lebègue uses it freely; and by the closing years of the century it is to be found practically everywhere. The "English cadence" survived in 18th-century France as a striking melodic-harmonic gesture: the composer supplied the "division" and left the cross-relation to the accompanist.

Montéclair's problematic passage may therefore be considered as part of a continuous French tradition which ran parallel to a tradition fostered in England. A document such as Blow's "Rules," thus has a certain amount of authority. In light of evidence that the "English cadence" was indeed part of the French musical vocabulary, I propose to accept Blow's solution, not just as a viable one for Montéclair's passage, but as the only possible solution.

Montéclair took the progression of Ex. 5 (or something very like it) as a point of departure for his passage in *La Fortune*, but he made the half cadence still more incomplete. In reducing it further, he scrapped the bass, leaving only the decorative "division"—the only one voice which is not essential to the half cadence. The melodic motive, even when taken out of its harmonic context, is still a striking and characteristic gesture. In *La Fortune* the motive is presented both as a self-sufficient tune and as a bass to be harmonized.[7] In the progression of *La Fortune*, or what is left of the progression,

[7]The reader will recall the stunning and dramatic effect in Act II of Monteverdi's *Orfeo* when the melody of the refrain "Ahi, caso acerbo" is suddenly used as the *bass* for the five-voiced restatement.

one non-essential part is made to stand for the whole of a well-known gesture—a personal and rather original idea on the part of Montéclair.[8]

It should now be possible to make a realization for Montéclair's problematic bass motive: a realization that will satisfy both the accompanist and the listener, in addition to being stylistically suitable. Either of the hypothetical figurings of Ex. 9 will serve the purpose. The figuring of Ex. 9b is simpler than that of Ex. 9a. It is also clearer. Whether we call the result a "sophisticated form of $\frac{5}{43}$ on g" or an "English cadence" makes little difference, so long as the able accompanist helps the composer by completing his gesture.

Example 9 "La douce esperance," mm. 30-33.

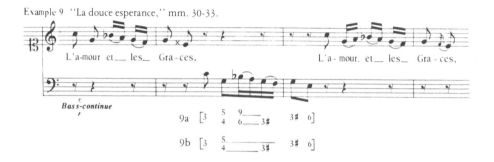

Montéclair's use of a mere fragment of an "English cadence" in place of the whole might suggest at least two things to the thoroughbass player. Having decided to *realize* Montéclair's gesture by supplying harmonies that will make it complete, he can point up the gesture still further by introducing another similar harmonic event in his accompaniment *before* Montéclair's gesture has occurred. The opportunity presents itself at measure 16 of "La douce esperance." The text "enchaîne les coeurs!" inspired the composer to do a bit of word painting: "enchaîne" is set to a melismatic sequence. The accompanist can underscore this word, and at the same time enhance the musical climax of the phrase by introducing an "English cadence" in his accompaniment. The "English cadence" not only fits in perfectly here, but it also helps to prepare for the gesture that is to come at measures 30-33. My proposed accompaniment is given in Ex. 10.

[8]He followed the same procedure in *L'Amour vangé* (*Cantates*, II [Paris, *ca.* 1717], p. 4, mm. 1-12).

Example 10   "La douce esperance," mm. 14-17.

En - chaf - - - - - - - ne, En-chaf - ne les coeurs!

Basse-continue

Having played two "English cadences" in the cantata, the accompanist might be tempted to see if the opportunity exists for introducing more of them. In "Non, non la Fortune volage," the cantata's closing air ["In Which The Moral Is Presented"], the familiar formula occurs at measure 38. In spite of the figuring of the bass, which seems to call for a diatonic sixth on the penultimate beat of the half cadence, I think the accompanist will wish to play a major sixth, making an "English cadence." The cross-relation will coincide with the word "esclavage" in the moralizing verses ("Et dans son funeste esclavage / tous nos plaisirs sont imparfaits'')—a bit of word-painting on the part of the accompanist.[9].

How did the "English cadence" achieve and maintain its place as a thoroughbass device in 18th-century France? I suspect that it was originally a "gimmick" used by organists and harpsichordists in their improvised harmonizations and that it had gained a status which was more or less legitimate by the late 17th century. The style of improvised harmonization is touchingly illustrated in an "arrangement" of Lully's march from *Thésée* (1675) which is preserved in a 17th-century anthology of keyboard pieces.[10]

---

[9]The accompanist may also wish to "complete the gesture" in—to choose but two examples"La Vivacité" (Couperin, Concert IX), m. 9, and the Prélude to Philidor's Sonata in d minor (ed. Hugo Ruf, *Hortus Musicus* 139), m. 11. Philidor's is a more complex form of the "English cadence". Ruf's realization is correct (according to the figures), but the cadence would gain in intensity and interest with the addition of the figures shown in brackets: $\begin{bmatrix}5\\3\end{bmatrix} \begin{smallmatrix}[7]\\ \flat\end{smallmatrix} \begin{bmatrix}5\\4\end{bmatrix} \begin{smallmatrix}7\\ [\#]\end{smallmatrix}$

[10]*Livre d'orgue attribué à J.-N. Geoffroy*, ed. Jean Bonfils (Paris, 1974), p. 109.

The original and the transcription are superposed in Ex. 11. Lully's brave and commanding tonic-dominant harmonies are replaced in the arrangement by incredibly gauche progressions which would have shocked Lully. The arranger evidently knew the march only as a tune, and in his arrangement supplied harmonies (including a full-fledged "English cadence") which seemed to him to be like those he had heard other keyboardists improvise.

Example 11   "La Marche". From J.-B. Lully, *Thésée* (Paris, 1688), I:viii.
A Lully's original setting, p. 146.

B An "arrangement" from Paris, BN, rés. 476, published as: *Livre d'orgue attribué à J.-N. Geoffroy*, ed. Jean Bonfils (Paris, 1974), p. 109.

A

B

The "English cadence" was never discussed by French theorists. Since it breaks well-known rules, there is no particular reason why they should *not* have mentioned it. They continually warned their readers about "non-harmonic relations" and "false relations." Their silence may be due to the peculiar custom of notating only part of the "English cadence." No cross-relation is to be seen in the notes themselves; it is introduced "accidentally" by the thoroughbass player; and the rules, although broken in performance, are still observed on paper.

CLEMENTI'S SELF-BORROWINGS: THE REFINEMENT OF A MANNER *

By Jerald C. Graue

Until recently, an objective assessment of the career of Muzio Clementi has been virtually impossible. The reputation of this once-illustrious composer, who was nearly universally praised by his contemporaries as the "father of the pianoforte," has gradually dimmed through generations of mystery and misinformation. Now there exist an exemplary catalogue of his works,[1] a major modern study of his life and music,[2] and a number of important smaller contributions that help to clarify his historical position.

The history of harsh pronouncements concerning Clementi can be traced to his pianoforte duel with Mozart in 1781, after which Mozart made some rather caustic remarks about Clementi in his letters. Mozart called his opponent "a charlatan — like all Italians," and " a mere mechanician," among other things.[3] As Mozart's correspondence later became known, his statements helped to shape the views of later generations toward Clementi, despite the fact that we now know that Mozart's contact with his opponent occurred at a very early, immature stage in Clementi's development, and that petty jealousy may have contributed to the severity of Mozart's remarks.[4]

Later critics have generally been somewhat milder in their views of Clementi's merit, but they have continued to reflect a grossly inadequate knowledge of the composer's work. Partial knowledge is surely responsible for some of the conflicts in statements made by generally trustworthy writers. Schumann, for example, referred to Clementi's "*contrapuntal*, often cold art,"[5] while more recently Charles Rosen has described Clementi's music as consisting of "loose, basically melodic structures."[6] We can only conclude that both writers knew only a small portion of Clementi's output. In other cases, a strong interpretive bias has led to false notions regarding Clementi's music. Philip Barford characterized Clementi's work as formalistic, repetitive, and, we must

---

*A version of this paper was presented at the Eastman School of Music on January 25, 1974, in the series, *Music in the 18th Century*.

[1] Alan Tyson, *Thematic Catalogue of the Works of Muzio Clementi* (Tutzing, 1967).

[2] Leon Plantinga, *Clementi: His Life and Music* (London, 1977).

[3] Emily Anderson, ed. and trans., *The Letters of Mozart and his Family* (London, 1966), II, pp. 793 and 850.

[4] For a well-balanced discussion of this conflict, see Leon Plantinga, "Clementi, Virtuosity, and the 'German Manner,' " *Journal of the American Musicological Society*, XXV (1972), pp. 303-330.

[5] Robert Schumann, *On Music and Musicians* (New York, 1969), p. 67.

[6] Charles Rosen, *The Classical Style* (New York, 1972), p. 454.

infer, unimaginative.[7] The fact that Clementi's best-known works — namely a handful of sonatinas and the *Gradus ad Parnassum* — are clearly pedagogical in their orientation has no doubt assisted in the preservation of a narrow and inaccurate picture of his music.

One additional feature of Clementi's posthumous reputation that should be noted is the simple fact that there has been progressively less attention given his music from the early 19th century up to the very recent past. He enjoyed stunning material success and high respect as an artist in his own lifetime, and yet his image faded rapidly in the 19th century. Sporadically, some sensitive writers have called for a broader appreciation of Clementi and his music, and they include John Shedlock, Eric Blom, and Georges de Saint-Foix,[8] but the brilliance of the great triumvirate of classical masters has effectively eclipsed Clementi from the attention of scholars and musicians generally. As a consequence of inattention and bias, there has been no basis for a comprehensive understanding of Clementi's development as a composer, and it is precisely that kind of understanding that is essential for an estimation of his real historical function and significance.

Now that a groundwork has been laid by recent scholarship, many basic questions need to be asked: was Clementi really as pedantic as he has sometimes been portrayed? What are the truly unique features of his style? Was he more interested in commercial appeal than in serious art? How does he relate to his contemporaries? What were his working methods? All of these questions cannot be treated in a brief essay, but I propose to contribute toward a reconsidered view of Clementi by exposing certain characteristic aspects of his working habits that serve to illuminate the nature of his growth as a composer.

The problem that I choose to deal with, then, is an extremely limited one: it is an investigation of the extent to which Clementi used his own published compositions as sketches, or sources, for subsequent works. My aim is to expose a facet of his creative process that seems especially consistent with his character as a man, and, because of this close coincidence between his personality and his music, the phenomenon is strikingly idiosyncratic. Before reviewing the musical evidence that bears on the argument, certain outstanding features of Clementi's personality must be considered. In order to achieve the high degree of success that he enjoyed as a composer, performer, teacher, publisher, and manufacturer, clearly he was a man of striking ability and uncommon versatility.

One of the keys to Clementi's success in business enterprises was a thriftiness that became almost legendary. So many stories of his penny-pinching habits were in circulation that a writer for the *Allgemeine musikalische Zeitung* in 1802 felt obliged to publish a defense:

[7]Philip Barford, "Formalism in Clementi's Pianoforte Sonatas," *Monthly Musical Record,* LXXXII (1952), pp. 205-208 and 238-241.

[8]John Shedlock, "Muzio Clementi," *Monthly Musical Record* XXIV (1894), pp. 171-173; Eric Blom in his *Classics Major and Minor* (London, 1958); and Georgoes de Saint-Foix, "Muzio Clementi," *Musical Quarterly* IX (1923), pp. 350-382.

I take the opportunity here to contradict a false notion concerning this master that has been spread in Germany: namely, Clementi is a great virtuoso, a great composer, but a shabby skinflint! That is what I had heard generally and indeed had also read. I was so much the more surprised when I became acquainted with the man himself. The first and second parts of that expression are certainly substantiated; and one might add: Clementi is a clever fellow, an intelligent man of the world, and also a mechanical genius: but the third part is false. Hopefully no one will find fault with the fact that he used the profits of his former situation when he gave private instruction; that he acquired a considerable fortune that he now possesses an instrument factory and music shop . . . that deserves attention; that he used the genuine brilliance of his position so much to the benefit of the good things of art . . . this deserves thanks.[9]

That Clementi was thrifty to the point of eccentricity still seems reasonably certain. Ludwig Spohr recounted in his autobiography that when he met Clementi with his pupil John Field in St. Petersburg in 1803, he once found the wealthy master and his student busily occupied washing their own laundry. Clementi pointed out to Spohr that washing in St. Petersburg "was not only very expensive, but the linen suffered greatly from the method used in washing it."[10] A third sample of Clementi's economy can be observed in the condition of the large collection of his manuscripts currently residing in the Library of Congress. The margins are trimmed so close to the musical text that identifying notes, tempos, clefs, and titles are often not to be found. Heinrich Simon, who was the first scholar to study those manuscripts, believed that the trimming was done by Clementi himself as an effort to conserve valuable paper.[11]

The inevitable impression left by such evidence is that Clementi was reluctant to waste anything unnecessarily. It is my hypothesis that this trait extended to his compositional thinking as well. However, an equally significant feature of his personality, for the issues at hand, is his impressive personal erudition. He spoke several languages fluently, he had a formidable knowledge of ancient Latin and greek literature, and he was keenly interested in the sciences as well as in the scientific aspects of music. At one point in the late 1780's following a disappointing love affair, Reichardt tells us that Clementi seriously considered giving up music entirely in favor of astronomy.[12]. Another premise essential to this view of Clementi's compositional methods is that his affinity for all things intellectual is reflected in the highly systematic working out of musical materials that can be observed in his compositions, both separately and collectively.

[9]Anonymous report, *Allgemeine musikalische Zeitung*, V (1802), cols. 196-197.

[10]*Louis Spohr's Autobiography* (London, 1865), I, pp. 39-40.

[11]See Heinrich Simon, "The Clementi Autographs at the Library of Congress," *Musical Quarterly*, XXVIII (1942), pp. 105-114.

[12]J. F. Reichardt, *Musikalische Monatschrift*, 2. Stück (August, 1792), p. 38.

The most important sources of evidence regarding Clementi's creative process are the various musical documents he has left us, although the interpretation of the documents is closely contingent upon the personal idiosyncrasies just described. Nearly all of his compositions were published in his own lifetime, so those authentic printed scores form one of the most important resources for a study of his style. The chronological ordering and relative reliability of the printed scores have been firmly established since the publication of Tyson's thematic catalogue in 1967, and all references to compositions in this essay follow Tyson's ordering.

The manuscript sources for Clementi's music are problematic. There are numerous autograph manuscripts, the largest collections being found in the British Library and in the Library of Congress, but most of them seem to be late revisions of previously-published compositions. It is symptomatic that when Breitkopf & Haertel began publishing the complete works of Clementi shortly after 1800, the composer seems to have undertaken a wholesale revision of his output, rather than permit the re-publication of his works from their authentic editions. Some of the surviving manuscripts were apparently intended for that complete edition. Consequently, the manuscript sources often represent after-thoughts rather than versions of works that antedate the first appearance of the work in print.

In addition to printed scores and manuscripts, a third resource that is helpful in evaluating Clementi's works is the small body of contemporary reviews and memoirs of Clementi that exists. The value of these documents can be seen most clearly when they transmit Clementi's own opinions regarding his compositions. For example, a memoir written by his business partner William Collard and no doubt authorized by the composer himself fails to include his opus 1 in the list of works. This fact, combined with other bits of evidence, supports the notion that Clementi came to regard his first published works as singularly unsuccessful.[13]

All of these contemporary sources provide a basis for an investigation of Clementi's creative process. But the focus of this study is not to explore *all* of the implications inherent in the sources; it is rather to examine his tendency to preserve what he perceived to be the most promising aspects of his style and to submit his musical materials to systematic refinement and elaboration.

If each successive composition is considered a potential source that the composer might draw upon in later works, then the meaning of the designation "self-borrowing" may be clarified. It is possible, obviously, to deduce or even to impose a seemingly logical scheme of evolutionary development upon the works of many composers, and one could easily discuss Clementi's development in just such terms. But self-borrowing has far more specific implications within his music. That is, in addition to the gradual refinement of general features of his style, Clementi frequently subjected particular, isolated ideas from one work to a re-working within another composition. The phenomenon of recasting definable fragments of music occurs most frequently among his early works, in which many aspects of his style are relatively unstable. He was rarely content to permit an attractive idea to languish in a flawed composition. The idea was often resurrected, transformed and improved, in a later work. Predictably some of the richest sources for such musical reincarnation are the compositions that Clementi

[13]Most of the relevant evidence is presented in Tyson, *op. cit.*, pp. 13-14, 16, and 33-35.

regarded as his worst. Very few of his compositions can be viewed as abject failures, but there is solid evidence that Clementi virtually disowned his opus 1, and the *Magazin der Musik* in 1784 reported that he regarded op. 3 as his worst opus.[14] Such clear statements of the composer's own views are admittedly scarce, but they firmly establish his self-critical attitude and underscore his penchant for revision.

As he matured artistically, Clementi's music offers progressively fewer instances of this selective resuscitation of details, and in order to link that phenomenon to a broader chronological view of his development, I might suggest a rough periodization for his career. The critical, formative phases of his growth occurred before 1791 and include his youth in Italy, his early years in Dorset and London, travels on the Continent between 1781 and 1784, and a period of professional re-evaluation in the late 1780's. In the 1790's Clementi's style was fully formed, and he worked productively until about 1802. Between 1802 and his death in 1832, he wrote very few new pianoforte works, although he did go on to produce the monumental *Gradus ad Parnassum*. His attention was increasingly occupied in his later years by pedagogical projects, symphony composition, and business ventures. Considering his career as a whole, many of his best works were written after 1790, but the earlier works hold a special fascination because they reveal the step-by-step formation of his style.

I do not want to suggest that in his early years Clementi had a finite stock of ideas that he presented and re-presented in various guises. His recycling techniques yield only a partial portrait of the growing composer; moreover, there are several distinct species of the phenomenon that should be differentiated. On the largest level he showed an occasional tendency to cultivate certain structural novelties that affect the organization of whole movements or whole sonatas. On a more detailed level, there are rare instances in which several ideas from one work reappear in an otherwise totally different composition. A more frequent pattern is the borrowing of a single detail from one work for a new treatment in another work. In most cases, the essential idea that Clementi re-uses is either a specific thematic design or a distinctive textural configuration that produces a characteristic sonority.

When a particular composition achieved significant notoriety on its own, it seems that Clementi preferred to revise the entire work without changing its identity rather than to submit isolated details to a revised treatment in different compositions. This is certainly the case with his famous C major sonata from opus 2, sometimes called "the Octave Lesson." It appeared in at least six different authentic editions, one of which was given a new opus number, op. 30, perhaps because the work was "modernized" by the addition of a slow movement. Similarly the Sonata in A major, op. 2, No. 4, appeared later as op. 31, newly furnished with a slow introduction according to current fashion.

A more radical operation was necessary to salvage the few parts of opus 1 that the composer viewed as having some modest merit. Almost ten years after opus 1 had been published in London, Clementi published another opus 1 — called *Oeuvre 1* — with Bailleux in Paris. The new opus 1 was an unabashed attempt to replace the earlier collection with works that would not embarrass their creator. The first four sonatas of

---

[14]*Magazin der Musik,* II (1784), p. 371.

Oeuvre 1 use some sections from the sonatas of the earlier opus 1, but the new collection is properly treated by Tyson in his catalogue as a wholly separate production.[15]

Normally, Clementi allowed his weaker compositions to die a much quieter death. It seems possible, for example, that he subtly attempted to replace his opus 3 duets and sonatas with the 6 sonatas of opus 4. It is probably an injury to Clementi's good name that the opus 3 duets are among the few of his works that are still easily obtainable in print. The entire opus unites modest technical demands with a structural sameness that blights the whole production. The main themes are simple, triadic, and essentially undifferentiated. Five of the six finales belong to the most rudimentary category of rondo. Some notion of the formulaic appearance of opus 3 can be gained by observing that each of the first movements in the three duets contains a third well-defined thematic idea that is characterized in each case by imitation (Example 1). The opus 4 sonatas are also modest works, but they reveal a variety of formal design that seems self-conscious and exploratory when compared to the monotony of opus 3. The most suggestive relationship between the two publications is the similarity of certain essential points in two sonatas in C major: op. 3, No. 6, and op. 4, No. 3. In the first movements, points of special resemblance are the second themes (Example 2) and the beginnings of the development sections. The opening themes of the finales are also clearly cut from the same cloth (Example 3). These similarities may be the most tangible evidence of the salvage operation that Clementi was attempting when he wrote his opus 4, and this relationship may be the most extreme instance of subtle substitution that can be observed among Clementi's works.

Perhaps the most consequential of the relationships under study here are the instances in which the structural techniques from an early work are revived in the organization of a later, more mature composition. An F major sonata, op. 2, No. 5, has special importance in this regard, and it is remarkable that this early work is among the least-

Example 1
Clementi: **Duets** Op. 3
Op. 3 No. 1
[Allegro spiritoso]

cont'd.

[15]Cf. Tyson, *op. cit.*, pp. 31-33.

Ex. 1, *cont'd.*

Op. 3 No. 2

Op. 3, No. 3

Example 2
Clementi: *Sonata* Op. 3 No. 6/i, second theme
[Allegro spiritoso]

Clementi: *Sonata* Op. 4 No. 3/i, second theme
[Allegro e spiritoso]

Example 3
Clementi: *Sonata* Op. 3 No. 6/ii
Allegro

Clementi: *Sonata* Op. 4 No. 3/ii
Allegro

discussed of Clementi's compositions. It is the best early example of the kind of motivic unity that became a norm in his mature style. Several scholars have asserted that Clementi learned the principle of thematic unification from the Haydn works he encountered in Vienna, yet Clementi's opus 2 already affords us an example of thoroughgoing thematic unity that predates Haydn's influential op. 33 string quartets by about three years, and of course it precedes Clementi's own visit to Vienna. The first movement of Clementi's sonata is dominated throughout by the first theme (Example 4). This theme forms the basis for a transitional section (4b), and it becomes, in diminution, the second part of the second theme (4c). The closing theme also reiterates the first theme in an undisguised variant (4d). Perhaps the most novel use of the thematic idea is its appearance in the second, final movement of the sonata. New variants of the motive appear at the ends of each of the contrasting episodes of the rondo, giving the motive genuine cyclic significance (one is shown in 4e).

Clementi's next use of a similarly cyclic design was in his three-movement sonata, opus 5, No. 3, which was also written before his visit to Vienna. The contour of the first

Example 4

Clementi: *Sonata* Op. 2 No. 5 (pianoforte only)

A. Allegro

first movement, transition

B. [Allegro]

first movement, last half of second theme

C. [Allegro]

first movement, closing theme

D. [Allegro]

second movement, "B" section

E. [Allegretto]

theme generates variants in the second theme and in the opening moments of each of the other two movements (Example 5). One of the noteworthy features of this sonata, however, is its use of dramatic contrasts of range and sonority that became enduring qualities in Clementi's music. Indeed, the effect of the double-octave opening was so pleasing to Clementi that he used it again for the opening of the second movement of his Sonata, op. 8, No. 3 (Example 6).

Several sonatas written later in the 1780's perpetuate the highly unified schemes that Clementi pioneered in op. 2 and op. 5. Among the most impressive of the later sonatas are the Sonata in G minor, op. 7, No. 3, and the Sonata in F minor, op. 13, No. 6. The G minor sonata is related to op. 5, No. 3, both in its tight motivic construction and in its

Example 5
Clementi: *Sonata* Op. 5 No. 3/i, beginning

Presto

second theme

[Presto]

Clementi: *Sonata* Op. 5 No. 3/ii

Andante

Clementi: *Sonata* Op. 5 No. 3/iii

Prestissimo

Example 6
Clementi: *Sonata* Op. 8 No. 3/ii

[Allegretto]

further exploration of colorful patterns and sonorities. Example 7 shows how the rhythmic relationships among the voices unify first theme, second theme, and closing theme. This particular configuration, in which the entries of the voices are staggered rhythmically, has more than casual significance. Clementi had tried it only once before, in the unprepossessing opening of the finale in Sonata op. 4, No. 5 (Example 8). The idea is given truly epic proportions in the op. 7 sonata, and the striving for richness of texture and sonority is an order of magnitude greater than the effects found in op. 5 (Example 9). The G minor sonata is Clementi's first sonata in a minor key, and it is easily his most powerful work up to that time (1782) in his career.

Example 7
Clementi: *Sonata* Op. 7 No. 3/i, first theme

Allegro con spirito

second theme

[Allegro con spirito]

closing theme

[Allegro con spirito]

Example 8
Clementi: *Sonata* Op. 4 No. 5/ii

Allegretto

Example 9
Clementi: *Sonata* Op. 7 No. 3/i, from development
[Allegro con spirito]

from development
[Allegro con spirito]

Clementi's F minor sonata, op. 13, No. 6, is closely related to the op. 7 sonata in several respects. It is no less impressive in its range of resources and techniques, it is equally cohesive in its formal construction, and it also derives thematic impulses from earlier works. The opening of the first movement can be traced to its source in the Sonata, op.11 (Example 10), but the opus 11 version lacks the highly effective alternation of duple and triple groupings that represents one of Clementi's "improvements" for the op. 13 version. The middle section of the slow movement of op. 13, No. 6, also looks back to a distinctive 9th-leap figure that served as a germ-motive

Example 10
Clementi: *Sonata* Op. 11/i
[Allegro con grazia]

Clementi: *Sonata* Op. 13 No. 6/i
Allegro agitato

for the Sonata op. 8, No. 1 (Example 11). Perhaps coincidentally, the ½ step-plus-leap idea that Clementi borrowed in this case also serves in another permutation to unify *all three* movements of the F minor sonata (Example 12).

Example 11
Clementi: **Sonata** Op. 13 No. 6/ii
[Largo e sostenuto]

Clementi: **Sonata** Op. 8 No. 1/i, from first theme
Allegro

Example 12
Clementi: **Sonata** Op. 13 No. 6
a. first movement
[Allegro agitato]

b. second movement
Largo e sostenuto

c. third movement
Presto

The manner in which thematic interrelationships are created in the F minor sonata gives us persuasive evidence of the increasing sophistication of Clementi's structural thinking. In the first movement, for example, the half-step motive is introduced first as an accompanying figure for the first subject (see Example 12). In the second subject the right-hand melodic figure is used virtually unchanged, but the accompanying figure is present only in its rhythmic profile (Example 13). Almost prophetically, that rhythmic idea happens to be the short-short-short-long made famous by a younger German composer some years later. Since it is the *intervallic* structure of the half-step motive that is most important in the unification of the entire sonata, Clementi's use of that motive as a *rhythmic* abstraction in the second theme is an especially impressive demonstration of the variegation of his structural techniques.

Example 13
Clementi: *Sonata* Op. 13 No. 6/i, second theme

Considered broadly, the F minor sonata may be Clementi's most impressive artistic statement before 1790. After that point, there is relatively less change in his stylistic orientation even though some of his most enduring works were written after that year. The technical mastery that he had acquired in his progress from op. 1 through op. 25 resulted in a much more consistent high level of quality in his later works, even in those designed for dilettantes. Consequently, the phenomenon of musical recycling is rather rare in his maturity. A number of new issues present themselves in the later works nonetheless. For example, beginning in 1794 with his op. 33 sonatas, strict canon and other contrapuntal techniques became frequent devices in his works. In fact, Clementi's last published composition was a canon dedicated to his pupil J. B. Cramer in 1830. However, the central core of his technique remained rather stable in his late works. There *are* occasional reminders of the trial-and-error progress of his early years, and the most fitting retrospective moment in his late works occurs in his last Sonata, op. 50, No. 3, in G minor from 1821. The opening of the finale of this work is an almost mystical recollection of the early masterpieces in G minor and F minor that have just been considered (Example 14). If one compares the op. 50 excerpt with the finale of op. 13,

Example 14
Clementi: *Sonata* Op. 50 No. 3/iii

No. 6, and the opening of op. 7, No. 3, the similarities are striking: each work is in a minor key, each is the last sonata in its opus, and each opens a movement with a triad-based theme placed in the upper-middle range of the instrument. The staggered eighth-note rhythmic support in the left hand in each case is another conclusive link in this coincidental but satisfying relationship.

The limitations inherent in this consideration of certain idiosyncracies in Clementi's growth as an artist preclude sweeping conclusions. On the other hand, the evidence that has been exposed seems sufficient to establish that in Clementi's case we encounter some close connections between the character of the man and the growth of the composer. It also seems safe to conclude that his progress toward maturity was marked by the most systematic self-critical examination of his methods and their results, to the degree that unsatisfactory works were often revised and good ideas were frequently revived. If such carefully calculated growth seems unromantic or callous as a background to such passionate works as the F minor sonata, we might take comfort from the words of another passionate artist, Edgar Allen Poe, who in an essay called ''The Philosophy of Composition'' wrote as follows:

> Most writers . . . prefer having it understood that they compose by a species of fine frenzy — an ecstatic intuition — and would positively shudder at letting the public take a peep behind the scenes . . . .

And in connection with the writing of his famous poem, ''The Raven,'' Poe tells us:

> . . . No one point is referable either to accident or intuition . . . the work proceeded, step by step, to its completion with the precision and rigid consequence of a mathematical problem.

This brief investigation of Clementi's creative workshop does very little injury to the profundity of his art; rather it exposes for greater appreciation the mental processes of one of the most consequential composers of the late 18th century.

SCHOENBERG RE-CYCLED

by Glenn Watkins

I

The continuing search over the last five hundred years for means of unification in compositions of large dimensions has led to a variety of solutions among which the cyclic principle has figured prominently. Indeed, it was precisely this principle which was invoked in the construction of the first large-scale musical edifice, the cantus-firmus mass of the fifteenth century.

The following centuries witnessed the rise and fall of forms alternately indebted to the practice or eschewing its organizational properties altogether. Its revival and near-canonization in the nineteenth century has important implications for musical developments in the twentieth, a century which increasingly reveals its Romantic origins. Whether the germ motif of Beethoven, the *idée fixe* of Berlioz, the *leit-motif* of Wagner, the thematic transformations of Liszt, or the cyclic proclivities of Franck, they were born of the prospect not only for development but for recognizable recurrence in large-scale structures. All such procedures were promoted by the composer's interest in nurturing intelligibility. Solutions by many early twentieth-century composers which are indebted to this nineteenth-century ideal can be observed readily in the string quartets of d'Indy, Debussy, Ravel, Berg, and Schoenberg all of whom followed in the tradition of their Romantic forbearers in their quest for unification through cyclic manipulation.

For the present, I would like to focus on the works of a single composer, Arnold Schoenberg, and briefly review his entire corpus from an angle that concerned him throughout his lifetime, that is to say, from the point of view of "comprehensibility," and attempt to indicate the role that the cyclic process played in its attainment.

II

Two works have appeared in recent years that have enlarged our view of Schoenberg: one, the revised and expanded version of *Style and Idea*,[1] a collection of essays by the

---

[1] *Style and Idea,* ed. by Leonard Stein with translation by Leo Black (New York, 1975).

master over a period of forty years; the other, an overview of Schoenberg by Charles Rosen.[2] The kind of writing indulged in by Rosen is of an order not normally utilized by Schoenbergians, which is to say for the most part, the composer-theorists. Rosen approaches the substance (if not the style) of Schoenberg's own writings about his music and is refreshingly lacking in any preoccupation with set theory and number analysis. By this I do not mean to imply that the latter is without value, only that it has had the better part of it until now, and that it is perhaps strange that such a level of discourse was the first to appear in an attempt to come to terms with Schoenberg. Perhaps it was "In-housekeeping," of value primarily to the composer who needed to know "how it worked" with the possible view of adopting certain aspects of the method, and who was little concerned with the listener's art.

Rosen's statement is valuable because it is an overview which addresses itself to issues other than those that are theoretically complex, and specifically because he attempts, among other things, to describe Schoenberg the neoclassicist. That he took such great pains to maneuver Schoenberg into a position which bespeaks a compatibility between serialism and the neoclassic aims of the 1920s is remarkable only because it had not been attempted before. The issue, verbally expressed by many but now treated for the first time at any length in print, is destined to be the object of even more rigorous assessment. A number of documents that still reside in the Schoenberg archives, a scrutiny of the Schoenberg cantata, *Der Neue Klassizismus*, curiously ignored by Rosen, and other works of the period will help us to sharpen not only our meaning of "neoclassicism," but also to understand the reasons for the fundamental antagonism born of this time and issue between Schoenberg and Stravinsky. For the present I would like to treat a formal issue that may be tangentially related to the subject of neoclassicism but which I suspect ought to be in the main separated from it. By so doing, the limits of the term may be somewhat clarified. The ideas proposed here should surprise no one even vaguely familiar with Schoenberg's music; yet it may be fair to claim that the emphasis placed on the relationship between two well-known quantities, cyclicism and the series, has hardly been made before.

The prominent attention which Schoenberg accorded the question of repetition and his views toward it have been largely responsible for encouraging the public to believe that his music moved to the most distant consequences of a stated idea too swiftly for the normal ear to comprehend. Under the subheading, "Repetition," in the essay *New Music, My Music* (c. 1930) he gave the critics all the ammunition they needed to pronounce his music unintelligible:

1. Substantially, I say something only once, i.e., repeat little or nothing.

2. With me, variation almost completely takes the place of repetition (there is hardly a single exception to this).

3. Not only are new sections, as so further developed, linked one to another or juxtaposed or lined up . . . but, particularly, almost the only aid to one's

[2]Charles Rosen, *Arnold Schoenberg* (New York, 1975).

perception of all these types of combination is logic and an acute sense of form.

Yet the composer continues in a vein which complements Berg's essay of 1925 concerning the difficulties in understanding Schoenberg's music:

> In general, music is always hard (not even relatively hard) to understand—unless it is made easier by repetition of as many minute, small, medium or large sections as possible. The first precondition for understanding is, after all, memory . . . The more easily graspable a piece of music is to be, the more often all its sections, small or large, will have to be repeated. Conversely, the fewer sections are repeated, and the less often, the harder the piece of music is to understand.[3]

Schoenberg regards the avoidance of exact repetition, the pursuit of immediate variation and continuing development as traits of his style, traits which he traces to the Brahms school. Schubert, Schumann and Wagner[4] are in his mind the great repeaters of melodic, harmonic, and rhythmic figure, the abusers of sequence (even if not so vulnerable as Tchaikowsky and Rimsky-Korsakof, whom he denigrates above all other in this regard). The issues for the paradox are set: 1) unvarying repetition is not to be admired; 2) music totally without repetition, and recognizably so, risks unintelligibility. The issue of comprehensibility obsesses Schoenberg throughout his life. The source of the obsession is to be seen in these two tenets.

III

The issue of repetition, which we have seen was sufficiently lively to spawn a large portion of an essay as late as 1930, relates in most of Schoenberg's writings to the idea of close-quarter restatement; a series of contiguous varied repetitions leads to the quality of developing variation which was dear to Schoenberg's heart. The idea of repetition at a sizeable distance, not in the developmental sense but with the aspect of recall, is an equally important issue which relates to larger issues of formal structure. In a word, an idea may in reasonably quick succession generate a dozen related ideas and provide a logical forward propellant, but in many musical forms there is a need to indicate a sense of return, and in such instances an additional development or variation even further

---

[3]*Style and Idea*, p. 102.

[4]In "Criteria for the Evaluation of Music," *Style and Idea*, pp. 128-130, Schoenberg asserts that the repetitious character of rhythm and motif in Schubert, Schumann and even Wagner "accomodated, probably instinctively, to the popular feeling." Brahms showed the way to the future when he "repeated phrases, motives and other structural ingredients of themes only in varied forms." Schoenberg continues, "A new technique had to be created, and in this development Max Reger, Gustav Mahler, and also I myself played a role. But the destructive consequences did not cease because of that. And unfortunately many of todays composers . . . produce compositions which become longer and broader only by numerous unvaried repetitions of a few phrases. I have made here the grave mistake of calling a criterion of compositorial technique 'destructive' as if it were now proven for all time to come that such a procedure is worthless."

removed from the original does not serve the composer's purpose. This requirement in a host of classical forms (sonata, song and trio, rondo, cyclic structures, etc.) was one that Schoenberg did not shy away from, and his early interest in delineating the structure of his works is mirrored in various analytical diagrams of works written in the first decade of the twentieth century. Berg, with the obvious approval of the composer himself, published an analysis of *Pelléas and Mélisande* (1903) as late as 1920, which elucidates not only the symphonic poem's dramatic structure but its compatibility with the design of a four-movement symphony. The final movement also functions as a recapitulation of the first movement and introduces cyclic elements through the incorporation of materials from interior movements as well. The same qualitites of double function and cyclic recall operate in the first string quartet (1905), which is provided with an analysis by the composer in the preface to the score. That similar principles of formal organization continued to prove fundamental in the music written before 1909 is observable in the *Kammersymphonie*, op. 9 (1906), which was also provided with an analysis by Berg along the lines of *Pelléas and Mélisande*. Speaking of the two views of the symphony's form (one large movement with recapitulation, or five movements cyclically related), Berg says:

> Whichever of these two explanations may be nearer the mark, it is in any case true that the work's form . . . results as much from the *constant* references back to earlier thematic components . . . as from the dovetailing . . . of the individual sections within this single long movement.[5]

The *Kammersymphonie* together with the *String Quartet No. 2* (1908) were crucial works in the composer's transition to such expressionist creations as *Erwartung* (1909) and *Pierrot Lunaire* (1912), wherein the formal principles of which we have just spoken are suddenly abandoned with threatening consequences. Yet the appeal of cyclic recall lingers on in the second string quartet, though not in a manner as thoroughgoing as before. Although the structure is in four separate movements, and the final movement fails to function as a recapitulation, Schoenberg in the preface to his score details for the listener the relationship between the theme for a set of variations (movement three) and the other movements, as follows:

> The theme consists of four motives which represent transformations of motives taken from the preceding movements. Motive I is taken from the 1st theme of the 1st movement; motive II from the 2nd theme of the 1st movement; motive III is from the 2nd theme of the Scherzo; and motive IV from the 1st movement theme of the subsidiary section.

All in all, it is tempting to see in the second string quartet and the *Drei Klavierstücke*, op. 11 (compare no. 1, mm. 1-2 with no. 3, mm. 24-5), evidence of the gradual dissolution of nineteenth-century structural principles on the eve of his entry into a world of music "from other planets," a last farewell to a perhaps somewhat shopworn formal aesthetic. Actually, the farewell proved to be only *Aufwiedersehen*.

---

[5]Published by Universal Edition, 1913.

IV

The so-called Expressionist Period (1909-15) of Schoenberg is marked by a brief catalogue of works—works which sparked a creative crisis and ultimate silence. They are by common consent Schoenberg's most radical works, and it is precisely in the area of thematic delineation, development, and restatement as much as in the question of tonality that we sense the crisis of these works. As Schoenberg stated:

> Intoxicated by the enthusiasm of having freed music from the shackles of tonality, I had thought to find further liberty of expression. In fact I myself and my pupils Anton von Webern and Alban Berg, and even Alois Haba believed that now music could renounce motivic features and remain coherent and comprehensible nevertheless.[6]

From this period Schoenberg left us a handful of masterpieces in which the creative spirit burned radiantly, but whose formal aspect was guided largely by intuition or a text. The ultimate rescue from his dilemma was provided by the discovery of the twelve-note series, but the rescue must be viewed as twofold: 1) by establishing an order of pitch succession for the total chromatic, a non-tonal terrain was encouraged; 2) in this same establishment of order resided the potential ingredients for the reintroduction of a more pronounced motivic content. Simultaneously, in Schoenberg's insistence that one and the same series serve as the basis for multi-movement compositions, the seeds for the reintroduction of cyclic phenomena were planted.

Even in the essentially non-serial *Serenade*, op. 24 (1920-3), written immediately prior to and contemporaneously with his first all-embracing serial ventures, we see the return to cyclic patterning. Because of Schoenberg's heavy reliance upon the suite and a variety of dance forms in other works of the 1920s, the *Serenade* has generally been viewed as related to works like the *Suite for Piano,* op. 25, and the *Septet,* op. 29. There are, however, larger formal properties at work that need to be stressed. A work in seven movements, the Finale is clearly audible as a recapitulation of the opening March movement. In addition there are thematic similarities between the several interior movements (the trio of the second movement, the first variation of the third movement, and the Waltz section of the Dance Scene, for example). Furthermore, the Finale serves not only as recapitulation of the first movement but introduces themes from earlier movements as well. The final gesture of the work (the coda to the last movement, *Poco Adagio*, m.149) simultaneously presents the Waltz theme (movement five) together with the principle theme from the *Song Without Words* (movement six) before closing with material common to movements one and seven. Schoenberg was also proud to claim relatedness between materials of different sections of the same movement, as witnessed by his remark:

---

[6]"My Evolution" (1949), *Style and Idea*, p. 88.

> The tones of the first measure of the Tanzscene appear—in a different order—as accompaniment in the Valse part. The clarinet adds the remaining six tones.[7]

While this statement undoubtedly reflects more of an awareness of proto-serial procedures than cyclic planning, Schoenberg might well have pointed to the thematic relationships in this work among the several movements and thereby suggested a backward-looking as well as a forward-looking aspect for the work. In any event, the cyclic principle was to prove of increasing importance for his immediately ensuing works. Less perceptible, perhaps, in the initial serial compositions such as the *Suite for Piano*, op. 25, and the *Woodwind Quintet*, op. 26, this quality becomes increasingly evident and audible in the *Septet*, op. 29, and is elevated to a major point of style in Schoenberg's final creations of the 1930s and 1940s.

V

There is no need to cite in detail the many works from Schoenberg's last period which demonstrate the overt re-subscription of cyclic procedures. It should be sufficient to suggest the most important of these pieces and to indicate the relationship of the operative formal components to the works of his first period. Four masterworks from the decades in question are ideal choices: the *Violin Concerto*, op. 36 (1936), the *Fourth String Quartet*, op.37 (1937), the *Piano Concerto*, op. 42 (1942), and the *String Trio*, op. 45 (1946).

At the beginning of the 1930s, in an essay intended for a proposed treatise on composition, Schoenberg reiterated once more:

1. One understands only what one can take note of.
2. One can easily take note of something only if it is
    a) clear
    b) frequently repeated
    c) not too long[8]

The issue of comprehensibility continues to haunt the composer, and toward this end he proceeds to make adjustments in his musical syntax, particularly with respect to phraseology and rhythm—adjustments that promote the objective of 2 a,b,c, above. The opening of the *Violin Concerto* illustrates this increasing propensity: the initial two-measure phrase structure is repeated four times, and its thematic identity is forged through interval (minor 2nd) and rhythm (dotted figure).

---

[7] "My Evolution," p. 90.

[8] "For a Treatise on Composition" (1931), *Style and Idea*, p. 267.

Example 1

In the fourth repetition (mm. 6-7) the rhythmic figure is already modified into a pattern which will identify the opening rhythmic material of the second movement: it is also projected in neatly-packaged, two-measure units.

In the opening of the third movement the ideas are also remarkably easy to grasp (clear, frequently repeated, not too long) and similarly laid out, in one of the most foursquare statements in all of Schoenberg.

Example 3
Movement III

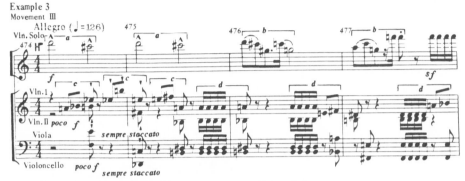

The four motives which constitute the opening of the movement are reworked and repeated throughout the movement and are subjected to various tranformations.[9] An additional motif is introduced which is reminiscent of both the first- and second-movement principal material and serves a prominent role throughout the course of the movement.

Example 4

In the final cadenza, a cyclic résumé of the entire concerto is worked out extensively, utilizing all of the motives mentioned above.

Example 5, (mm. 647-650 and 666-669)

[9]For a discussion of these transformations see the author's ''Understanding Schoenberg,'' *Perspectives of New Music*, forthcoming.

Example 5 *(contd.)*

© G. Shirmer, 1939; renewed by Gertrude Schoenberg, 1967. Used by permission.

It is one of the most elaborate formal recalls in any of the large-scale works of Schoen-berg, and because the individual ideas are trenchant, the cyclic aspect is readily grasped.

The remaining three works from this period which were alluded to above also show a return to premises of unification employed by the young Schoenberg. Thus the *Fourth String Quartet,* op. 37, in addition to the single series which unites all movements, discloses a similarity of basic shape between principal materials of the first and third movements that directly recalls the relationship between the same movements of the *Second String Quartet,* op. 10.

© 1939, G. Schirmer. Used by permission.

© 1912, Universal Edition; renewed 1940 by Arnold Schoenberg.
Used by permission of Belmont Music.

In a similar fashion the *Piano Concerto* and the *String Trio* return to the idea of the double-function form which had been utilized in the *First String Quartet* and the *Kammersymphonie,* op. 9. Thus, in his last and most mature works, the composer

80

furthers not only the development of his serial technique but concurrently forges a link between it and the cyclic principles of his youth. That the serial idea was deemed so compatible with the cyclic principle says something about the notion of the series as Schoenberg viewed it. It could be used as the basis for developing variation and yet, through the retention of the same series for all movements of multi-movement compositions, serve as the natural agent for cyclic recall.

The appeal of the cyclic idea and multiple function structures is visible not only in the works of Schoenberg. Berg, Bartok and Ravel were equally obsessed with the idea at about the same time. Interestingly Ravel's cyclic *String Quartet* (1902-3) and *Sonatine* (1903-5) parallel Schoenberg's own formal solutions of that time, and his *Concerto for the Left Hand* (a double-function one-movement work), first performed in 1932, is analogous to Schoenberg's own contemporaneous concerti.

When the history of the first half of the twentieth century comes to be written with the vision that only additional distance can bring, it may be increasingly related how nineteenth-century structural premises momentarily faded in the second decade of the twentieth century only to be resurrected with a renewed vigor by a host of its major composers in the third and fourth decades. The vitality as well as the breadth of this re-subscription suggests that it cannot all be explained under the banner of neoclassicism.

AN INTRODUCTION TO ALLESANDRO SCARLATTI'S *TIGRANE*

By Michael Collins

Signori e Signore:
    Sentireste dell'impegno d'amore, e
    Fede, vanto dell'onore e di gloria,
    Ascoltate la favola del core
    Del gran Tigrane dell'alta memoria.

"If you would hear of the bonds of love and fealty, the vaunt of honor and glory . . ."
So might a poetic prologue capture the imagination of an audience about to hear
Tigrane, ovvero l'egual impegno d'amore e di fede, libretto by Domenico Lalli and
music by Allesandro Scarlatti, performed at Teatro S. Bartolomeo in Naples, on
February 16,1715.

The stirring fanfares of the *Sinfonia* subside, and the curtain rises to reveal a sump-
tuous pagan temple in which stands an enormous image of the god Mars, adorned with
trophies of war, and a sacrificial altar upon which lies the carcass of a stallion from which
protrudes a gleaming scimitar. A procession is in progress: Tomiri, Queen of the
Scythians, on a golden chariot drawn by slaves, is preceded by a chorus of ceremonial
dancers, and the chariot is surrounded by courtly retainers and custodians of the temple,
one of whom bears a gilded basin containing a severed head. He will place the basin on a
base on which an inscription reads, "This is the head of Ciro, fallen to the strong arm of
Tomiri." To shouts of "long live our great Queen," Tomiri sings that she is commemorating the anniversary of her great victory over Ciro. She commands:

> Attend there! Light the pyre, and consume that ferocious steed in its great
> flames, that his ashes may rise to the great deity.

And then in dramatic accompanied recitative she offers this prayer to Mars:

> Thunderbolt of war, fear of legions, invincible leader of armies and warriors,
> and great terror of the whole world, humbly I offer thee the head of mine
> enemy Ciro, slayer of my son, severed by mine own hand, as a gift on thy
> awesome altar.

What an auspicious beginning! The audience is entranced by the ceremonial
splendor. There is a grand sweep and the ring of truth, although the tale that is to
unfold is based on only the tiniest kernel of historical veracity, if indeed Herodotus
reports something more than legend.[1] The rest is pure operatic fabrication, invented as

---

[1] *Herodotus*, with an English translation by A. D. Godley, Vol. I, *The Loeb Classical Library* (London, 1921).
Subsequent references to Herodotus are drawn from the same source.

the aftermath of the slaying of the Persian Emperor Cyrus the Great by Thomyris, Queen of the Massagetae.[2]

The Massagetae were, according to Herodotus, a nomadic Scythian tribe dwelling on the plains to the east of the Caspian Sea. They prized bronze and gold for their adornments: all their spear-points, arrowheads, and battle-axes were of bronze, and gold adorned their headgear, belts, and girdles. Their horses were adorned in the same manner, the forehands with bronze breastplates, the reins, bits, and cheekplates with gold. They worshipped the sun god and made sacrifices of horses to him, for the reason that he is the swiftest of the gods, and they therefore offer him the swiftest of mortal things.

Desiring the kingdom of the Massagetae, Cyrus wooed the widowed Thomyris, and upon her refusal he attacked her land. Cyrus was victor of the first skirmish through trickery: he crossed the river Araxes, made camp, and then, leaving behind only those who were useless, he marched his army back across the Araxes, leaving a great spread of food and wine. The Massagetae attacked those left behind, slew them, and seeing the banquet, they feasted and drank. When they had fallen asleep from the affects of the food and wine, Cyrus swooped down on them, killing many, and taking many prisoners, among them Spargapises, leader of the Massagetae and son of Thomyris. The Queen, apprised of the disaster, sent a herald to Cyrus with this message:

> Bloodthirsty Cyris, be not uplifted by this that you have done; it is no matter for pride if the fruit of the vine--that fruit whereof you Persians drink even to madness, so that the wine passing into your bodies makes evil words to rise in a flood to your lips--has served you as a drug to master my son withal, by guile and not in fair fight. Now therefore take this word of good counsel from me: give me back my son and depart unpunished from this country; it is enough that you have done despite to a third part of the host of the Massagetae. But if you will not do this, then I swear by the sun, the lord of the Massagetae, that for all you are so insatiate of blood, I will give you your fill thereof.

Cyrus ignored her message, and meanwhile the captive Spargapises did away with himself. A great battle ensued, in which the Persians were defeated and Cyrus himself was killed. According to Herodotus, Thomyris filled a skin with human blood, and put the severed head of Cyrus into it, speaking these words to her victim:

> Though I live and conquer thee, thou hast undone me, overcoming my son by guile; but even as I threatened, so will I do, and give thee thy fill of blood.

So much for history. We now turn to the *Argomento* of the libretto of *Tigrane*, which recounts that Tomiri had lost both of her infant sons (neither of whom was named Spargapises). The first, Archinto, had been kidnapped by a pirate and sold to the Prince of Armenia, who had taken him to his heart, renamed him Tigrane after his own

[2]Cyrus reigned from 558 to 529 B. C., and it is worthy of note that the Shah of Iran, who claimed to celebrate the 2500th anniversary of the founding of his dynasty in 1971, was actually commemorating the death of his ancestor at the hands of the bellicose Thomyris.

deceased, beloved son, and on his deathbed had made him heir to his Principality. The second son, Seleuco, had in the course of time been slain in battle by Cyrus--a point of contact with historical account. Having been able to avenge herself for this second loss, Tomiri had enlisted the aid of two kings, Policare of Lydia and Doraspe of Damascus, one of whom she had promised to choose as her husband on the first anniversary of her victory. The events of the opera all take place on that fateful day, thus fulfilling the Aristotelian unities of time, place, and action. We find Tomiri procrastinating because of her secret love for the leader of her armies, the Armenian Prince Tigrane, whom in any event she could not marry because he is not of royal lineage.

Now Tigrane had formerly been at the court of Cyrus, where he and Cyrus' daughter Meroe had secretly exchanged vows of betrothal. But with the death of Cyrus, he had been forced to flee. He believes his beloved Meroe to be dead, because she had caused false news of her demise to be spread abroad so that she could come in secret to wreak vengeance upon Tomiri for the death of her father.

When Meroe, disguised as a gypsy fortune-teller, reveals herself to Tigrane, he is caught upon the horns of the sort of dilemma that is the grist for *opera seria:* love demands that he aid Meroe in her quest for vengeance, while honor requires his allegiance to Tomiri. The Aristotelian crux occurs when Tigrane foils Meroe's attempt to assassinate Tomiri and is himself left holding the dagger. In the face of flagrant evidence to the contrary, he can only proclaim his loyalty to Tomiri, secretly protecting his beloved Meroe. Honor binds him to silence, and he is condemned to death. Honor even commands him to remain captive when the love-torn Tomiri offers him an avenue of escape. As may be seen, Tomiri has at this juncture sacrificed both duty and honor to *Amore.*

As Tigrane is about to be slain by the arrows of his own archers, Meroe rushes forth in royal garb, reveals her identity, and confesses her own guilt. She, too, is honorable. But as she is being bound to the stake in Tigrane's stead, Policare bursts upon the scene with word brought by a messenger, sent by the dying pirate, that Tigrane is in reality the long lost son of Tomiri. The denouement is truly Aristotelian, as proof of Tigrane's identity is revealed by the royal Scythian tattoo on his right arm that no one seems to have noticed until this moment.[3] Tomiri's attraction to Tigrane is explained as the famous, 18th-century *voix du sang.* The plot unravels precipitately: Tomiri pardons Meroe and approves her betrothal to Tigrane, Meroe lays aside her lust for vengeance, Tomiri gives her promise of marriage to Policare who brought about the joyous reunion, and Dorilla, the queen's lady-in-waiting yields to the suit of Orcone, the servant of Meroe. These turns of events leave Oronte, Captain of the Guard, to exclaim what a happy day it is, and Doraspe to suffer in peace his misfortune. All join in praising loyalty and honor, the epitome of true virtue.

Tomiri appears to be the only historical personage in the libretto except for the late

---

[3]According to Aristotle in the *Poetics*, signs and marks are the least effective means to unravel an impossible dramatic situation, and their use shows lack of imagination on the part of the dramatist. Nevertheless, it was one of the most common means in 18th-century opera, and was, of course, still being parodied by Gilbert and Sullivan.

Cyrus. There were, however, several Tigranes in history, although Herodotus does not mention any of them in connection with the story of Thomyris. The librettist seems to have brought him into the story from Xenophon's *Cyropaedia*, where he is in fact described as the son of the King of Armenia, who became a general in the army of Cyrus.[4] Xenophon makes no mention in his writing of Thomyris. Our Tigrane is a figment of the librettist's imagination, adopted by a king of Armenia and named for that king's deceased son.

The same use of names culled from a few scraps of historical fact occurs in another libretto, the main character of which is Thomyris, the very queen of the Scythians we have in *Tigrane*. This libretto, *Thomyris, Queen of Scythia*, is by Peter Anthony Motteux (London, 1707), who writes in the preface:

> Tho' all the Airs of this Opera are by the famous [Alessandro] *Scarlatti* and [G. B.] *Buononcini,* except a few by other great Masters [Albinoni, Gasparini, and Steffani], neither the Words, the Thoughts, nor the Design owe anything to *Italy* , except the Advantage of the Musick; to which with more Pleasure yet than Pain, I have endeavour'd to make 'em subservient: I hope those who would not have Sense sacrific'd to Sound, nor the Mind despleas'd while the Ears are entertain'd, will consider the Difficulties in working so many Airs of different Kinds into one Subject, and in putting Words wholly different from the *Italian*, to Songs so full of pathetick Notes and nice Graces, in a Language perhaps too manly for such Composures, if not manag'd with the utmost Art . . . As for the Recitative, Mr. *Pepusch* is known to be so great a Composer, that there is no doubt but he has also done his Part in that, and in adding such Ritornels, and other Musick, as were necessary to make the whole a Compleat Opera.

Interesting comments on the art of translation and the making of a *pasticcio*. Pepusch produced this opera at the Theatre-Royal in Drury Lane in 1707.

The central events of *Thomyris* are the two battles between the Scythians and Persians recounted above from Herodotus, except that the son of Thomyris is called Orontes, not Spargapises, or Seleuco for that matter. He is in love with Cleora, captive niece of Cyrus, who loves him in return. She is, however, affianced by Cyrus to his ally, Tigrane, King of Armenia! In this opera he is certainly no son of Thomyris, but her enemy. The central events, as mentioned above, are the two battles that precede the events of *Tigrane*, and the following lines from Act III, Scene ii of *Thomyris,* in which Orontes is found in chains, reveal their origin in Herodotus:

---

[4]Xenophon, *Cyropaedia,* with an English translation by Walter Miller, Vol. I, *The Loeb Classical Library* (London, 1914), Book III, pp. 1-43.

Orontes: Ha! sure I dream — What objects strike my Eyes!
            To arms — My Sword — Ha! Chain'd — *Tigranes*
            here! — My Fellow Soldiers —
            Ah! ch'io sogno — che remiro — strano oggetto!
            all'armi, all'armi. La mia Spada — Ahi! son
            legato — Qui Tigrane! — Miei Soldati! — [5]

Tigranes: Surpriz'd, like you, Death, or your Chains they
            share. Retreating *Cyrus*, press'd by
            you, His Camp did to the Foe resign, With Dainties
            stor'd, and treach'rous Wine, Your *Scythians*
            to subdue. Lethargic Drugs, mix'd with the
            generous Juice Soon did to Sleep your wearied Troops
            reduce: With Ease a Grave they found in every Bed;
            Buried in Wine and Sleep, already like the Dead.

Orontes: Oh! Fraud alone of Vict'ry cou'd deprive 'em.
            Kill me! Why shou'd I survive 'em?
            Coll'arte sol tu vincergli potevi
            Se l'opra vuoi compir, me pure uccidi!

The second battle, that of Thomyris against the forces of Cyrus in revenge for what she believes to be the death of her son, brings about the death not only of Cyrus, but also of Tigranes. In a reversal of history, Orontes, son of Thomyris, lives to wed Cleora.

Other librettos with the title *Tigrane*, which prove to be about another historical character entirely — Tigranes the Great, King of Armenia (reigned 95-c.56 B.C.) — are based on Francesco Silvani's libretto *La virtù trionfante dell'odio e dell'amore* of 1691, first composed by Ziani in 1691, refurbished by an unknown Neapolitan poet in 1723, and revised and retitled by Carlo Goldoni in 1741.[6]

---

[5]As a point of interest, the "contra-tenor" role of Orontes was sung by "Signior Valentino," who was the only member of the cast to sing in Italian. The libretto gives the English lines followed by the Italian that he sang.

[6]The following listing is from Sonneck's *Catalogue of Opera Librettos:*
    Tigrane, music by Hans Leo Hasse detto il Sassone, for S. Bartolomeo, Naples, November, 1723.
    Tigrane, by Bartolo Vitturi, music by Giuseppe Antonio Paganelli, for Teatro di Sant'Angelo, Venice, Carneval, 1733.
    Tigrane, by C. Goldoni, music by Arene, for Teatro di San Giovanni Grisostomo, Venice, 1741.
    Tigrane, for the fair at Crema in 1743. Apparently an unknown opera by Gluck.
    Tigrane, for the Real Teatro di SanCarlo, Naples, November 4, 1745. Arias marked by S. are by Sig. Gio Adolfo Asse detto il Sassone, as well as music for scene ii of the third act; all the recitatives, sinfonia, and some arias are by Antonio Palella, maestro di cappella napolitana, direttore dell'opera.
    Tigrane, by C. Goldoni, music by Lampugnani, for Teatro di Sant'Angelo, Venice, Ascensione, May 10, 1747.

One further opera that is in fact based on the same story as our *Tigrane* is *Die grossmüthige Thomyris*, libretto by J.J. Hoe, composed for Hamburg by Reinhard Keiser in 1717.[7]

Scarlatti's libretto of *Tigrane*, then, seems to have originated with Domenico Lalli, who himself was a person of some interest. The following quotation details his biography in capsule form:

> Lalli's real name was Sebastiano Biancardi. He was born at Naples in 1679 and died at Venice in 1741. Apparently his position as clerk in a Naples bank proved to be too much of a temptation for him: he was accused of embezzlement, and we may assume that he was guilty since he left the city, his wife and fifteen children, travelling about Italy with a Neapolitan friend. As a further precaution he changed his name to Domenico Lalli, settling at Venice about 1710. He became acquainted with Zeno, who helped him financially and professionally, for Lalli embarked on a vigorous though at times ethically questionable career as a poet. Eventually he became an Arcadian, thus acquiring another name, Ortanio. He also secured the friendship of Metastasio and Goldoni. A second marriage took place at Venice, resulting in fifteen more children. Thus, according to one eighteenth-century writer, "it is not surprising that, having to support himself and so numerous a family by force of poetry, he concluded his life in poverty."[8]

Lalli was in fact a notorious plagiarist and purveyor of identical or quasi-identical works under different dedications or titles. He was evidently an acquaintance of Nicola Grimaldi, called Nicolini, who as we shall see sang the title role in the first performance of *Tigrane*, for during the 1726 season, when Nicolini was in Venice, Lalli dedicated to Nicola Grimaldi his *Sette Salmi della penitenza*. The *Salmi* were reprinted in 1739, with a new dedication to Cardinal Stampa, Archbishop of Milan, and a third printing exists with a dedication to a Baron d'Assebourg that is identical to the original dedication addressed to Nicolini.[9]

Tigrane, by Cigna-Santi (Goldoni), music by Niccolò Piccini, for the Regio Teatro di Torino, Carneval, 1761.

Tigrane, by Goldoni, music by Antonio Tozzi, for Teatro di Sant'Angelo, Venice, for Ascensione, May 19,1762.

Tigrane, author and composer unknown, for Teatro di via della Pergola, Florence,Carneval, 1771.

Tigranes, by A Filistri De Camarandani, music by Vincenzo Righini, for the Royal Theater, Berlin, January 20, 1800.

[7]Reinhard G. Pauly, "Alessandro Scarlatti's 'Tigrane,' " *Music and Letters*, 35 (1954), p. 345.

[8]*Ibid.*, p. 344.

[9]*Ibid.*, p. 345.

A further fraud on Lalli's part concerns the libretto for *Tigrane* itself. In 1715, for the same Carneval season for which *Tigrane* was performed in Naples, an opera called *L'Amor di figlio non conosciuto,* music by Tomaso Albinoni and libretto by Lalli, was presented at the Teatro di Sant'Angelo. Pauly discovered that the librettos are indeed almost identical. The name of Meroe's confidante, Orcone, is changed to Latiro, and the part of Dorilla is cut, probably because there are no comic scenes in the Venice libretto. This libretto is compared in greater detail with that of *Tigrane* below.

Yet to be discussed are the three comic scenes in *Tigrane* mentioned above, which are completely independent in nature; that is, they are neither integrated with respect to the time and place of the *seria* plot, nor are they themselves unified by plot. The two roles in these comic scenes are, however, taken by very minor characters from the *seria* plot in which they have very few lines, but sometimes engage in sarcastic asides to the audience. During the comic scenes, which comprise the final scenes of Acts I and II and Scene xiv of Act III just preceding the five scenes which present the denouement of the seria plot, Dorilla and Orcone engage in outrageous flirtation, Orcone playing the flatterer and Dorilla the coquette.

The scenes take place in the present, that is, in 1715. In Act I, Scene xviii, Orcone retains his sorcerer's costume from the preceding scene, and the byplay concerns the conjuring of monsters and furies from the nether world. Orcone identifies himself as a Bolognese, Dorilla as Bergomasca. Act II, Scene xviii finds Orcone dressed as a Parisian fop and Dorilla in a German regional costume. Orcone refers to her as his Columbine, so we can assume that he plays Columbine's usual companion in the *commedia dell'arte.* After considerable flirtation in very corrupt German, they address themselves to the audience as vendors of cosmetics especially designed for aging ladies and Parisian dandies. The following dialogue gives an example:

> Dorilla: You're selling to men?
> Orcone: Yes, men still delight in cosmetics. If only I had as much cash at my
>   command as there are men who use makeup.
> Dorilla: (What refined diversion!)
> Orcone: At least, where is the man that you don't see made up?
> Dorilla: *You* are certainly covered with it.
> Orcone: Custom absolves everyone, and the defect becomes a whimsey. You
>   plain and I powdered, to each his own.

This scene ends with a mock love scene in extravagant language.

In Act II, Scene xiv, Orcone appears as Dr. Graziano, the pompous Bolognese academic of *commedia dell'arte* fame, while Dorilla is dressed as Zaccagnina from Bergamo.[10] When not flirting with her in his special brand of Latin hyperbole — *Radiantis Occellulis; vestram lucem perbellulam, mirificam, scintillosque perbellulis, faciunt te plusquam bellam et magnificam. Questo intender no'l puoi, ch'è stile proprio Ciceroniano* — the two converse in Bolognese dialect:

---

[10]Zaccagnina is the counterpart of Zaccagnino, in the *commedia dell'arte,* a comedian from Bergamo. There is also a valley near Bergamo called Zaccagnina from whence came the *Zanni* (zanies or clowns) of the *commedia dell'arte.*

Orcone: Cara la me bellina, cosa fàla? Comod stàla? Cosa dìsla? Cos'hàla?
La digga la me bella Zaccagnina.
Dorilla: Ah dig mi, che stò bè; mà desìm ù tantì, desìm, che vò volìd'ol
fagh me?
Orcone: Cosa disìvu mò? No sgnora ch'las lassa pur srvir; mi son servitor sò;
mi n'ho lengua pr dir quant' a sippa ubbligà a un ezzes aqsi grand
dlà sò buntà.[11]

The Music

Tigrane represents Alessandro Scarlatti at his best. The arias are definitely High Baroque, not unlike Handel in style, full of melodic, harmonic, and rhythmic variety. They are suffused with the concerto principle with respect to the relation between singer and orchestra; that is, the orchestral *tutti* (*ripieno*) plays during the ritornelli and while the voice is silent, while the *soli* (*concertino*) accompany the voice.

There are several purely instrumental numbers besides the usual three-part *Sinfonia*. The raising of the curtain brings a *Marcia* and *Ballo* in which on-stage oboes and bassoons participate. Act II opens with an instrumental *Marcia* and *Ballo* with double reeds on stage again. These are followed by two mock battle pieces — *Sonata per la lotta* and *Sonata per la zuffa de' gladiatori* — and the comic scene inserted in Act III ends with a *Ballo* and *Menuet*. All these numbers are no doubt intended to accompany ballets. A grand *Ritornello* accompanies the splendid cortege that opens Act II, Scene xiv. It is scored for two *corni da caccia*, oboes with bassoon, and strings. *Tigrane* has long been renowned as the first opera in which horns were employed. Other numbers featuring that instrument are the *Sonata per la zuffa de' gladiatori* and Tigrane's grand aria "All'acquisto di gloria," Act I, Scene iv, the longest aria of the opera by 75 measures and the only number in which the horns have an independent part.

Three of the arias have obbligato parts for unusual instruments: "Al girar d'un suo bel guardo" (Act I, Scene iii), in which Policare is accompanied by two *violette* (tenor viole da gamba) and solo violoncello; "Care pupille belle" (Act II, Scene xvii), in which Policare is accompanied by a viola d'ez'ore playing full chords; and "Chi mi dice spera?" (Act III, Scene xiii), Policare again, with an offstage echo and singing of a nightingale (a part presumably improvised by a whistler). This "Echo" aria has a long operatic genealogy reaching back to the "Eco" of Cavalieri's *Rappresentazione di animo e di corpo* and the lament "Voi vi doleste, o monti" from Monteverdi's *Orfeo*.

The usual Baroque aria types (cantabile, bravura, etc.) are represented. The lilting 12/8 Siciliano, for which Scarlatti is justly famous, is found twice in Act II: in Scene v, "Ma qual core," an Andante in G minor sung by Tigrane, and in Scene xi, "Se mai ti punse il core," an Adagio in E minor sung by Policare. The latter is particularly rich in Neapolitan harmonies.

[11]Orcone: *Cara la mia bellina, cosa fa lei? Comoda sta lei? Cosa dice lei? Cos'ha lei?*
Dorilla: *Dico che sto bene: ma ditemi un tantino, ditemi, che voi volete del fatto mio?*
Orcone: *Che dite voi a me? No Signora, che lei si lascia pur servir; io son servitor suo; io non ho lingua per dire quanto io sia obbligato a un eccesso a così quanto io sia obbligato a un eccesso a così grande della sua bontà.*
I am indebted to Prof. Vanni Bartolozzi of the University of California, Berkeley for his invaluable help with the dialect.

An aria of unusual style appears in Act I, Scene ix. "Prova eccelsa è di grandezza" is an Allegro in A minor and 3/8 meter bearing the direction "a modo di cantar zingaresco" and featuring cross relations and repetitious figures moving within minor thirds. The style would seem to support the direction to sing in gypsy style, whatever that might be. The aria is sung by Meroe, who is described as being disguised as an Egyptian fortune-teller, which at that time still meant a gypsy, thus giving Scarlatti an opportunity to insert a bit of local color.

Of the 45 arias and seven duets, 39 and five respectively are full-fledged da capo arias with ritornelli. Five arias and two duets present only the "A" section of a da capo aria. Only one, "Bella costanza e fè," Act I, Scene xvii, has a unique form; it is binary with repeat signs, preceded and followed by ritornelli.

The number of arias given each character in *Tigrane* reflects the importance of both the role and the singer who sang it at the first performance. The statistics appear in the following table:

Role	Solo Arias	Aria Segments	Duets	Total
Tigrane	10	1		11
Tomiri	7	2	2	11
Meroe	7	1	1	9
Policare	7		2	9
Doraspe	4		1	5
Orcone	2		4	6
Dorilla	2		4	6
Oronte	1	1		2

The arias and duets for Dorilla and Orcone appear only in the comic scenes, and they are in an advanced style featuring the leaps of octaves or fifths and motivic repetitions, as well as other stylistic characteristics, of the *intermezzi*, of which Pergolesi's *La serva padrona* of 1733 is often considered the prototype.

The First Performance

The first performance of *Tigrane* took place at the Teatro di S. Bartolomeo in Naples, February 16, 1715. The set designer was Sig. Ruberto Clerici, a protégé of the famous Bibiena family, and the ballets were choreographed by Sig. Antonio Piccinetti of Venice. The cast as it appears in the libretto was as follows:

Tomiri:	La Sig. Marianna Benti Bulgarelli, detta la Romanina
Tigrane:	Il Sig. Nicola Grimaldi, Cavaliere della Croce di S. Marco
Meroe:	La Sig. Angiola Augusti
Policare:	La Sig. Giovanna Albertini, detta la Reggiana
Doraspe:	Il Sig. Gaetano Borghi
Oronte:	Il Sig. Nicola Ippolito Cherubini
Dorilla:	La Sig. Santa Marchesina
Orcone:	Il Sig. Gioacchino Corrado, Virtuoso della Regal Cappella di Napoli

Nicola Grimaldi, called "Nicolino" or "Nicolini," one of the most renowned castrati of the first quarter of the 18th century, was born at Naples in 1673.[12] At the tender age of twelve he made his debut at the Teatro S. Bartolomeo in the role of Armello, page of Stellindaura, which Francesco Provenzale had inserted into his *Stellindaura* especially for the young singer. During a career that spanned 46 years Nicolini created an incredible number of roles.[13] In 1705, for his creation of the title role in Francesco Gasparini's *Antioco* at S. Cassiano in Venice, he was given the title "Cavaliere della Croce di San Marco." His first of many triumphs in London, Addison in *The Tatler* and *The Spectator* notwithstanding, was in Alessandro Scarlatti's *Pirro e Demetrio* in the season of 1701-1709.[14] Charles Burney reports the following about Nicolini's performance as Pyrrhys:

> The performance of this drama forms an aera in the annals of our lyric theatre, as it was the first in which the celebrated *Cavalier* Nicolino Grimaldi, commonly known by the name of Nicolini, appeared. This great singer, and still greater actor, was a Neapolitan; his voice was at first a *soprano*, but afterwards descended into a fine *contralto*.[15]

Of Nicolini's portrayal Sir Richard Steele had the following to report:

> For my own part, I was fully satisfied with the sight of an actor, who, by the grace and propriety of his action and gesture, does honour to a human figure, as much as the other [a tumbler who did not appear that evening] vilifies and degrades it. Every one will easily imagine I mean signior Nicolini, who sets off the character he bears in an opera by his action, as much as he does the words of it by his voice. Every limb, and every finger, contributes to the part he acts, insomuch that a deaf man might go along with him in the sense of it. There is scarce a beautiful posture in an old statue which he does not plant himself in, as the different circumstances of the story give occasion for it. He performs the most ordinary action in a

---

[12]E. Faustini-Fasini, "Gli astri maggiori del 'bel canto' Napoletano," *Note d'archivio per la staria musicale*, XII (1935), pp. 297-316. Faustini-Fasini establishes the birth date by baptismal record dated April 5, 1673. Erroneous reports of Nicolini's birth around 1680 in Venice stem from Choron's *Dictionnaire* of 1810 and Fétis' *Biographie Universelle des Musiciens*, Vol. IV (1837). Unless otherwise noted, details of Nicolini's career are taken from Faustini-Fasini.

[13]The Appendix lists the operas in which Nicolini sang leading roles. They are drawn from Taddeo Wiel, *I Teatri musicali veneziani del settecento* (Venezia, 1897), Emmett L. Avery, *The London Stage 1660-1800* (Carbondale, Ill., 1960), and Faustini-Fasini, *op. cit.*

[14]Otto Erich Deutsch, *Handel, a Documentary Biography* (New York, 1955), p. 35: "This opera [Pirro e Demetrio] . . . was based on a libretto by Adriano Morselli, translated by the manager, Owen Swiney, with Italian lyrics by Niccolò Francesco Haym [Nicolini, Valentini, Margherita de l'Epine, and the Baroness sang their roles in Italian; Mrs. Tofts, Mr. Cook and Mr. Ramondon theirs in English], the music, augmented from Scarlatti's *Rosaura*, arranged by Haym."

[15]Charles Burney, *A General History of Music* (London, 1789), IV, p. 207.

manner suitable to the greatness of his character, and shows the prince even in the giving of a letter, or despatching of a message. Our best actors are somewhat at a loss to support themselves with proper gesture, as they move from any considerable distance to the front of the stage; but I have seen the person of whom I am now speaking enter alone at the remotest part of it, with such greatness of air and mien, as seemed to fill the stage, and, at the same time, commanded the attention of the audience with the majesty of his appearance.[16]

A humorous quotation of Addison in *The Spectator* gives an idea of the approbation Nicolini received from London audiences:

> It is observed, that of late Years, there has been a certain Person in the Upper Gallery of the Play-house, who when he is pleased with any thing that is acted upon the Stage, expresses his Approbation by a loud Knock upon the Benches or the Wainscot, which may be heard over the whole Theatre. . . .
>
> It has been remarked, that he has not yet exerted himself with Vigour this Season. He sometimes plies at the Opera; and upon *Nicolini's* first Appearance, was said to have demolished three Benches in the Fury of his Applause.[17]

Further documentation of Nicolini's powers as both a singer and an actor come again from Burney. He quotes Galliard, the translator of Tosi's treatise on singing, as saying in reference to a singer named Valentini, ''though less powerful in voice and action than Nicolini, he was more chaste in his singing.'' ''What a felicity,'' Burney continues quoting Galliard, ''would it be to possess both [singing and acting talents] in a perfect degree? . . . Nicolini had both qualities, more than any that have come hither since. He acted to perfection, and did not sing much inferior. His variations in the airs were excellent; but in his cadences he had a few antiquated tricks.''[18]

It is certain that by as early as April 28, 1710, Nicolini was about to achieve even intercontinental fame, as we see from the *Daily Courant*, on April 26:

> Comment [on a performance of Mancini's *L'Idaspe fedele* to be given on April 28]. For the entertainment of Four Indian Kings lately arrived from America. Tee Yee Neen Ho Go Row, Emperor of the Six Nations. Sa Ga Yean Qua Rash Tow, King of the Marques. K Tow oh Koam, King of the River Nation. On Nee Yeath Tow no Riow, King of Granchjoh-Hore.[19]

---

[16]*The Tatler*, 115 (London), Jan. 3, 1710, p. 240.

[17]*The Spectator*, II (London), Nov. 29, 1711, pp. 198-199.

[18]Burney, *op. cit.*, p. 208.

[19]Avery, *op. cit.*

One can imagine the wonderment of the Indian kings upon seeing *Idaspe*, for this is the opera in which the famous combat between Nicolini and the lion takes place. Even the English were bemused:

> Many likewise were the Conjectures of the Treatment which this Lion was to meet with from the Hands of Signior *Nicolini*; some supposed that he was to subdue him in *Recitativo*, as *Orpheus* used to serve the wild Beasts in his time, and afterwards to knock him on the Head; some fancied that the Lion would not pretend to lay his Paws upon the Hero, by reason of the received Opinion, that a Lion will not hurt a Virgin; Several, who pretended to have seen the Opera in *Italy*, had informed their Friends, that the Lion was to act a Part in *High-Dutch*, and roar twice or thrice to a *Thorough Base*, before he fell at the Feet of *Hydaspes*.[20]

Indeed this scene must have been ridiculous. Hogarth, in his *Memoirs of the Musical Drama*, writes:

> This scene must have had a most whimsical effect on the stage. Hydaspes addresses the lion in a long bravura song, ''Mostro crudel, che fai?'' full of divisions and flourishes; first calling on the ''cruel monster,'' in a tone of defiance, to come on, and then telling him, with a sentimental air, and in a *largo* movement in the minor key, that he may tear his bosom, but shall not touch his heart, which he has kept faithful to his beloved. The exhibition of Nicolino, alternately vapouring and gesticulating to a poor biped in a lion's skin, then breathing a love-tale in the pseudo-monster's ear, and at last fairly throttling him on the stage, must have been ludicrous in the extreme, and sufficient to throw ridicule on the Italian opera.[21].

The lion, in fact, seems to have had more admirers than Nicolini himself, for Addison felt he had to rise to his defense:

> I have often wished, that our Tragaedians would copy after this great Master in Action. Could they make the same use of their Arms and Legs, and inform their Faces with as significant Looks and Passions, how glorious would an *English* Tragedy appear with that Action, which is capable of giving a Dignity to the forced Thoughts, cold Conceits, and unnatural Expressions of an *Italian* Opera.[22]

---

[20]*The Spectator*, I (London), March 15, 1711, pp. 40-41. Addison's well-known satire of Nicolini's battle with the lion appears in Oliver Strunk, *Source Readings in Music History* (New York, 1950), pp. 514-517.

[21]George Hogarth, *Memoirs of the Opera in Italy, France, Germany, and England* (London, 1851), Vol. I, p. 202.

[22]*The Spectator*, I (London), March 15, 1711, pp. 42-43.

Rinaldo, of 1711, was the first of two Handelian operas that Nicolini introduced in the title role at the Haymarket; the second was *Amadigi* in 1715. Addison's comment on *Rinaldo* was, "How would the Wit of King *Charles's* Time have laughed, to have seen *Nicolini* exposed to a Tempest in Robes of Ermin, and sailing in an open Boat upon a Sea of Paste-Board? What a Field of Raillery would they have been let into, had they been entertain'd with painted Dragons spitting Wild-fire, enchanted Chariots drawn by *Flanders* Mares, and real Cascades in artificial Land-skips?"[23] However, his criticism was aimed at the opera, not at Nicolini, for when it was announced in June, 1712, that Nicolini was leaving for Italy forever, he wrote as follows:

> I am very sorry to find, by the Opera Bills for this Day, that we are likely to lose the greatest Performer in Dramatick Musick that is now living, or that perhaps ever appeared upon a stage.[24]

Not everyone was so sorry to see Nicolini depart, and Hawkins quotes a satiric poem published in Steele's *Miscellany*, which he says, "bespeak]s] the general sentiments of the English with regard to the Italian opera and singers":

> Begone, our nation's pleasure and reproach!
> Britain no more with idle trills debauch,
> Back to thy own unmanly Venice fail,
> Where luxury and loose desires prevail;
> There thy emasculating voice emply,
> And raise the triumphs of the wanton boy.
> Long, ah! too long the soft enchantment reign'd;
> Seduc'd the wife, and ev'n the brave enchain'd;
> Hence with thy curst deluding song! away!
> Shall British freedom thus become thy prey;
> Freedom which we so dearly us'd to prize,
> We scorn'd to yield it — but to British eyes.
> Assist ye gales, with expeditious care,
> Waft this prepost'rous idol of the air;
> Consent ye Fair, and let the trifler go.
> Nor bribe with wishes adverse winds to blow:
> Nonsense grew pleasing by his syren arts,
> And stole from Shakespeare's self our easy hearts.[25]

Apparently many did not share Steele's bitterness, among them Queen Anne herself, who presented Nicolini with a very precious gift on his departure, nothing less than the

[23]*Ibid.*, March 6, 1711, p. 17.

[24]*Ibid.*, III, June 14, 1712, p. 260.

[25]Sir John Hawkins, *A General History of the Science and Practice of Music* (London, 1776), V, pp. 133-134.

staff of St. Joseph, which was said to have burst into bloom on his marriage to the Holy Virgin.[26]

Nicolini, however, returned to London again in 1715, after the performance of *Tigrane*, in Naples, on February 16. Burney is in error when reporting that Nicolini returned to London for a revival of *Rinaldo* on January 4, 1715.[27] If this were so, he could not have been present for the premiere of *Tigrane*. As a matter of fact, the first performance of *Rinaldo* in the 1714-1715 season took place on December 30, 1714, with Signora Diana Vico in the role of Rinaldo.[28] Presumably she continued in this role on January 4, 8, 15, 22, 27, 29, and February 5, 12, and 19, for surely special notice would have appeared for the return of so famous a singer as Nicolini. And indeed such notice did occur when he sang *Idaspe* on May 7, a date allowing him ample time to return from Naples. Coleman's *Register* reports of the May 7 performance: "Il Sig.ʳ Cav. Nicolino Grimaldi, being come again to England perform'd ye part of Hydaspes, ye House extraordinary full."[29] Performances of *Idaspe* with Nicolini were given on May 11, 14, and 21, preceding the premiere of Handel's *Amadigi* on May 25, with Nicolini singing the title role.

Further notice of Nicolini's return appeared in the *Weekly Packet* of June 25, 1715, on the occasion of a special performance of *Rinaldo* with Nicolini:

> Signior Nicolini's Quail-Pipe continues to lug the Nobility and Gentry by the Ears, who have gone very far on his last Benefit-Night, towards equipping him for another purchase at Venice, he having already built a stately Edifice there, near the Rialto, upon which is written in Characters of Gold, VILLA BRITTANNICA, as a Testimony that Scaliger's Saying, that we are Hospitibus Feri, is downright Untruth, and falsly imputed to our Nation.[30]

Nicolini sang throughout the 1716-1717 seasons, and then left England, never to return.

After fifteen years of successful seasons in Venice, Naples, and Milan, Nicolini returned to Naples in December of 1731 at the age of 58 to prepare a performance of Pergolesi's *Salustia* at S. Bartolomeo. He was to have sung the role of Marziano, father of Salustia and supreme commander of the imperial armies, but on the point of entering the stage for the first performance, he collapsed, and a few days later he died, on January 1, 1732.

Marianna Benti-Bulgarelli, our Tomiri, was born in 1684, in Rome, where she also died in 1734, four years after she had returned there in retirement. She made her debut

---

[26]Faustini-Fasini, *op. cit.*, p. 305.

[27]Burney, *op. cit.*, p. 250. The error is repeated in Otto Erich Deutsch, *op. cit.*, p. 66.

[28]Avery, *op. cit.*

[29]*Ibid.*

[30]*Ibid.*

in Rome in 1703, and ended her career in Venice in 1729. In addition to *Tigrane*, she sang several roles in partnership with Nicolino: *Eumene* of Albinone in Venice, 1717; *L'Astianatte* of A. Bononcini in Venice, 1718; *Arsace* of M. Gasparini in Venice, 1718; *Arsace* of Sarro in Naples, 1718; a *Serenata* of Leo in Naples, 1719; *Didone abbandonata* of Sarro in Naples, 1724; *Didone abbandonanta of* of Albinoni in Venice, 1725; *Siroe Re di Persia* of Vinci in Venice, 1726; and *Siface* of Porpora in Venice, 1726.[31]

Hogarth claims that she was the greatest singer and actress of her time. Quantz claims to have heard both Benti-Bulgarelli and Nicolini during the season of 1726, in Venice (no doubt in Vinci's *Seroe*), and he praises both artists for their acting ability, while stating that Nicolini's voice was in decline.[32]

In 1724, while in Naples, she became the patroness of the young and destitute Pietro Metastasio, who in two years had dissipated the fortune of 15,000 crowns he had inherited in 1718 from his patron, the unmarried and childless Roman lawyer Gravina. She maintained a constant affection for Metastasio until her death. It was she who caused Metastasio to write especially for her his famous *Didone abbandonata*, first set to music by Domenico Sarro and first performed at Teatro S. Bartolomeo at Carnevale in 1724, with Benti-Bulgarelli as Dido and Nicolini as Aeneas. In 1725 she accompanied Metastasio to Vienna, and in 1728 sang in Breslau and Prague. At her death she left Metastasio 25,000 *scudi,* which he renounced in favor of her widower, Bulgarelli, who Schmidl suggests no doubt accepted the sum philosophically.[33]

Giovanna Albertini, one of the famous singers of her time, was born in Reggio Emilia around 1688. She sang the role of King Policare and must have been a contralto, since the part is notated in alto clef. She sang in Teatro del Sole of Pesaro in the autumn of 1718, in Pallavicino's *Vespasiano*, the performance in honor of the exiled pretender to the English throne, James III (Stuart), brother of the late Queen Anne, who was living in Pesaro at the time.[34] Gaetano Borghi, our Doraspe, was a tenor, born in Bologna in 1686. After singing in many important opera houses in Italy, he was employed in Vienna from 1720 to 1740, under the Emperor Charles VI and then under Maria Theresa. He died on January 18, 1777, at 91.[35] The other singers of the cast must have been of lesser importance, for they do not appear in biographical sources.

There were two additional performances of *Tigrane*. The first of these took place in Innsbruck on the occasion of a visit by the Elector of the Palatinate, 1715. The libretto

---

[31]Wiel, *op. cit.*

[32]Ludwig Gerber, *Historisch-Biographisches Lexicon der Tonkünstler* (Leipzig, 1790), I, col. 547.

[33]The details of Benti-Bulgarelli's life are drawn for the most part from G. Schmidl, *Dizionario universale dei musicisti* (1926). Hogarth, in his chapter on Metastasio's life, gives a somewhat different picture of the relationship between Benti-Bulgarelli and Metastasio, who was also on good terms with her husband. The three of them, in fact, lived together in Rome. Hogarth quotes in full the letter Metastasio wrote to Bulgarelli renouncing the fortune.

[34]Schmidl, *op. cit.*

[35]*Ibid.*

(there is no extant score for this performance) is the same as for the Naples performance except for a few cuts: Policare loses two arias (Act I, Scene xiii and Act III, Scene xii, the beautiful echo aria), and Tigrane loses two (Act I, Scene xvii and Act II, Scene v, his Siciliano). The entire comic scene is cut from Act III, perhaps so as not to interrupt the action. The corrupt German is cut from the comic scene of Act II, for the obvious reason that it would not have amused the Elector of the Palatinate.

The third and final performance of *Tigrane* was given at Livorno during the Carneval season of the following year, 1716, in Teatro di S. Sebastiano. The cast for this performance, as it appears in the libretto, follows:

Tomiri:	La Signora Margherita Zani di Bologna
Tigrane:	Il Signor Francesco de Grandis Virtuosi di S. A. S. di Modona [*sic*]
Meroe:	La Signora Anna D'Ambreville Virtuosa di S. A. S. di Modona [*sic*]
Policare:	Il Signor Gio: Carlo Bernardi di Siena
Doraspe:	Il Signor Gaetano Mossi di Roma
Oronte:	Il Signor Sio: Maria Morosi di Volterra
Orcone:	Il Signor Ipolito Maria Cigna di Volterra

One notices that Dorilla is no longer listed and that Orcone is superseded by Oronte. The reason for this is that the comic scenes are entirely eliminated. With these gone, there is no necessity for a Dorilla, and Orcone, although still essential to the plot, loses all of his arias.

Although no score exists for this performance, it is apparent from the libretto that many of the arias from Naples were replaced or cut. These differences are accounted for by the fact that the roles of Tomiri and Tigrane were taken by considerably less famous singers in Livorno, while the role of Meroe was sung by the renowned Anna D'Ambreville,[36] Thus three of Tigrane's arias are cut altogether (I, iv, "All'acquisto di gloria," the grandest aria in the Naples score; II, v, "Ma qual cor," the Siciliano; and III, viii), five of Tomiri's are substituted and have shorter texts (I,i; I,x; II, ii, vi, xvii), while all seven of Meroe's arias are substituted and have longer texts (I, vi, ix, xiv, xvi; II, vii, xviii; III, vi). Other substitute arias exist for Tigrane (II, xvi), Policare (II, xviii; III, iv), Doraspe (I, ii; III, v), and Oronte (I, viii; II, viii).

A comparison of the Naples libretto with that of the Lalli-Albinoni *L'Amore di figlio non conosciuto* shows that the recitatives are essentially identical. There are, however, fifteen fewer arias, and nineteen of the aria texts are different, although often they are paraphrases of those in the Naples libretto. Tigrane loses three arias, Tomiri two, Meroe one, Doraspe one, and Policare a grand total of six. Latiro (Orcone in Naples), because

---

[36]There is confusion concerning Anna D'Ambreville in the biographical dictionaries. Schmidl gives a rather lengthy biography, listing performances and the fact that, from 1721 to 1740, she was in the service of the Austrian court, under the married name of Ambreville-Perroni, where she was joined by her sister, the singer Rosa d'Ambreville-Borrosini. Gerber (1790), however, lists only Rosa d'Ambreville, wife of Peroni, who had a sister named Eleonora. Choron (1810) also lists only Rose, wife of Peroni, and says she had a sister named Eleonora d'Ambreville-Borosini!

there are no comic scenes in which he can sing arias, has been given two arias at the expense of other characters, and Oronte has an additional aria. The role of Dorilla is not present. The most surprising aspect of the Venetian libretto is the drastic reduction of Policare's role from seven arias to one, especially since it is he who wins the hand of Tomiri. He even loses the text "Se mai ti punse il core," for which Scarlatti composed the beautiful Siciliano. That text is given to Doraspe. This reduction leads one to suspect that Lalli wrote *Tigrane* for Scarlatti before adapting it for Albinoni.

The Scores

Four complete manuscript scores exist for *Tigrane*. Although not an autograph, the one in the Conservatorio S. Pietro a Majella in Naples is certainly the most closely related to the first performance, as the title page reads:

> Il Tigrane / Musica del Sig.^r Alessandro Scarlatti, at. 3 / In Napoli L'Anno 1715.

The text of this score follows the libretto very closely. Only rarely is a single word or two different, probably having been changed for musical reasons during composition.

Pauly has suggested that this is not the score for the first performance, his reasoning based on false testimony from Fétis, who describes the singer Nicola Grimaldi as a bass![37] Since the libretto lists Grimaldi as singing the role of Tigrane, and the score gives this role in soprano clef, Pauly assumes that the score must have been used for a subsequent performance with a castrato in the part. There can be no doubt, however, that the Naples score was that of the first performance, with the castrato Grimaldi in the role of Tigrane.

Two other scores are to be found in England, one at The British Library, the other at the Birmingham University Library. Neither of these bears a date on the title page. Neither of them can have been used for performance, because of the many uncorrected errors. The Birmingham score is an especially careless copy, with five different hands alternating in the copying. There is reason to believe that they were both made from a no-longer extant copy, because they appear more closely related to each other than to the Naples copy in the following ways:

1. Both regularize the barring in several recitatives in order to eliminate unmarked 2/4 or 3/2 bars in the Naples score.

2. Both label the aria "Al girar d'un suo bel guardo" (I, iii) as Andante instead of Allegro.

3. Both label the aria "Un solo sospiro" (I,xiii) as Vivace instead of Andante.

4. Many errors in both are identical.

5. Preceding "Care pupille belle" (II, xviii) both have a ten-measure solo for viola d'amore and violoncello. The bass is given, but the viola d'amore part is to be improvised. The Birmingham copy gives the first measure written out for the viola

---

[37]Pauly, *op. cit.*, pp. 341-342. The error of Fétis occurs in his *Biographie Universelle des Musiciens* (Paris, 1837), and is repeated by Schmidl (*Dizionario*) and Allorto e Ferrari (*Dizionario di musica*). Burney, Hawkins, Choron, Gerber, and others correctly describe Grimaldi as a castrato.

d'amore. The British Library copy has only the instructions "suonerà ad Arbitrio suo sopra questo basso."

The Birmingham score has the following notation on the title page: "con l'ajuto del Sig.r Alesandro Gordoni / Inglese." The phrase is in a hand different from that of the rest of the title page, and my suspicion that it was written by an Alexander Gordon is confirmed by the following excerpt from a communication received from Winton Dean:

> [Alexander Gordon] had an extraordinary career, beginning as a teacher in Aberdeen and ending as a land-owner in South Carolina. He sang as a tenor in Italian opera houses, including Naples in 1716-18 and later under Handel in London. Presumably he brought the Barber MS [Birmingham copy] of *Tigrane* back from Italy. He had a reputation for dishonesty: hence no doubt his claim to a share in *Tigrane*.

Since the short viola d'amore solo mentioned above is not in Gordon's hand, nor are any of the copyists' hands his, I conclude that the attribution of help from Gordon is meaningless.

The fourth full score lies in the Conservatorio di Musica L. Cherubini in Florence. It bears the same date, "In Napoli l'anno 1715," as the Naples score, and appears to be a late 18th-century copy in a very neat hand; for example, the barlines are measured off equi-distantly on each page. I believe that it was copied directly from the Naples score.

The Bibliothek des Bischöflichen Priesterseminars in Muenster contains a manuscript that includes the comic scene from Act III under the title "Scena Giocosa / Orcone da Cottor Graziano, e poi Dorilla da Zaccagnina / Musica / Del Sig.r Allessandro Scarlatti."

The only known performance of *Tigrane* since 1716 in Livorno, took place in Basel in 1969. The production was a joint effort of the Basel University and the Stadttheater. The score was prepared from the Naples copy under the direction of Hans Oesch, Paul Zelter conducted, and the part of Tigrane was taken by counter-tenor Paul Esswood. The opera was sung in German translation except for the comic scenes.

A modern edition of *Tigrane* under my editorship is forthcoming from Harvard Publications in Music, in the series *The Operas of Alessandro Scarlatti*, General Editor, Donald Jay Grout. One hopes that American audiences may soon hear this and other operas of Alessandro Scarlatti from an era that at present is dominated solely by those of George Frederic Handel.

APPENDIX

The singing career of Nicola Grimaldi (Nicolini). The list includes first performances only, not repeats in the same year or revivals, unless exceptional.

La Stellindaura (Provenzale), S. Bartolomeo, Naples,1685.
Tullo Ostillo (G. Bononcini), Rome, 1694.
Xerse (G. Bononcini), Rome, 1694.
La caduta de' Decemviri (Scarlatti), S. Bartolomeo, Naples, Dec., 1697.
Muzio Scevola (Scarlatti), S.Bartolomeo, Naples, Feb., 1698.
Tito Manlio (Pollarolo), S. Bartolomeo, Naples, Feb., 1698.
Il prigieniero fortunato (Scarlatti), S. Bartolomeo, Naples, Dec., 1698.
Partenope (L. Manzo), S. Bartolomeo, Naples, Feb.,1699.
Gli amici (Albergati-Capacelli), T. Malvezzi, Bologna, Aug., 1699.
Il duello d'amore e di vendetta (Ziani), T. San Salvatore, Venice, June, 1700.
La pace generosa (Ziani), T. San Salvatore, Venice, Jan., 1700.
Le due Auguste (Aldovrandini), T. Formagliari, Bologna, Aug., 1700.
Venceslao (Pollarolo), S. Gio. Grisostomo, Venice, 1703.
Antioco (Gasparini), S. Cassiano, Venice, Aug., 1705.
Ambleto (Gasparini), S. Cassiano, Venice, Carn., 1705.
La Partenope (Caldara), S. Gio. Grisostomo, Venice, Carn., 1707.
Un selvaggio eroe (Caldara), S. Gio. Grisostomo, Venice, 1707.
Alessandro in Susa (Manza), S. Gio. Grisostomo, Venice, 1708.
Pirro e Demetrio (Haym-Scarlatti), Queen's, London, Dec., 1708.
Camilla (M. A. Bononcini), Queen's, London, Jan., 1709.
Clotilda (pasticcio), Queen's, London, Mar., 1709.
Thomyris, Queen of Scythia (Scarlatti et al.), Queen's, London, Nov., 1709.
Almahide (G. Bononcini?), Queen's London, Jan., 1710.
L'Idaspe fedele (Mancini), Queen's, London, Mar.,1710.
Etearco (Gasparini), Queen's London, Jan., 1711.
Antioco (Gasparini), Queen's London, Dec., 1711. (See Venice, 1705.)
Rinaldo (Handel), Queen's, London, Jan., 1711.
Le gare generose (Albinoni), S. Cassiano, Venice, Aut., 1712.
La verità nell'inganno (Gasparini), S. Cassiano, Venice, Carn., 1713.
I veri amici (Paulati), S. Cassiano, Venice, Carn., 1713.
Artaserse (Mancini), R. Palazzo, Naples, Oct., 1713.
Porsenna (Lotti), S. Bartolomeo, Naples, Nov., 1713.
Il gran Mongol (Mancini), S. Bartolomeo, Naples, Dec., 1713.
Scipione nelle Spagne (Scarlatti), S. Bartolomeo, Naples, Jan., 1714.
Amor generoso (Scarlatti), S. Bartolomeo, Naples, Oct., 1714.
Arminio (Scarlatti), S. Bartolomeo, Naples, Dec., 1714.
Vincislao (Mancini), S. Bartolomeo, Naples, Dec., 1714.
Tigrane (Scarlatti), S. Bartolomeo, Naples, Feb., 1715.
L'Idaspe fedele (Mancini), King's (formerly Queen's), London, May, 1715.
Amadigi (Handel), King's, London, May, 1715.
Rinaldo (Handel), King's, London, June, 1715.

Lucius Verus (?), King's, London, Feb., 1716.

Pirro e Demetrio (Haym-Scarlatti), King's, London, Mar., 1716.

Clearco (?), King's, London, Apr., 1716.

Rinaldo (Handel), King's London, Jan., 1717.

Eumene (Albinoni), S. Cassiano, Venice, Aut.,1717.

L'Astianatte (A. Bononcini), S. Gio. Grisostomo, Venice, Carn., 1718.

Arsace (M. Gasparini), S. Gio. Grisostomo, Venice, Carn., 1718.

La fede ne' tradimenti (Sarro), S. Bartolomeo, Naples, May, 1718.

Rinaldo (Handel), R. Palazzo, Naples, Oct., 1718.

L'Andromeda (a Serenata) (?), P. Palazzo, Naples, Oct., 1718.

Arsace (Sarro), S. Bartolomeo, Naples, Dec., 1718.

Cambise (Scarlatti), S. Bartolomeo, Naples, Feb., 1719.

Serenata (Leo), R. Palazzo, Naples, 1719.

Rosiclea in Dania (Bononcini), R. Palazzo, Naples, Oct., 1721.

Arianna e Teseo (Leo), S. Bartolomeo, Naples, Nov., 1721.

Lucio Vero (Sarro), S. Bartolomeo, Naples, Jan., 1722.

Bajazette (Leo), R. Palazzo, Naples, Aug., 1722.

L'Arminio (Pollarolo), S. Angelo, Venice, Aut., 1722.

Timocrate (Leo), S. Angelo, Venice, Carn.,1723.

I veri amici (Paulati), S. Angelo, Venice, Carn., 1723.

Siface (Leo), S. Bartolomeo, Naples, May, 1723.

Silla dittatore (Vinci), R. Palazzo, Naples, Oct., 1723.

Tigrane (Hasse), S. Bartolomeo, Naples, Nov., 1723.

Amare per regnare (Porpora), S.Bartolomeo, Naples, Dec., 1723.

Didone abbandonata (Sarro), S. Bartolomeo, Naples, Feb., 1724.

Antigona (Orlandini), S. Cassiano, Venice, Aut., 1724.

Didone abbandonata (Albinoni), S. Cassiano, Venice, Carn., 1725.

Arsace (Brusa), T. Ducale, Milan, Aug., 1725.

Seroe Re di Persia (Vinci), S. Gio. Grisostomo, Venice, Carn., 1726.

Siface (Porpora), S. Gio Grisostomo, Venice, Carn., 1726.

I rivali generosi (Vignati), S. Samuele, Venice, Ascension, 1726.

Siroe Re di Persia (Porta), T. Ducale, Milan, Dec., 1726.

Girita (Vignati), T. Ducale, Milan, Jan., 1727.

Arianna e Teseo (Porpora), S. Gio Grisostomo, Venice, Aut., 1727.

Argene (Leo), S. Gio. Grisostomo, Venice, Carn., 1728.

Ezio (Porpora), S. Gio Grisostomo, Venice, Aut., 1728.

Onorio (Campi), S. Gio Grisostomo, Venice, Aut., 1729.

Catone in Utica (Leo), S. Gio Grisostomo, Venice, Carn., 1729.

Semiramide riconosciuta (Porpora), S. Gio. Grisostomo, Venice, Carn., 1729.

L'abbandono di Armidia (Pollarolo), S. Gio. Grisostomo, Venice, Carn., 1729.

Didone abbandonata (Sarro), S. Gio. Grisostomo, Venice, Aut., 1730.

Idaspe (Brosci), S.Gio. Grisostomo, Venice, Carn., 1730.
Artaserse (Hasse), S. Gio. Grisostomo, Venice, Carn., 1730.
Mitridate (Giai), S. Gio. Grisostomo, Venice, Carn., 1730.
Siroe Re di Persia (Vinci), S. Gio. Grisostomo, Venice, Carn., 1731.
Massimiano (Orlandini), S. Gio. Grisostomo, Venice, Carn., 1731.
La Salustia (Pergolesi), S. Bartolomeo, Naples, Dec., 1731 (prepared but not performed due to death).

WOLFGANG ROBERT GRIEPENKERL AND
BEETHOVEN'S NINTH SYMPHONY

by David B. Levy

The nineteenth century, perhaps more than any other era, has left for posterity a rich body of interpretive literature on music. No other period turned as frequently to the written word for insights into the workings of the creative musical mind as did the generations of the first half of the 1800s. One need not search long to recollect many famous examples from relevant literary genres. E.T.A. Hoffmann alone produced many prime examples that include, among others, *Ritter Gluck, Don Juan, Beethoven's Instrumental Music.* and *Rath Krespel.* The list can be augmented by including Eduard Moericke's *Mozart auf der Reise nach Prag* and Jean Paul's *Hesperus.*

Our histories of music for the nineteenth century rarely fail to emphasize the literary leanings of many composers, most notably Berlioz and Schumann, and we would be negligent to ignore the ideas that were common to musicians and writers alike. Familiarity with both spheres of activity, literary and musical, serves us well in our attempt to reconstruct a true and comprehensive picture of the first half of the nineteenth century.

Another figure who wrote literature on musical subjects and whose name should be added to those already listed is Wolfgang Robert Griepenkerl (1810-1868). The relative obscurity of his name and achievements today belies the high repute and influence that he enjoyed throughout his career. Consider, for example, the following endorsement of his critical abilities from no less a man of letters than Hector Berlioz:

> I am much indebted to the artists and music lovers of Brunswick. I owe a great deal too to the leading music critic, Robert Griepenkerl, who in an erudite pamphlet . . . gave what seems to me a very accurate idea of my music and of the force and direction of the musical impulses that drive me on.[1]

Berlioz wrote this in a letter to Heinrich Heine that dated from the time when Berlioz was touring Germany (1841-1842), and it was subsequently published in his *Mémoires.* Griepenkerl's admiration for the Frenchman found its fullest expression in the "pamphlet" entitled *Ritter Berlioz in Braunschweig, Zur Charakteristik dieses Tondichters* that was published in Braunschweig in 1843.[2] It was Griepenkerl's recognition, in particular, of Beethoven's influence on Berlioz that gave rise to this enthusiastic acclaim.

---

[1] *The Memoirs of Hector Berlioz*, trans. and ed. by David Cairns (New York, 1975), p. 314.

[2] Wolfgang Robert Griepenkerl, *Ritter Berlioz in Braunschweig, Zur Characteristik dieses Tondichters* (Braunschweig, 1843).

What credentials could Griepenkerl offer as a writer on musical topics? Part of the answer lies in the musical activities of his father, Friedrich Konrad (1782-1849). The elder Griepenkerl, like his son, was principally a man of letters who studied and taught literature, philosophy, and language. But among his teachers was Johann Nikolaus Forkel, with whom he studied organ, keyboard, and music theory at Goettingen.[3] After settling in Braunschweig in 1821, he organized a *Singakademie* for the purpose of performing J.S. Bach's choral works. In 1837 he began his activities as an editor of Bach's works for keyboard and organ for the publishing house of Peters. To this end, the elder Griepenkerl, although not as celebrated or influential as Mendelssohn and Zelter, must be credited for furthering the "revival" of J.S. Bach's music.

It is clear then that Wolfgang Robert Griepenkerl came from a musical background. We have, however, no indication that he had any formal musical training. But he did have a gift for writing and a fertile imagination combined with, as will be demonstrated, a solid familiarity with musical current events and with some of the major musical figures of his time. In 1847, Griepenkerl was invited to give the keynote address to the *Tonkünstlersversammlung* in Leipzig. On that occasion he spoke to the audience of professionals on *Die Oper der Gegenwart*.[4]

Griepenkerl's musical-cultural hero was, beyond all doubt, Ludwig van Beethoven. The vehicle for his adoration of this hero was a *Novelle* entitled *Das Musikfest oder die Beethovener*. The work stems from the period of 1837-38, when Griepenkerl was a contributing editor for Schumann's *Neue Zeitschrift für Musik*.[5] His association with that magazine offered him the opportunity to publish excerpts or *Bruchstücke* from *Das Musikfest* before its appearance in completed form in 1838.[6] The book was reissued in 1841, expanded by a preface and a musical *Zugabe* that comprised a song by Meyerbeer based on a poem from Chapter 5 of the book.[7]

At first glance, *Das Musikfest* invites dismissal as being merely a freely-drawn exercise in extra-musical fiction. Its literary style can hardly be deemed first-rate, despite heavy borrowings or imagery and character types from Hoffmann and Jean Paul. But Griepenkerl certainly did not stand alone in that department. A review of the book by C.F. Brendel that appeared in volume 10 of the *Neue Zeitschrift*, 1839, faulted Griepenkerl for, among other things, his loose, disjointed style:

[3]Heinrich Sievers, "Griepenkerl, Friedrich Konrad,"*Die Musik in Geschichte und Gegenwart* (Kassel und Basel, 1956), V, col. 908.

[4]Wolfgang Robert Griepenkerl, *Die Oper der Gegenwart. Vortrag zur ersten Tonkünstlersversammlung in Leipzig im Saale des Gewandhauses am 14. August 1847, gehalten von Wolfgang Robert Griepenkerl* (Leipzig,1847).

[5]Perhaps his most interesting contribution to the Leipzig *Neue Zeitschrift für Musik* was his "Musikalisches Leben in Braunschweig," VI (1837), pp. 57-58, 60-61, 65-66, 69-70, 74.

[6]Wolfgang Robert Griepenkerl, *Das Musikfest oder die Beethovener* (Leipzig, 1838).

[7]Wolfgang Robert Griepenkerl, *Das Musikfest oder die Beethovener. Zweite, mit einer Einleitung und einer musikalischen Zugabe von G. Meyerbeer vermehrte Ausgabe* (Braunschweig, 1841).

Even taking poetic framework into account, I miss the strength of thought connection. It relies too much on isolated, if meaningful remarks. The way in which they are founded is obscured. No connection can be found between the musical work and the explanation. Much that is said, albeit striking in itself, such as the comments on the Adagio of the Ninth Symphony, seems unfounded, grabbed from thin air and simply visions of the fantasy, while in fact a more thoughtful concept is required.[8]

Brendel's criticisms are undeniable, although I believe that there are some striking "connections" that he did not recognize, particularly regarding some observations on music from the pen of Jean Paul.

The premise of *Das Musikfest* is as follows: a grand musical festival is planned to take place in an unnamed town in Germany. A young, enthusiastic Count, Adalbert von Rohr, is summoned by his friend to participate in the organization and management of the festival. Adalbert comes into contact with the local organist, who is an especially sensitive Beethovenist named Pfeiffer, and with the cynical, music-loving clergyman, the Vikarius. Adalbert also encounters the anti-Beethovenists: Siebert, Dr. Ganz (the editor of the local newspaper), and Funk. These three businessmen have no time for modern art-music, especially music by Beethoven. Adalbert and his friends insist that their hero be fully represented on the program and choose for performance the "Eroica" and Ninth Symphonies. They succeed in securing the backing of the wealthy Baron Mellin, whose beautiful daughter, Caecilie, studies piano with Pfeiffer.

Despite attempts on the part of the businessmen to undermine the proceedings, the Beethovenists succeed in amassing the necessary forces to place the symphonies into rehearsal. Sadly, the music's effect on various characters, most notably the contrabassist, Hitzig (who will be discussed later), combined with the devious plots and scandals perpetrated by the businessmen, brings the whole affair to a tragic conclusion.

What interests the modern-day reader is the book's exposition of attitudes toward and interpretations of Beethoven and his works and their place in musical, and even world, history. Little more need be said about the pedestrian plot, which merely serves as a vehicle for Griepenkerl to express his opinions (although we cannot alway ascertain that they are his *own* views in all cases). Each character (or group of characters in the case of the businessmen) represents a particular point of view. In turn, each point of view may be seen as symptomatic or idiosyncratic for larger elements of the musical or social thought of the period.

Theodor W. Werner[9] has correctly observed that there are three principal types of interpretation set forth in the book, each with its personal representative or spokesman. Adalbert is the symbol for a socio-political point of view. Pfeiffer represents a more purely artistic-philosophical attitude. The Vikarius proposes a theological and humorous interpretation of Beethoven. Each character is strongly influenced by Beethoven, but, at

[8]C. F. Brendel, "Bücher," *Neue Zeitschrift für Musik*, X (1839), pp. 161-62.

[9]Theodor W. Werner, "Wolfgang Robert Griepenkerls Schriften über Musik," *Zeitschrift für Musik-wissenschaft*, 2. Jahrgang, Heft 6 (März, 1920), pp. 361-76.

the same time, each brings strong extra-musical associations to his understanding of the music. Many of their ideas are shared, and their specific associations are identifiable. All three men see a close connection between Beethoven and Shakespeare, for example. "Beethoven is Shakespeare's brother" shouts Adalbert in a moment of enthusiasm.[10] A linking of Beethoven with the Bard is introduced even earlier in the text. In the first chapter, Funk denounces them both in a single stroke of disgust:

> Yes, these Beethovenists are all madmen. In L. I was in the company of such idiots. Nothing but Beethoven's compositions was presented. Four bearded brothers played a quartet that they called Hokus Pokus 95. Immediately thereafter the assembly sprang to their feet as if possessed, threw their chairs to the floor, and grabbed each other by the arms. One pulled out his hair and swore that he was nothing, completely nothing. Another bellowed his rapture into the score, but couldn't read any notes because his eyes were full of tears . . . A fourth compared Beethoven to a certain Shakespeare, an English composer, whose oratorio, *Delire*, supposedly the greatest in the world, had many similarities with this quartet.[11]

Another more earnest comparison of Beethoven with Shakespeare occurs in Chapter 5 during a conversation among Adalbert, Caecilie, and Pfeiffer. Adalbert differentiates Beethoven from all other composers by the "one strong hue of his spirit, his humor. Humor in the sense that only Shakespeare and Jean Paul had portrayed it."[12] One can find references to a Beethoven-Jean Paul connection elsewhere. Ernst Ortlepp, for one, proposed the same thesis in his article, "Über Jean Paul und Beethoven," that appeared in his anthology, *Grosses Instrumental und Vokal-Concert*,[13] in 1841. In this brief essay, Ortlepp confesses that he could comprehend neither Beethoven's music nor Jean Paul's writings until he approached both bodies of works simultaneously. Through Jean Paul he learned about humor and "found in it the key to Beethoven."[14]

The concept of humor is one of the central ideas that Griepenkerl presents in *Das Musikfest*. Werner counts him among the first writers to have investigated this attribute in music.[15] But did Griepenkerl agree with Ortlepp as regards Beethoven and Jean Paul? A statement taken from one of Griepenkerl's articles in the *Neue Zeitschrift* (1837) helps to clarify the issue:

[10]Griepenkerl, *Das Musikfest . . .*, p. 81.

[11]*Ibid.*, pp. 20-21.

[12]*Ibid.*, p. 77.

[13]Ernst Ortlepp, "Über Jean Paul und Beethoven," *Grosses Instrumental und Vokal-Concert. Eine musikalische Anthologie. Herausgegeben von E. Ortlepp* (Stuttgart, 1841), 11. Bändchen, pp. 10-15.

[14]*Ibid.*, p. 11.

[15]Werner, *op. cit.*, pp. 364-65.

His [Beethoven's] minuets, his scherzos are not comparable to the lighter, sylph-like dance that Haydn had produced for us. It is that Proteus, humor, and not the lyrical type of Jean Paul, rather the dramatic kind of Shakespeare that holds up its mask here.[16]

How does Griepenkerl understand the term "humor?" Werner posed this question and cited a reference by Griepenkerl himself taken from his *Kunstgenius der deutschen Literatur*:

Humor is not the comic, it is just as much the sublime; humor is not the sublime, it is just as much the comic; It is the concrete unity of both (for concrete is that which unifies in itself opposing notions).[17]

Humor, then, can wear several different guises, and in Beethoven it can be very grim indeed. This definition of humor is central to Griepenkerl's interpretation of Beethoven's music. What he perceives as sharp juxtapositions of opposite moods create, and add to, humor.

Humor lies at the very core of the Vikarius' existence. It is his own true element. In the rehearsal of the "Eroica," the Vikarius, who until that point had been vociferous in his enthusiasm, sits quietly through the Scherzo "only because the spirit that reigned here coincided with his own to the letter."[18] Consistent with his character, the Vikarius had his own peculiar way of enjoying the Adagio from the Ninth Symphony:

The Adagio produced the same effect on all those present throughout the hall. Only the humor of the Vikarius was not in agreement. But what did this man do secretly? He reopened his score and read, not the Adagio—no—he read the Scherzo and enjoyed it now for the first time, goaded by the contrast that he could not find during its performance. In this sense he did not only enjoy the Scherzo, but also the Adagio, into whose heaven he entered belatedly.[19]

In keeping with his ecclesiastical profession (although the reader cannot but conclude that he is a most unusual clergyman!) the Vikarius also does not fail to introduce religious symbolism into his view of Beethoven's music. Nowhere is this more clearly demonstrated than in his long speech on the meaning of the opening moments of the first movement of the Ninth Symphony. This scene occurs in Pfeiffer's apartment:

"Vikarius, what did Beethoven mean to say with these fifths?"
"Nothing, Organist!"

[16]Griepenkerl, "Musikalisches Leben in Braunschweig," p. 70.

[17]Quoted in Werner, *op. cit.*, p. 365.

[18]Griepenkerl, *Das Musikfest . . .*, pp. 161-62.

[19]*Ibid.*, pp. 197-98.

"Nothing! A lovely beginning for a work like the Ninth Symphony," said Pfeiffer, smiling.

"From nothing God created the world! Did you know that, Organist? Now this nothing may have been true nothingness, or, in light regarded as a small something. Simply, that from which God created the world is brought about in music by such murmuring fifth-whisperings. But, Organist, I turn the sentence around and say thusly: God created the world to nothing! For nothing is more easily made from something than something from nothing."[20]

Here the Organist questions the Vikarius on the biblical correctness of his assertion. The Vikarius continues:

"The devil, Organist, I say. God created the world to nothing! And I fault Beethoven greatly that he did not close his symphony as nothing. He begins well with his fifths . . . but in the last movement he believes, you see, Organist, and that was dumb. As he began with his fifths, so should he have ended with his fifths. Beginning and end of all things is—nothing."[21]

Pfeiffer, who is the true tragic hero of the story, can not resist sentimentalizing his feelings toward Beethoven's music. Griepenkerl leaves no doubt in the reader's mind that Pfeiffer is nothing less than a brilliant performer at the organ and piano. But he is a sentimental romantic who feels compelled to use literary analogy, especially poetry, to illuminate music. Griepenkerl casts him as the author of poetical texts inspired by works such as the "Moonlight" Sonata. The reader can find these poems interspersed throughout the book. Pfeiffer sees art as a true mirror of nature. He believes that it is "the beautiful law of nature that everything grows upward towards heaven."[22] He elaborates on this thought in a lesson with Caecilie, whom he secretly loves:

It is the duty of art to imitate beautiful nature. This idea of sublimity, as it is called, works with greater power in music than in any other art because where it works, its entire strength is as direct and as unintentional as is nature's. What means does true music, that is, instrumental music, have to put this idea into focus?[23]

This question echoes E.T.A. Hoffmann's *Beethoven's Instrumental Music* and anticipates Wagner's *Artwork of the Future*.

Another reflection of Pfeiffer's unabashed romantic nature may be found in the manner of his death. His death is also a fulfillment of the Vikarius' statement regarding the "end of all things." Pfeiffer knows that Caecilie is in love with Adalbert. During

[20]*Ibid.*, pp. 138-39.

[21]*Ibid.*, p. 139.

[22]*Ibid.*, p. 30.

[23]*Ibid.*, p. 32.

the rehearsal of the Adagio from Beethoven's Ninth Symphony, Pfeiffer suffers the sharpest pains of unrequited love. The day following the rehearsal, the scene shifts to the local cathedral, where Pfeiffer improvises at the organ on themes from Beethoven's symphonies. Suddenly he plays an open fifth, *fortissimo,* and dwells on it. Gradually the volume diminishes until no further sound is heard. Pfeiffer is found dead at his instrument.

In this instance, Jean Paul may be called upon to find the key to Pfeiffer's behavior. A selection of aphorisms on music by Jean Paul can be found in Ortlepp's anthology. Two of these are relevant to Pfeiffer's death in *Das Musikfest*:

> When I am overcome by a feeling that needs to be portrayed, it does not lean toward words, but toward tones, and I will express it at the keyboard.

> Nothing exhausts and stirs me more than fantasizing at the keyboard. I could fantasize myself into death. All sunken feelings and spirits arise—my hand and my eye and heart know no boundaries. Finally I close with ever-recurring, but all-powerful tones. One can, indeed, tire of listening to music, but not of making music; and every musician could, like the nightingale, warble himself to death.[24]

One can only marvel at how paradoxically "romantic" it all is! Music expresses the inexpressible, while words are intoned to express the meaning of music.

If Pfeiffer's egoism is passive, then Adalbert can be viewed as his perfect foil. Adalbert is a world-mover, a figure deeply involved with lighting political fires. For him, Beethoven is a mirror of the new feelings of the time. Adalbert believes that Beethoven's music is intimately tied to political history and events—most notably to the French revolution. He is of like mind with the Vikarius and Pfeiffer in placing Beethoven at the pinnacle of musical creation "in a world-historical meaning." He accepts the management of the festival because it affords him the opportunity to become the shaper of events, the opportunity to proselytize his doctrine — a doctrine that makes Beethoven the symbol of a new age:

> "The symphony," cried Adalbert, "is the most sparkling product of the newer art, and those by Beethoven are the all-truest mirror of our time . . . You cite Haydn, Mozart! But they were only the predecessors of the true Messiah. Indeed Mozart tore at the old forms; but Beethoven burst them open. His art is the daemonic celebration of this stroke of power."[25]

The "Eroica" and Ninth Symphonies, according to Adalbert, are the highest achievements of the "sparkling product of the newer art." He elaborates his thesis in a conversation with Caecilie and Baron Mellin:

[24]Found in Ortlepp, *Grosses Instrumental und Vokal-Concert*, 4. Bändchen, pp. 46-47.

[25]Griepenkerl, *Das Musikfest . . .*, p.13.

These Beethoven Nine Symphonies are, unchallenged, the greatest examples of what music has to offer. Nine fearsome movers of the thundering era, driving all the hidden, wild motives of the centuries . . . Art . . . has ceased being a thing of play.[26]

Thus is art no longer the bell of conscience of selected individuals, but the grand toll of nations resounding throughout the centuries, announcing the secular evangelist . . . It is the conflicts of world history that art should portray . . . Beethoven is the first . . . to raise true music, that is, instrumental music, to the height of self-understanding, so that one has no doubt about the true colors of his intentions. All these carry the character of our time, whose directions he recognized in his prophetic spirit. Anticipating the great drama of the July revolution, played behind a curtain, that was held down only with great difficulty, of the stirred stage of the people, he condemned light play with forms. In art, his symphonies were the first battle cry of that occasion. One should travel to Paris to see how this audience sits there and listens to these works. One would have to say that in Beethoven's symphonies, chords are struck that are as powerful as the blustering wings of the period itself. Then the result there is enormous, almost unbelievable. I saw an entire auditorium spring to its feet as if smitten by a magical stroke, and with a cry that one could call a cry of horror as much as a cry of enchantment. Where has one ever seen music, oft-neglected music, arrive at that? With Beethoven, the first epoch of this art in world-historical meaning begins.[27]

Adalbert's information about the reaction of the Paris audience is correct. All accounts of the *Concerts du Conservatoire* under Habeneck are in agreement.[28] This does not tell us much about the music itself, one must admit, but it does indicate something about how Beethoven's music was perceived. For Adalbert, Beethoven's symphonies are the bible of a new universal religion—a religion that dictates that the individual ego should yield to the general good. By citing the case of the Paris audience, the reader is prevented from interpreting Adalbert's statement as a "Young Germany" doctrine.

Later in the text, Adalbert clarifies his personal philosophy as it relates to the festival:

Here one learns to subordinate the individual to the large entity. The proud feeling of a self-controlled egoism can unite thousands. Is that not beautiful and a true blossom of humanity?[29]

[26]*Ibid.*, pp. 58-59.

[27]*Ibid.*, pp. 60, 62-63.

[28]In addition to the contemporary reviews from Paris in various music journals, see Anton Schindler, *Beethoven in Paris* (Muenster, 1842). Leo Schrade's remarkable study, *Beethoven in France: Growth of an Idea* (New Haven, 1942) also provides insight into this area.

[29]Griepenkerl, *Das Musikfest . . .*, pp.89-90.

110

Adalbert's tragedy lies in the fact that his egoism, his personal interpretation of music, is not self-controlled. He becomes so self-involved and carried away by his beliefs that he ignores, and ultimately alienates, all those around him. Consequently he loses everything; the festival falls into ruin, and Caecilie (who is completely ignored by him) becomes so grieved that she can no longer hold on to life.

One further character in Griepenkerl's *Novelle* deserves special attention. He is Hitzig, "the principal contrabassist of the great Italian, a man of strength, the Atlas who balances the heaven of an entire symphony on his shoulders."[30] The "great Italian" is Spontini, who comes to the festival to conduct the "Eroica." Hitzig is a madman who comes directly from a Hoffmanesque mold. He is a field general in the battleground of symphonic music. His weapons are his instrument, "der alte Luizi," and his bow that he keeps handy in his boot and wields like a threatening sword whether he is playing or not. He is a Beethovenist with a vengeance. The mere mention of Beethoven's Ninth Symphony in his presence produces violent reactions:

> "What? The Ninth Symphony? May twice 25 contrabasses rob you of your meager senses! Mensch, who are you? What is your name? I must love you because you speak like a trombone! Little brother, little brother, tell me first—to what end do you speak here about the Ninth Symphony? The thought has something behind it. The thought has twice 25 contrabasses behind it."[31]

> "The Ninth Symphony," cried Hitzig frightfully. "Hurrah, fire, brimstone pool of hell. Sound the attack, sound the alarm! Heaven is reeling, bring supports, good carpenter, bring supports—so, so! Hear the 'Freude,' the cry of enchantment. Bow down, Millionen—ha, ha, ha! May twice 25 contrabasses rob you of your meager senses."[32]

Hitzig offers the comic relief in the *Novelle*, without which the book would be unbearable. A memorable moment is the first confrontation between Hitzig and his long-lost hunchback son, Amadeus:

> "Who here is the great contrabassist, Hitzig?" asked the dwarf in high discant.
> "I am," thundered the besought from his lofty height. "What does this worm want?"
> "Oh father, father, dear father," the little man gesticulated, "finally I see you face to face."
> "What ails you young soprano? I your father? No, nature doesn't make this great an error."

[30]*Ibid.*, p. 47.

[31]*Ibid.*, pp. 45-46.

[32]*Ibid.*, p. 49.

"Yes, but believe it and rejoice. I am your living son, the little timpanist, Amadeus Hitzig."

"Remove yourself from me, young capon. I'll have none of you. By all nine symphonies, I would have done it better!"[33]

The end for Hitzig can only be tragic. He fights his last and greatest battle in the rehearsal of the Ninth Symphony, but it "robs him of his meager senses" and his insanity turns itself loose in full force. He smashes his instrument with his foot, suffers a total nervous breakdown, and, finally, destroys himself, Samson-like, by bringing the pillars of a building down on himself.

At this point it is reasonable to inquire for whom Griepenkerl wrote the book. Did *Das Musikfest* offer new insights into the music itself? In what way could a reader benefit from reading it? Finally, how are we to appraise the book's impact on musical comprehension in the 1830s and 1840s?

Brendel[34] did not find the book "opening a new path of understanding." Karl Nef[35], on the other hand, believed that the book offered several fresh insights into Beethoven's symphonies. But he also faulted Griepenkerl for contributing to the confusion surrounding the meaning of the finale of the Ninth Symphony, a confusion between *Freude* and *Freiheit*. The passage in question comes in Chapter 11 of the book, where the Vikarius exclaims that Beethoven had revealed in the finale the true meaning of Schiller's ode. It is underscored by the author's footnote that reads, "It was freedom."[36] Werner[37] concludes that Griepenkerl and his contemporaries could not appreciate the finale in any other light. It is true that many did, and still do, believe that freedom was the message. But here one must inquire as to the sort of freedom that is to be understood—political, spiritual, or artistic. Adalbert, the Vikarius, Pfeiffer, and Hitzig all pay too dear a price for the reader to conclude that Griepenkerl fully endorsed unqualified freedom.

The fact that Griepenkerl published *Das Musikfest* as a *Novelle* argues for the thesis that he attempted to reach a large audience of readers that would encompass non-musicians as well as professionals. The non-musicians were the ones who needed some frame of reference in order to comprehend Beethoven's works. The professionals could deal directly with the music's technical attributes. If this assessment is correct, then it is reasonable to propose that Griepenkerl may have been offering his readers a warning to avoid false or dogmatic interpretations of Beethoven's music. If it is true that Griepenkerl's characters are symbolic of attitudes toward Beethoven, then it may be wrong to conclude that he wished his readers to adopt these attitudes for themselves. In

[33]*Ibid.*, p. 100.

[34]Brendel, *op. cit.*, p. 161.

[35]Karl Nef, *Die Neun Sinfonien Beethovens* (Leipzig, 1928), pp. 316ff.

[36]Griepenkerl, *Das Musikfest . . .*, p.206.

[37]Werner, *op. cit.*, p. 373.

Hitzig's words we may ask, "Who gave you the right to judge this work?"[38] But we cannot have any doubts that Griepenkerl was, himself, a Beethovenist.

The author also demonstrated solid knowledge of music's technical side. Chapter 11 is dedicated to a description of the rehearsal of the Ninth Symphony. Each character is afforded an opportunity to voice his interpretation of each section of the work. But the reader also finds an analytical account of the music. The analyses are remarkable for their accuracy and clarity—clarity found wanting in many analytical articles about the work found in professional journals. Furthermore, Griepenkerl's inclusion of several musical personalities such as Spontini, Mendelssohn (who conducts the rehearsal of the Ninth Symphony), Friedrich Schneider (identified only as the "Dessauer Kapellmeister"), Ludwig Spohr, Heinrich Marschner, a group of music enthusiasts from Leipzig identified as "Davidsbündler," and Georg Friedrich Bischoff,[39] indicates that he was in touch with current musical events. His choice of Mendelssohn to conduct the Ninth Symphony was especially timely, since Mendelssohn was acknowledged as the greatest interpretor of that work in Germany. The list is impressive.

Das Musikfest oder die Beethovener was, for the readers of its day, a pleasant means of entertainment and musical edification. It may be faulted for occasionally failing to find a successful balance between the entertaining and the didactic. At least one critic, namely Brendel, found several flaws in it. But Brendel was a professional, trained musical journalist and his criticisms of a book aimed at a more diverse audience should be viewed with that in mind. The fact that *Das Musikfest* was republished in a second edition with the addition of a song by a composer of the caliber and repute of Meyerbeer should attract our attention today, as it must have at the time. As for our assessment of this *Novelle* nearly 140 years later, *Das Musikfest* offers an unusual and fascinating glimpse into the feelings and attitudes of the first few decades after Beethoven's death. It illuminates the spirit of an era that was struggling to come to terms with its politics, its need for freedom, and its art. If the lessons of history have taught us that any fulfillment of their dreams would be long in coming, we may still recognize in Wolfgang Robert Griepenkerl another significant piece of that very great puzzle.

---

[38]Griepenkerl, *Das Musikfest . . .*, p. 176.

[39]The Sibley Music Library of the University of Rochester's Eastman School of Music owns an autographed copy of the 1838 edition of *Das Musikfest*. The autograph is accompanied by the following quote taken from page 104 of the book: "Hoch lebe der Stifter der deutschen Musikfeste! Der deutsche Mann Bischoff lebe hoch!" This copy was apparently a gift from the author to Bischoff.

TRADITION AND ACCULTURATION:
A VIEW OF SOME MUSICAL PROCESSES

by Frank Harrison

The word "tradition" has become, in the vocabulary of people concerned with cultural matters, a linguistic maid-of-all-work. In many discussions of these matters, including discussions about musical events and processes, the word is currently used in a number of imprecisely differentiated senses. While one or more of these senses may be valid in the contexts concerned, the real meaning and import of many statements in which the word "tradition" is used are often clouded and confused, since it is unclear to which of the various connotations that the word has acquired the reader or listener is being referred. This situation may perhaps be understood when one finds that a standard historical dictionary of the English language has examples of its use in six more or less distinct meanings.[1] Disregarding those uses that are peculiar to legal terminology and to the terminologies of certain religions, it seems possible to distinguish four current uses of the word "tradition" that are relevant to cultural situations in general. These are: first, the action of transmitting, or "handing down" something from one person to another, or from one generation to another; this something is described as "statements, beliefs, rules, customs or the like," especially those transmitted by word of mouth, or by practice without writing. The word is used in this sense chiefly in such a phrase as "by tradition." Although the action of transmitting is said to be from one *person* to another, the phrase "from generation to generation" implies repeated transmission over a period of time. An example of transmission of rules and customs by word of mouth might be that of the oratorical and acting techniques handed on by teachers and producers at the *Comédie Française* in Paris. Transmission by practice may be witnessed at almost any meeting of non-writing musicians; for example, at an Irish Fleadh Cheoil, the three-day gatherings where players and singers sometimes desert the official competitions for an opportunity to acquire from another musician a tune they do not know.[2]

A second dictionary sense of "tradition" is the something that is handed down, the content of that which is transmitted from generation to generation, whether statement, belief or practice, especially if it is transmitted orally. An example of this is the use of haggis, whisky, and Scottish bagpipe music in the celebration of Burns night in Scotland and where Scotsmen gather. A third dictionary definition is of use by quasi-personification, or what may be termed an anthropomorphic use, where beliefs or practices are said to be communicated by an agent called "tradition," as in the phrase

[1] *A New English Dictionary on Historical Lines,* ed. Sir James A. H. Murray et al. (Oxford, 1926), X, s.v., "tradition."

[2] John Healy, "The Fleadh Cheoil," *Comhaltas 1968* (Dublin, 1968), p. 22.

"tradition tells us that so-and-so happened." A fourth meaning has again the sense of content, but here used more vaguely, the word connoting a relatively long-established and now generally accepted custom, or method of procedure, having almost the force of law. Such customs or methods are sometimes referred to as "immemorial" usages, whose origin is thereby implied to have been anterior to any written or otherwise recorded documentation. In this meaning the word "tradition," to quote the dictionary, is used "of the body of, or any one of, the experiences and usages of any branch or school of art or literature, handed down by predecessors and generally followed." The dictionary example of this use quotes an English newspaper as observing that a certain proposal was "contrary to Conservative traditions"—with a capital C!

Viewed in a musical framework, these definitions may be considered to describe three distinct but related factors: transmission, the content of transmission, and an attitude taken up toward its content. They suggest that what we habitually call a "musical tradition" may be defined in terms of three corresponding concepts of musical acts and processes. In this view, what we call a "musical tradition" may be more precisely described as: (1) acts of communication of and about organized non-linguistic sound; (2) the materials and practices which are thus communicated; and (3) the process by which, in the course of time, part at least of these materials and processes becomes solidified, and in some cases petrified, is accepted without further documentation or demonstration, and becomes in a certain sense sacrosanct, and hence impervious to doubt and questioning.

Some examples of the use of the word "tradition" in current musical terminology show that it is used more or less indiscriminately in any or all of these senses, and occasionally in others. When, for example, a certain genre of Japanese music is said to have "a long history of continuous performance, making it the oldest autochthonous tradition in Japan," the word is used for the relation between a musical genre and historical time. The genre in question is not, in fact, an unwritten tradition, or more precisely, its mode of transmission is not entirely oral, for two kinds of notation are used for it, one for voices and one for instruments. The further information that "traditionally, the performance should last from twilight until the following morning" concerns a social usage, whether prescribed in writing or carried in memory; while the fact, here anthropomorphically put, that "the tradition of the court musicians recognizes" in the genre concerned "a single mode with a fixed generating tone" is a comment on the performers' view of a music, again without reference to its mode of transmission. In the course of the same discussion the word tradition occurs in the sense of specific sets of musical practices, in the expressions "vocal tradition" and "the separate tradition of the accompanying instruments," and it also is used in the information that "the use of falsetto is proscribed in the tradition." Here the implication is of certain petrified elements in a corpus of constantly re-performed music. This is not to make a critique of the content of the very informative article from which these phrases are quoted,[3] but quite simply to isolate an inexact terminological usage common to discussions of this kind at the otherwise most competent level. Another present-day writer on Japanese music has remarked in the course of an admirable article on certain

[3]Robert Garfias, "The Sacred Mi-Kagura of the Japanese Imperial Court," *Selected Reports* (Institute of Ethnomusicology, University of California, Los Angeles), I, 2 (1968), pp. 150-178.

115

seventeenth-century events that a particular Buddhist temple "was known for its active musical tradition."[4] Here the sense is of a certain body of material and practice, orally transmitted, that was over a certain period of time observed to be actively cultivated. The sleeve-notes of an undated but *c.* 1970 disk of "Ragas of South India" that presents "a technique of performing *raga* that is commonly associated with the *vina* in the South Indian tradition" gives in the same paragraph the information the "the selection and order of the *ragas* . . . is governed by tradition."[5] In the final paragraph of the same sleeve-note any precise meaning that the writer may have hitherto attached to the word vanishes with the *raga*-sound, when he comments: "There is a point where movement ceases, where sound fades into silence, where the active individual melts into the passive tradition."

The concept of tradition which implies the existence of a generally accepted and relatively solidified corpus of musical material and practice is probably the one most often used currently. However, such a corpus can over a period of time be only relatively stable. The innumerable changes and variations which occur within its framework do not invalidate the integrity of a tradition; they are in practice, if not necessarily in theory, an essential part of its working. Leaving aside changes which may be generated by pressures within comparatively small social units, it is difficult to define the extent to which alien musical elements, dialects, or even languages may be assimilated into a tradition without changing it radically. Such a definition, if taken on musical grounds alone, must often be arbitrary. More precise determination in specific cases must take other criteria into account, criteria that are partly historical and partly anthropological, having to do with changes within and conflicts between societies. Some anthropologists are accustomed to distinguishing between two kinds of social conflict and hence between two kinds of social change. The conflicts and changes that operate within the existing normative framework of a social system or unit may usually be resolved in terms of shared sets of values, and therefore offer no challenge to the existing institutions. An example in a musical context is the quickening of tempo on the part of Imperial Court musicians in Japan; this has the result of shortening the present day performance-time of music which should "traditionally" last all night to a performance-time of seven hours. The second kind of change in a social system is change in the character of the system itself. This is structural or "radical" change. The conflicts to which it gives rise are considered not to be resolvable in terms of the existing values of the society. They are new kinds of conflicts, and "tradition [in the nominative] provides neither precedents nor cures for them."[6] Correspondingly the various levels of musical tradition within a society or social unit may remain basically undisturbed, although absorbing "un-traditional" elements from other musical languages and systems, so long as these elements can be utilized in terms of the existing contexts of musical practice. But where the contexts of music are radically changed, due to structural changes in the social

[4]Willem Adriaansz, "The Yatsuhashi-Ryu: a Seventeenth Century School of Koto Music," *Acta Musicologica*, XLIII (1971), p. 58.

[5]*The Pulse of Tanam*, Nonesuch Explorer Series H-72032; sleeve-notes by Nageswara Rao and Jon K. Barlow.

[6]John Beattie, *Other Cultures* (London, 1966), pp. 246-247.

system, musical materials and practices may become subject to basic technical changes of a more or less rapid kind in a process for which it is convenient to use the term "acculturation." In the broadest sense, acculturation implies a process of adjustment of one relatively definable set of elements to another set, a process in which the degree of accommodation of static tradition to dynamic acculturation is infinitely variable as between one observable situation and another.

It has been a commonplace, for example, to discuss some of Handel's music in terms of its relation to certain English so-called "traditions" that he encountered. In specific terms, Handel worked out his personal musical acculturation in his Chandos anthems, where he accustomed himself to using the established elements and available forces used in the "verse-anthem" of the English cathedrals and the ceremonial "odes" of charitable societies and universities. In Northwest Europe from the ninth to the twelfth centuries it seems very probable that the uses of in-church sequences and out-of-church lais by certain social units were not merely innovations and interpolations in the formal and structural sense, but, more fundamentally, resulted from a process of accommodation to alien elements and practices, whose practitioners and promoters were in a position to force this degree of acculturation on certain strictly codified religious and social rituals.[7] There are many others among the sets of musical events commonly researched by musicologists which might usefully be discussed in terms of the content of a tradition and the partial acculturation of its practitioners.

Though patterns of musical acculturation vary with the specific circumstances and elements involved, the acculturation process is rarely total. In some cases it is partial in the sense of resulting in fusions or new combinations of elements. In other cases some alien and some pre-established practices and genres co-exist in relatively unchanged forms, both in time coming to be regarded as equally "traditional" elements. Again, depending largely on the nature of the social system which has undergone structural and "radical" changes, an intermediate unit of society may cohere and be definable. This was the case with Anglo-Irish society during the eighteenth century, whose social usages, including music, were not only identifiable, but became highly influential in the country's social and political development.

The rarity of attempts at total acculturation, whether made from outside as in the case of some American Indian communities, or voluntarily, as in much of present-day urban Japan, was remarked on a moment ago. There is a remarkable first-hand account by a Bavarian Jesuit missionary of the enforced total musical acculturation that the Jesuit missionaries to Paraguay in the seventeeth century effected on those Indians who accepted conversion and membership in the firmly controlled religious and social organization of the Jesuit missions. Father Anthony Sepp told in vivid letters sent back to Augsburg of the musical acculturation of the three thousand musicians who functioned in the twenty-six Jesuit missions, which were called *reductiones*. The date of this letter is 1691.

> Who taught these Indians to sing (he asked rhetorically), to play the organ, to blow the trumpet and shawms, the bassoon, and so on? Reverend Fathers,

[7]Eric Dobson and Frank Harrison, *English Medieval Songs* (in the press).

those who taught these poor forsaken people to live the Christian life, to say the Lord's Prayer, to bake bread, to make clothes, to cook, to mill, to cast bells, to make an organ, a cornett, shawms, trumpets, harps and many more such things, and to make accurate clocks which chime the quarter-hours and all the hours—those who taught them these things also taught them music and every other art, artifice and craft. I mean the first missionary fathers, our saintly forerunners, particularly certain Netherlands fathers, whose trouble and toil are here still kept in blessed remembrance. These, I say, have with the greatest trouble and toil taught the Indians to sing.

Father Sepp then went on to describe the method of music-transmission the earlier missionaries had used:

> As concerns their compositions [i.e., those of the missionaries], these were not the products of professional musicians, but they had only the few they had improvised, and the few that they wished to teach the Indians they sang to them, with the greatest trouble and toil, so often that they were finally driven into those hard skulls, and still to the present day, *per traditionem,* every man and woman in church on Sundays sings them all *choro pleno.* [8]

It is clear that Sepp was here using the phrase *per traditionem* in the sense of oral transmission, in this instance oral transmission of a restricted repertory of apparently uncomplicated though polyphonic choral music. Further observation of the musical practices of the acculturated Indians of Paraguay could not be made after the year 1767, when Charles III banished the Jesuits from Spain and the Spanish dominions. The European-dominated organization of the *reductiones* soon fell apart, and their buildings disintegrated.

Present-day observation of the effects of a comparable situation is still possible, however, in other parts of Latin America, for example in southern Mexico. The Tzotzil-speaking Indians of the municipality of Zinacantan have an elaborate socio-religious organization in which the use of three distinct kinds of music, all transmitted without writing, has been documented. In one of these kinds, the stringed instruments played and the music-structures involved are demonstrably of late sixteenth- to early seventeenth-century Spanish origin, and the process of the Indians' acculturation to these elements must have taken place at or not long after that time. A second musical usage, three-hole pipe and drum music for the office-exchanging ritual dance of cargo-holders in the socio-religious hierarchy, seems to be of similar origin. [9] However, the social context of both kinds of music has some elements in common both with the Spanish

---

[8]RR. PP. Antonii Sepp und Antonii Böhm, *Reissbeschreibung wie dieselbe aus Hispanien in Paraquariam kommen* (Nuremberg, 1697), pp. 253-254; text and English translation in Frank Harrison, *Time, Place & Music* (Amsterdam, 1973), pp. 97-113.

[9]Frank and Joan Harrison, "Spanish Elements in the Music of Two Maya Groups in Chiapas," *Selected Reports* (Institute of Ethnomusicology, University of California, Los Angeles), I, 2 (1968), pp. 7-18. Notations on pp.22-36, 41-43.

religious practice of the sixteenth and seventeeth centuries and with pre-Hispanic rituals of the Aztec and Mayan peoples. These parallels have as yet hardly been researched. It is known that flutes and drums were used in pre-Hispanic temple rituals and at Moctezuma's banquets.[10] In present-day Chiapas, however, the flute is a European three-hole pipe and the drum is a European Renaissance type (the music-stucture also has European prototypes). In Spain these instruments had a secular dance connotation, even though they may have been used in extra-liturgical religious festivities on fiesta days. In present-day Chiapas they are used primarily for the dance of cargo-holders entering or relinquishing a cycle of ritual duties. Between the pre-Hispanic and post-Hispanic ritual usages there seems thus to have been a shift of instruments, though not of sound-types, within related, though not identical socio-religious situations. A third sound usage in this community shows no evidence of acculturation: the *teponaztli* (two-note wooden slit drum) and gourd and frame rattles used in non-Christian rituals involving animal disguise and the reverencing of pine-dressed crosses are pre-Hispanic. The "traditional" musical practices of this community are thus a complex of elements, of which some are at present identifiable and some are not.

Reference was made earlier in this paper to the existence in eighteenth-century Ireland of a cohesive Anglo-Irish social unit. The musical culture of this land-owning society had elements in common with urban societies, particularly Dublin, whose musical orientation was to England and the European mainland, and to some extent with the continuing orally-transmitted music of the rural people. There were, in addition, the bilingual people who were economically mainly dependent on the Anglo-Irish estate owners, and those living in economically depressed conditions in the Western parts of the country, whose only language was Irish. Itinerant musicians like the harper-poets Turlough Carolan (1670-1738) and Arthur O'Neill (1737-1816), both of whom were blind, were dependent on the estate owners. Two paragraphs from the memoirs of Arthur O'Neill give a good idea of his life in the year 1792, when he was returning home from the first Belfast meeting of harpers where Edward Bunting put many of their pieces into notation:

> I went to Broughshane, from that to Cushendall . . . and then went to Ballycastle to Archibald MacDonnell's . . . where I remained about three weeks. From thence I went to New Ferry to Henry O'Neill's . . . where I was well received and used. From thence I went to Castle Dawson, and stopped a week there with Dr. Shields. From that to Moneymore, which I might then justly call Moneyless, as I was uncommonly bare of money. From that I went to Hugh Stuart's of Ballymena, from thence to Dungannon, and then home to my brother Ferdinand's at Glenart, where I remained in the usual manner as after my different peregrinations.
>
> After remaining with my friends as usual for some time, I left my brother's and came to Mr. Stewart's of Acton, County Armagh, and on leaving that gentleman's house I met Mr. Edward Bunting as I was going

---

[10]Juan de Torquemada, *Los veintiún Libros rituales y Monarchia Indiana* (Madrid, 1723; original print, Seville, 1615), I, Book II, p. 229; text and English translation in Frank Harrison, *Time, Place & Music,* pp. 25, 37.

towards Newry, where he brought me, with whom I spent as agreeable a fortnight as I ever spent in my life. He took some tunes from me, and one evening at his lodgings he played on the piano the tune of 'Spéic Seóigheach,' and I sung with him. There was at that time in Newry a gentleman in disguise who called himself Mr. Gardiner and lodged near Mr. Bunting's, whose lady was looking out of her window and heard us. She spoke to my landlord to induce me to spend the evening with her and her husband, which I did and was uncommonly well used; and on coming away this Mr. Gardiner (who was no other but the Scotch Earl of Galloway in disguise) slipped me a guinea, and what his motives were for disguising himself I never could learn.[11]

It is possible to gather from music-notations and other written sources something of the hybrid nature of the harpers' musical practices. Its main components were instruments and instrumental techniques which had some elements at least three centuries old, with which they played music drawn from or imitated from at least three repertories: (1) that of the entirely Irish-speaking peoples; (2) that of the hybrid Norman-Gaelic-English governing groups; and (3) that of the urban societies, whose music-orientation then was chiefly towards contemporary Italian art-music. A sampling from the relatively few tunes by Carolan that were printed in the eighteenth century (the date of this print is thought to be *c.* 1750) may illustrate the process of three-way acculturation that was taking place in this area of Irish music.

One of the Carolan tunes in this *c.* 1750 print was named after Betty O'Neill, an estate owner's daughter in whose honour Carolan made a poem in Irish which appears to belong to this tune.[12] The poem has five four-line stanzas, while the tune has five four-bar units; notes and syllables match exactly. The tune's range of an octave and a seventh is easily within the compass of the contemporary Irish harps, though relatively extended for a voice. However, its rhythm (in which it has some similarity to the kind of dance-tune called a Scottish measure)[13] and its fiddle-style figures give it the character of an oral-tradition dance-tune allied to a patron's praise-song.

A "shifting-drone" implication is pervasive in a minuet-like tune composed for John Drury,[14] son of a landowner whose family was descended from one of Queen Elizabeth I's Lords Deputy in Ireland. The tune's series of pitches clearly implies a basis alter-

[11]"The Memoirs of Arthur O'Neill," in Donal O'Sullivan, *Carolan* (London, 1958), II, p. 175.

[12]Tune printed in *ibid.,* I, p. 202; poem *ibid.,* II, p. 58.

[13]See George S. Emmerson, *Rantin' Pipe and Tremblin' String* (London, 1971), pp. 122-129.

[14]Donal O'Sullivan, *op. cit.,* I, p.187.

nating between *g* and *f*. This implication, which is very common in oral-tradition dance-tunes and is observable in some notated tunes from the twelfth century onwards, co-exists here with minuet-rhythm and with elements of sequence and recurrence common in minuets. The tune's unit-symmetry and balance should presumably be restored by adding a last bar on *g,* though it should be pointed out that many Irish dance-tunes end on the second degree of the mode in which they appear to stand. Some tunes in this *c.* 1750 group seem oriented neither to oral tradition nor to urban art-music; they have units which are tune-conceived, without either shifting-drone or harmonic implications.

The tunes in this group that have Italianate harmonic implications to some extent are nevertheless not completely orthodox in this respect. Both sections of Michael O'Connor's March and Jig, for example,[15] have occasional shifting-drone implications. The Jig called O'Flinn again has this,[16] and also, at times, a half-bar rhythm consisting of two sixteenth-notes and two eighth-notes which is more indigenous than Italianate.

Though the eighteenth-century social boundaries have virtually disappeared from contemporary Ireland, two of the repertories of that time have kept their distinct character—that of urban art-music, and that of the largely rural people whose first language is Irish. At the latest census the number of these was less than fifty thousand, and was still decreasing. Yet another repertory, not primarily attached to the Irish language, also retains something of the eighteenth-century character of landed-gentry music, though its determinants are now less matters of social usage than of technical factors like transmission-methods and playing-techniques. This may be illustrated by two examples of present-day fiddle playing. In the first example three children of an Irish army officer play together a tune named "Blind Mary,"[17] probably by Carolan, which he may have composed for a blind female harper. These players probably acquired the tune from the notation printed in Donal O'Sullivan's book on Carolan,[18] though there is a significant difference in the rhythm of the first two complete measures. The first playing is in unison; the second is in quasi-faburden improvisatory style.

There are distinctive tunings and bowing, and many regional styles of performance among Irish fiddlers. County Clare, in the middle south-west of the country, is notable for the number and distinction of its instrumentalists. Though Irish was spoken there late in the nineteenth century, this is no longer so. The instrumental music, however, still currently has many of the usages and characteristics of an indigenous non-Italianate repertory. A second example of present-day fiddle-playing, a reel played by the sixty-year-old County Clare fiddler Bobby Casey,[19] is structured in three main sections, each containing two tune-units disposed in the following way:

[15]*Ibid.,* p. 227.

[16]*Ibid.,* p. 232.

[17]Unnumbered tape in the Sound-archive of *Comhaltas Ceoltoiri Eireann,* Dublin.

[18]Donal O'Sullivan, *op. cit.,* I, p. 267.

[19]Unnumbered tape in the Sound-archive of *Comhaltas Ceoltoiri Eireann,* Dublin.

Section I	Units ABABAB
Section II	Units CDCDCD
Section III	Units EFEF

Music notation, apart from showing this design and conventionalized pitch and rhythm outlines, is an inadequate vehicle for discussion and analysis of the other factors involved. Casey's intonation of the note b', which is the seventh degree in the scale series of section I and the fourth degree in that of sections II and III, seems on aural evidence to be rarely either a decided b'-flat or a decided b'-natural in tempered scale terms. The instrument's tuning, in the absence of detailed documentation, not available with the field recording, is judged to be in fifths, pitched a full tone lower than from the usual g, i.e., $f\,c'\,g'\,d''$, or possibly with the third string tuned to a', i.e., $f\,c'\,a'\,d''$. Casey constantly varies the tune elements, so that the usual notation for repeats and recurrences of units is not usable; each of the sixteen units must be shown separately in a transcription. Besides tune-pitch variations there are at least five other observable kinds of variation in Casey's performance: (1) double stopping; (2) anticipations and immediate repetitions of sixteenth-note length, relatively unstressed; (3) appogiaturas; (4) pitch-slides; and (5) playing the first of two eighth-notes which are theoretically equal slightly longer than the second. Tempo variation is minimal—predictably so for a dance-tune. Casey plays this reel at a virtually rock-steady $\downarrow$=104; he quickens the tempo slightly in the first D unit, but from the second C unit to the end it is again $\downarrow$=104.

In general, Casey uses pitch-variation most often in either the first or the second half-measure of a one-measure element, much less often in both, and he occasionally puts together two previously separated half-measure elements. This type of element use and recurrence is analogous to some surviving notated medieval dance-tunes, and also to some medieval *lais* and sequences.

Every tune may be described as an organized non-linguistic sound-process in, so to speak, horizontal time. Its pitch-successions may also, however, have some so-to-speak vertical implications which may be heard as interval situations in a simultaneous sense. Unit A of this tune, for example, has a drone-c' implication, which is reinforced by the intermittent double-stopping with c' as the lower note. Most of unit B has the implication of an alternation between a'-d'' and c''-e''-g''. Unit C has a hexatonic choice of notes, from f' downwards to a with the omission of b', e' and b. In unit D there is an alternation, in orthodox terms, of tonic and dominant in f until the modal cadence upwards to d'' in the eighth and sixteenth measures. This cadence is made by an element which has also been used in section C. The interval implications of section E are a shifting drone between c' and d' with an f-drone below, while section F resembles section D in this respect.

Observations of this kind on present-day Irish performance suggest that the repertories typified by these two examples still maintain some distinctive elements of tune-idiom and performance-technique. The evidence of some semi-official publications, such as those of the Government-sponsored *Comhaltas Ceoltóirí Éireann* (Society for Irish Music) in Dublin, shows that now these two repertories, along with other current repertories, are considered to constitute "Irish Music." A contribution to one of the

122

publications of *Comhaltas Ceoltoiri Eireann* in the spring of last year had the title "Irish Traditional Music and the Common Market."[20] Its writer did not believe that commercial union with the European mainland would have a harmful effect on non-urban Irish music. He wrote:

> If we prepare properly Irish culture will receive such an infusion of new ideas that our traditional culture will be revitalized. We should not expect it to be unchanged, but those who have ever attempted to define tradition will know that it must change or die.

This writer was also aware that in any outward movement of a culture the nature of its presentation is a critical concern:

> Assuming that traditional music is useful, what is its sphere? Should it pervade all the media or is it, by its nature, best suited to, say, personal performance? If we decide that it is limited, that it cannot, for instance, be convincingly presented on television, do we decide to invent a new traditional form which can be? Certainly it seems better that the form of presentation should stem from those who have a tradition of music rather than from people whose only interest is in the presentation. Or do we have to stick to the old forms with their limitations? Will they survive unchanged?

Even if one has reservations about such concepts as "traditional music," "a tradition of music," or the apparently paradoxical intention to "invent a new traditional form," one still sees the cogency of this writer's dilemma. Some of the current happenings in Bulgarian music show a similar dilemma; this is apparently inescapable, given the requirements of presentation, both within and outside the country, to large audiences in situations far removed, whether culturally or geographically or both, from those in which the music was originally produced. Something of the resulting process of so-to-speak deliberate acculturation, of change purposely exercised on musical repertories by members of society who are nevertheless intent on the conservation of some recognizable national elements, may be shown in three musical items. The first is from the spring maiden rituals done on St. Lazarus day, in this case in the village of Bistritsa, near Sofia.[21] Two pairs of women sing antiphonally a diaphony in which one maintains a drone and the other sings a restricted-ambitus tune at a minor second above or below the drone or in unison with it. At the end of each unit the two singers join in the drone, overlapping the beginning of the other pair's unit.

In the region of the Pirin Krai, in the south-west corner of Bulgaria, women sing various ritual and social songs, including *lazarski*, in diaphony whose intervals are most often seconds, thirds, fourths or fifths, with occasional upward *glissando* whoops at a

[20]John P. Moulden, "Irish Traditional Music and the Common Market," *Treoir*, III (1971), pp. 10-11.

[21]*Bulgarian Ritual Folk Songs*, Balkanton BHA 1045; recorded in the field; sleeve-notes by Raina Katsarova; items 2a¹, "White flowers, i Lazare, which blossom early," which is sung upon entering the courtyard, and 2a², "Mari Maline, Maline," which is sung to a new couple.

fourth, fifth, seventh or indeterminate interval. This repertory and other music of the Pirin region has been arranged for presentation in Bulgaria and abroad by the Pirin State Ensemble, whose arrangements, to quote the sleeve-note of one of their disks,[22]

> follow the lines of diaphonic harmony and its varieties characteristic of the Region. A keen insight into the nature of this folklore on the part of the music specialists in charge of the Ensemble has made it possible to draw on the most beautiful and typical works created by the genius of the people.

One of the items on this disk is sung by women in alternating two-voice and more-than-two-voice sections. The diaphony of the two-voice sections has minor seconds, though rarely, and occasional sounds of indeterminate pitch, though these are less robust in sound than whoops. The harmonic texture and rhythm of the more-than-two-voice sections recall those of state groups from the Soviet Union which have presented Russian ensemble vocal material in other countries. An item for women's singing ensemble from the repertory of the Bulgarian State Ensemble for Folk Songs and Dances, which was founded and is directed by the composer and People's Artist Philip Koutev, shows a closer acculturation to non-Balkan, in this case partly at least to western European and North American commercial ways of presentation.[23] The modal tune, which has two repeated sections, is sung in unison, in two to three parts, and in three or four parts. It is also sung a fourth higher, and its second section is sung a fourth higher in major mode. Though the arrangement sounds thoroughly non-indigenous, or is perhaps, to adopt the Irishman's phrase, part of a process of inventing a new tradition, the voice-timbres still have something of the regional sound, though noticeably less so than those of the Pirin Ensemble. This timbre-remainder and the regional elements in the tune still seem to be sufficient to transmit to members of other societies and cultures a sense of the special characteristics of some Bulgarian music.

The specific repertories discussed during this paper may have reinforced the opening contention that the word "tradition," as part of the terminology of musical investigation, is both over-worked and under-defined (one can think of others; the chronically imprecise term "influenced by," for example, still in common musicological use, might well be abandoned). The concept of "acculturation," however, seems in the musical context both under-employed and susceptible to reasonably precise use. Research in the change-processes of any music-repertory involves the identification and analysis of its components and usages, both current and, as far as is ascertainable, past, and the sifting out of specific technical elements which can be more or less clearly differentiated in technical terms. It might then be possible to co-ordinate, and view in specific time-and-place situations the history, content, and current practice of a music-repertory and the relevant analytical data drawn from these.

[22]Balkanton BHA 512, The Pirin State Ensemble for Folk Songs and Dances, Director Kiril Stephanov; side 1, band 2, titled 'Pismo ti e doshlo'.

[23]Balkanton BHA 1103, Performances by the State Ensemble for Folk Songs and Dances, Artistic Director People's Artist Philip Koutev; side 1, band 1, titled "Hey Kalina, you red apple."

The musical usages of some of the indigenous peoples of Mexico, for example, indicate that the repertory of Spanish in-church liturgical music to which they were purposefully and rapidly acculturated in the sixteenth century has finally been totally abandoned by them. A considerable part of their current repertory is outdoor ritual music whose usage-matrix (though not content) was common to them and to their Spanish conquerors. This has apparently been a more significant factor in repertory-maintenance than the few identifiable technical similarities that can be deduced from the historical evidence. On the other hand, the repertories of Irish music over the past three centuries are, taken broadly, those of a part of a people (the mainly Irish-speakers) on whom no acculturation was even attempted. One may here note briefly the striking difference from the earlier Anglo-Norman colonizers of Ireland, many of whom became so Gaelicized that they were said to be *ipsis Hibernis Hiberniores*—more Irish than the Irish. From the seventeenth century onwards many of the native Irish were merely removed to remote parts of the country, and virtually ignored by their English colonists. Some of their distinctive, and voluntarily acquired and conserved music-repertory is still in use, amid purposeful though only partly successful attempts by their de-colonized fellow-countrymen to forestall its extinction by acculturating it to an overall repertory of "Irish music," The lack of preoccupation on the part of the users of the indigenous Irish repertory with its outward movement and with the questions of presentation involved is in strong contrast to the actions of Bulgarians who take their music to be one of the main vehicles for solidifying and communicating a national identity. In this instance, identifiable changes in music repertories and practices, many of which are unique and seemingly of great antiquity, are deliberately being made in the context of internal social changes and of the requirements of outside theatrical presentation. Our cursory attention to processes of acculturation in some of the music of three regions for which material is available suggests that research into such processes, and the acquisition and conservation of significant current evidence, might be a rewarding activity for musicologists, whether their subject be identified for academic purposes with the prefix "ethno-" or not.

HAS MUSICOLOGY DESTROYED THE HISTORICAL PROCESS?

by Imogene Horsley

Almost every musicologist, at some time or other, has been accosted by a young composer and berated for bringing more music of the past into the repertoire. The implication is that if all past music were only removed from the musical scene, then audiences would hear just contemporary music, and our musical culture would return to a normal, healthy state. Before the nineteeth century, old music was continually abandoned for the new so that living composers provided and continually replenished the concert repertoire. This is the state that our composers understandably long for, and most of us musicologists still think of this as the natural state of a musical culture, even while we concentrate on bringing to light more and more music from the past.

We can hardly take all the blame for the present state of affairs, however. The change really began early in the nineteenth century, before the onset of musicology. The music of the Viennese classicists never did drop from the repertoire. The music of Beethoven, Mozart and Haydn remained; works of new composers were added and many of these also remained; then, beginning with the Bach revival, the constant addition of rediscovered works from the past accelerated the expansion of the repertoire. Next, musicology entered the field and, thanks to our energetic labors, this accretion continues in increasing volume today. By bringing more and more old music to publication and performance we are certainly giving formidable competition to composers, but have we really given the *coup de grâce* to the natural historical process?

We must surely plead guilty to changing the musical situation. But let us turn the question around and ask if we have not exacerbated the situation in a different way. For while we have been disturbing the old order, have we not at the same time created the myth that this old order was the natural one—that continual progress and change are characteristic of all valid musical creativity? By deriving all our patterns and terms from our studies of the growth of European music, have we not projected that as the norm for the present and the future? Do we not continually impress upon all who will listen to us that this is the natural state of affairs, that the important dates in the history of music are those when the most radical changes in style have taken place, that the main thing to remember about a composer is what he has done beyond the accomplishments of his predecessors? Without consciously trying to do so, we have managed to create a time-value theory in regard to musical composition which puts those composers who accept it under constant pressure to produce something radically new or to abandon what they are doing to follow the latest innovation of another composer.

There is nothing inherently bad in originating a theory. Most theories were not true in the absolute sense of the term, and yet they have generated valid works of art. Like other theories—such as the medieval *musica mundana, humana*, and *instrumentalis* (which supported the idea that music must be basically consonant), or the late stress on the physical law of probability (which has given birth to aleatoric music), the theory that a work composed in the latest segment of time must be innovative to be valid has brought

126

forth a great number of novel and brilliant works. This present-day valuation of newness and uniqueness, coupled with the widely expanded repertoire of available music from the past and other cultures, has produced, however, great strains in our musical culture—strains which are felt in all aspects of our professional life.

We have now progressed to the stage where the time-value scale has been removed from real time and can act as an absolute indicator in imaginary time. Recently, I was present at a discussion centering upon two composers in our area. Both had been actively composing during the year, simultaneously in real time. The older man had been using the most recent techniques, while the younger one had been experimenting with techniques that were first used several decades ago. When we asked about the works they had just completed, we were told that the older man's work was much farther ahead on the time-continuum. And there was no question in anyone's mind as to what was meant!

As a scholar well versed in other time-based evaluations born of my studies in the history of western music, I was reminded that in this history it was the composer who turned away from the accepted theories of his day who became important in starting a new trend. I suggested that, by analogy, today's radical might be the one who refused to accept valuation based only on time, wherein a compositional procedure originating earlier in time was, for that reason alone, considered less valid than the one more recently devised. While I was only half-serious, I was taken seriously, and the rebuttal was based upon another time-delineated value that we musicologists have promoted, the *Zeitgeist*. By turning away from the very latest approach, the composer was committing the sin of not expressing the spirit of his time. I decided to refrain from prolonging the discussion by bringing in two other theories that gained prominence a few years ago—what one might call the "counter-*Zeitgeist*" (that instead of expressing the spirit of an age, the arts provide what is lacking in it), and the "future-pointing *Zeitgeist*" (that the arts are most influential on the cultural climate of the age that follows their appearance, since it takes time for ideas to permeate society).

It is not my intention to imply that these terms are ridiculous or fallacious, but only that they refer to certain situations in the past, and cannot be taken as universally valid. Nor do I think that we musiclogists have erred in our ordering of the past, or that our work has been unimportant. I will admit that most of my research has been done because it was fun and because I enjoyed working with music in all its aspects, rather than from a conviction that it was significant or necessary. But now I am beginning to wonder if our work may not have been vastly more important than we realized, that we may have been engaged not only in preserving musical masterpieces of the past, but that we are also engaged in the recording of a unique phenomenon, and that what we have thought of as the historical process is not a natural law, but a special occurrence, localized in time and space.

For some time, in a series of articles, Leonard B. Meyer has been pointing out to musicologists what has long been known to historians in other areas, that continuous progression and change in a forward direction have not been characteristic of most musical cultures.[1] He has also shown that a state of stasis has been more common in

---

[1] Collected in: Leonard B. Meyer, *Music, the Arts and Ideas* (Chicago, 1967) Part II.

127

other cultures than progress, and he speculates that a state of stasis characterized by the coexistence of a number of different styles, rather than by one main style undergoing change in the progress of time, is likely to be characteristic of the future.

As scholars who have spent many years working within an historical framework, most of us find it hard to conceive of such a state existing in our own culture. Yet, for the musical listener this is already the state of affairs. We find him existing blissfully in an ambiance overflowing with different musical styles and forms; he can choose music coming from different points in time and in geographic space, and from different levels within both local and faraway cultures. If he so desires he may spend his leisure time listening alternatively to Schubert, Machaut, Yoruba drums, Stockhausen, and the songs of whales. If he is musically sophisticated he may speak of the different styles he enjoys according to their origin in time or in a particular cultural-aesthetic milieu, such as Gothic, Romantic, or Eskimo. But for him each of these styles satisfies an aspect of his aesthetic nature in the present. It is being manifestly proved that, as far as the listener is concerned, music that has originated at different points in time and under the aegis of vastly different cultures can find acceptance and evoke an intense response here and now.

We have already seen on a larger scale the appeal of a strongly individualized, personal style at two different times in widely different cultures, where a similar experience had taken place. The French in the late nineteenth and early twentieth centuries—once proud conquerors of Europe—had undergone humiliating defeat at the hands of the Germans. At this time, as Leo Schrade has shown in his brilliant book, *Beethoven in France*,[2] Beethoven's music became almost a cult in France. A few years ago, when the Japanese nation was recovering from a similar war experience, we found numerous stories in the press quoting Japanese who proclaimed that only Beethoven's music could truly express the Japanese soul.

It would appear, then, that the listener does not naturally follow what we have considered to be the natural order as seen in the past, either in finding the music written by his contemporaries the only acceptable expression of his aesthetic nature, or in wanting to hear only compositions in the latest style. Today's performers also have broadened the range of music which seems akin to their nature, some specializing in works of a particular time, others ranging widely through the available literature. Only the composer feels that he must continually stay abreast of progress in his field if his music is to be valid. Most musicologists would agree with the composer (even though they do not always listen to the latest compositions), but even we do not keep to this pattern: when listening or performing we also act outside what we consider to be the natural historical process.

Of course, music is not alone in this curious state. A comparable situation obtains not only in the other arts, but also in the realms of cuisine, of clothing, and of styles of living. We are simply moving into a new age—what our confrere, Walter Wiora, has

[2]New Haven, 1942.

128

called in his book, *The Four Ages of Music*,[3] the "Global Industrial Culture."[4]

As historical musicologists, most of us have been working within what Wiora calls the Third Age,[5] which encompasses the development of western music. We could as well call it "The Age of the Historical Process" for, while historians have long agreed that time in itself is not causative and that steady progress has not been characteristic of most cultures, they do recognize that during this era Western man's conviction that progress was the normal state of things did result in a long age characterized by notable forward progress in most areas. Although the term "historical process" must be stripped of the accompanying adjectives "natural" or "normal" (since it is no longer considered to be a natural law) it can very well be used as a special term to delineate a unique occurrence in world history.

While it applies well to the whole of western history, the period is particularly well-defined in the history of our music. Coinciding roughly with the beginning and end of the general historical periods, we have in music significant changes which bracket the musical ages in time. In Carolingian times there was the turning to polyphony as the new musical dimension and the coincident development of a graphic notation system which made it possible for composers to work out and preserve the complex forms developed within this new dimension. Composition took on, for the first time, a leading function in musical life, and it is primarily in this realm of musical creation that we observe the steady growth and working out of forms and procedures that represent, for us, the historical process in music.

The present age, with its highly developed technology and global communication, again has had a special impact on musical life. This time it was the listener who was liberated. The ability to record music so that it could be replayed at any time, always available, and—later—the ability to broadcast it over enormous distances had a revolutionary impact on the listener. It was this change, which gave him freedom of choice as to when and what he would hear, that made the decisive break with the order of the past. Musicologists—ethno- and historical—made it possible for music from different times and places to compete on equal footing with contemporary music, but without this technological change the old balance would not have been so rapidly upset.

Now we also have a drastic change taking place in the technology of composing and preserving a musical composition. For more than twenty years a composer has been able to record, edit, and create directly on tape without needing a graphic score. Now, he can also create a composition directly in computer-generated sound, preserving it in a computer program that is not visually representative of sound, as well as by recording it on tape. This is a much more complex technique and involves an entirely new way of training composers; both techniques represent a clear break with the past. As long as human performers enjoy performing, graphic notation will probably not be abandoned, but for the composer it is now an optional choice.

It is striking to note that, along with this change in technology, we have again the

[3]Trans. M. D. Herter Norton (New York, 1965).

[4]*Ibid.*, pp. 147ff.

[5]*Ibid.*, pp. 123ff.

introduction of a new dimension into music, roughly paralleling the introduction of polyphony at the beginning of western music. In addition to extending the possibilities within the aspects of sound that composers have been working with for centuries— duration, pitch, timbre, dynamics—we can now, by means of complex computer programming, multiple tape tracks, and multiple speakers, add to a sound the effect of virtual movement in space in relation to the listener.[6] I have heard only two works using this technique, both composed in the Spring of 1971. In one, the listener hears single tones coming at him from different points in space and at different speeds.[7] In the other, three melodies chase each other through space in a sort of twentieth-century *caccia*.[8] There are other complex sound images as well, but it is the movement in space that is essentially new.

One is tempted to "explain" the historical significance of these two pieces by correlating them with examples of early polyphony. It is easy to make a parallel according to the apparent difficulty of the musical use of the new technique in the two works. Both are, of course, already far beyond the point where one might bring in a reference to anything so simple as parallel organum, but we could compare the first, with its impartation of movement to single notes, to perhaps free or melismatic organum, and the other, naturally to the fourteenth-century *caccia* or the *Sumer* canon.

Then, moving on to the next step, we might point out that it took at least a couple of centuries to encompass the growth from melismatic organum to accompanied canon. But at this point the parallel breaks down. It is not just that the computer works were produced concurrently, but that time does not have the same meaning in the two cases. In the past development of our music, time had primary significance; this is, in fact, the significance of the term "historical process." The complex techniques developed through many centuries required new, imaginative musical concepts as well as the techniques necessary to create them within the accepted musical system. One step in this development led to the next, and the ordering necessarily took place in time.

If the technique of moving tones in imaginary space were being introduced into a musical culture like the classical music of India and there were no other cultures using harmonic or polyphonic procedures, then there might be a slow development in time. But, thanks to musicologists, composers have an overwhelming number of models and procedures which can be enriched by the new dimension and can also serve as analogues in the conception of entirely new effects and procedural modes.

There is also, now, a new relationship between practice and theory. During the past age, most of the forms and stylistic procedures grew up in the process of composition without a pre-existent model—a step-by-step building up encompassing several generations of composers, each step necessarily depending upon the advances made in the step preceding it. Only when a new procedure was clearly taking form did the theorists abstract the stereotype from the works of practical composers and rationalize it.

[6]John M. Chowning, "The Simulation of Moving Sound Sources," *Journal of the Audio Engineering Society*, 19, No. 1 (Jan., 1971), pp. 2-6.

[7]Steve Martin, *Three Movements for Computer* (1971), III.

[8]Chowning, *Sabelithe II* (1971).

These idealized models usually appeared when the techniques and forms themselves were no longer in the forefront of actual composition.

Now, when each composer may work out his own prototype, the situation is entirely different. Any variants will be made *after* the prototype, a strikingly different relationship. Just as the two pieces using the new technique of projecting movement in imaginary space were created concurrently, so numerous variants of other compositional procedures can appear at the same time, totally independent of each other. Here, the composer has freed himself from one essential aspect of the historical process.

He may also have made the historical musicologists irrelevant when it comes to working with the music created by composers of the future. Concepts that are our stock-in-trade, such as "transitional," "led up to," "intermediate stages," "incipient," "pre-____," "post-____," and the like, can have little meaning in a situation where a great number of sophisticated and fully mature works radiate simultaneously from an already perfected model—though perhaps such terms as "variant," "derivative," and "deviate," will still be useful.

At any rate, there is no need to toss accusations back and forth. The fact remains that, however complex the causes, the Age of the Historical Process is rapidly receding from view. When the next generation or two of musicologists has finally completed the sorting out and recording of the history of Western music, it may be that people will look upon that process itself as having aesthetic value. For in it we find a rare and harmonious interlocking of composer, performer, audience, and theorist. At times one of these might move slightly ahead of another, but the composer did not outrun his audience or performer for long, nor did the audience or performer lose their composers. The progress was steady, but very slow. The coalition was the result of isolation, limitation, rigidity, of being bound together by social and economic forces that no longer exist.

Once the bonds were broken, each element gained its freedom from the restrictions placed upon it by the other, but at the same time it ceased to be bound up with the other. Today's composer who longs for a captive audience should remember that under the old regime the composer was also the captive of his patron and hence of his audience. When he broke away, he gained his freedom, but he also began to outpace his listeners. When he gained his freedom in the early nineteenth century, the music of past composers became an essential part of the concert repertoire. Then, when twentieth-century technology further freed the listener from time-old limitations, the musicologists helped to increase the repertoire, and the gap between the creator of music and the listener to that music increased.

Since both the present age and that which is fast receding into the past have no known antecedents in world history, we have no basis for predicting what the future will be. Nor can we say that the relation of composer and audience in the past was more normal than that which is in effect now, but it is certainly more pleasant when the composer and listener have a mutual interest and appreciation during the same segment of the time continuum. Perhaps as the musicologist loses his function as recorder of the historical growth of composition he may have the pleasure of observing and detailing the rap-prochement of the listener and composer on some new basis during the passage of future time.

THE FINAL CODA IN BEETHOVEN'S STRING QUARTET IN F MINOR, OPUS 95 *

by Ernest Livingstone

The final coda in Beethoven's String Quartet, Opus 95, at first glance, seems to have nothing in common with the quartet itself. In the literature[1] only a few superficial relationships have been pointed out, while Vincent d'Indy did not know what to do with this coda, criticizing it sharply to the effect "that no interpretation could palliate this error of a genius and that this coda is without interest or utility of any sort."[2] This paper attempts to show that such criticism is totally unjustified and that this coda is a closely related and integral part of the whole quartet.

This problem comes closer to a solution if one considers the F-major chord, marked ppp, in IV 132, as already belonging to the final coda despite the *following* double line, new key and new meter signatures (Ex. 1). This F-major chord is a "bridging chord", very similar to the diminished-seventh chord, which joins the second with the third movement. If we now consider the two measures following this F-major chord, we find the following melodic line in IV 132-134: F-F♯-G-G♯-A-E-F-D-C-D-E-F, which

Example 1

cont'd.

*A version of this paper was read at the Internationaler Musikwissenschaftlicher Kongress der Gesellschaft für Musikforschung, Berlin, September, 1974.

[1] Joseph Kerman, *The Beethoven Quartets* (New York, 1967), pp. 182 ff. D.G. Mason, *The Quartets of Beethoven* (New York, 1947), p. 159. Philip Radcliffe, *Beethoven's String Quartets* (London, 1965), p. 97.

[2] Quoted in Mason, *ibid.* from the article "Beethoven" in *Cobbett's Cyclopedic Survey of Chamber Music* (London, 1929), I, p. 97.

cont'd.

133

Ex. 1, *cont'd.*

corresponds to the main theme of the whole quartet, I 1-2: F-G-A♭ -G-F-E♭ -D♭ -C-D♮ -E♮ -F (Exs. 1 and 2). The first 12 tones of the coda constitute a turn away from and back to the tonic F just as the 11 tones of the main theme constitute a double turn from and to F. But there exists an even greater similarity a little later in the first movement; in I 18-21 we have the same melodic line as in IV 132-134, except that each tone is ornamented by a turning figure, derived from the main theme, I 1. The ornamentation of the F lasts longest, which corresponds to the longest note value of the F (♩.) in IV 132; then comes the turn on G♭ , a little shorter, again corresponding to the somewhat shorter note value of the F♯ (♩) in IV 133. Then we have a sixteenth-note run up from G, the goal of which is A♭ , I 20-21, corresponding to the accelerated progression G-G♯ in the coda, IV 133.

The first high point of the melody in the coda is A, while that of the corresponding passage in the first movement is A♭, I 21. This could be explained by the fact that the coda is in F major while the first movement is in F minor; however, in the recapitulation Beethoven actually carries the melody through A♭ , after some intervening measures, to the climactic A♮ in I 95-96 (Ex. 7).

The major or minor sixth, characteristic for the two passages just compared, is an important feature of the main themes of all four movements depending on whether they are in major or minor. The introductory measures of the second movement in the cello constitute a descending minor sixth (D-F♯, II 1-3), which are then answered by an ascending minor sixth in the main theme (D-B♭ , II 5-8) (Ex. 3a). In the third movement we have the descending sixths A♭ -C (III 5-8, 107-110) and C-E♮ (III, 17-19 et al.) and in the fourth movement the ascending sixth F-D♭ (IV,11-12 et al.) (Exs. 4 and 5).

The chromatic line, which we have just discussed, also appears quite clearly in the second movement in the opposite direction. In the fugato part of the second movement (Ex. 6) the viola begins with the notes (A)-D-C♯-C♮ , then has B♭ on the heavy first beat of the next measure and finally descends to its lowest note A (II 34-39). In the first answer played by the second violin we have (D)-A-G♯-G♮ , then F♯ and F♮ , both ornamented by turning figures, which, in retrograde, is almost exactly the melodic line of the coda theme and of the recapitulation in the first movement (II 38-41).[3] The same melodic line is found at the end of the second movement: A-G♯-G♮ twice, then F♯ also twice followed by F♮ in the viola in the bridge chord leading to the third movement (II 184-192) (Ex. 4).

In the scale runs of the coda we have the range of a major or minor ninth in various places: from low C to high D (IV 134-136), from high F to low E and back to high F (IV 145-148), and from low E to high F in the very last scale runs (IV 172-175) (Ex. 1). This idea of alternating major and minor ninths (or seconds) has been introduced right at the beginning of the whole quartet through the major and minor seconds D♭ -C-D♮ (7th, 8th and 9th notes of the main theme in I 1). The same idea appears in the cello whole-notes G♭ -A♭ -G♮ against the notes D♭ -(G♭)- C♭ -D♭ - C♮ in the first violin (I 7-

---

[3]This relationship was pointed out to me by Professor Charles Warren Fox, whose brilliant course on Beethoven's String Quartets inspired me to do more detailed research in this field.

Example 2

136

Example 3b

9) and the transposition of the main theme in the cello up a minor ninth from F to G♭ (I 1 and 6) (Ex. 2).

That this idea is important enough to appear frequently in many places may be demonstrated by a few examples: the ascending minor ninth G-A♭ followed by the descending major second A♭ -G♭ (I 20-21) (Ex. 2); the main theme of the second movement likewise contains a minor ninth, at first only implied in the range from low A in the cello to the first high point B♭, later clearly spelled out in the recapitulation through the addition of the up-beat figure A-B-C♯ in the first violin (II 4-8, 115-119); but it also contains a major ninth from D to the second high point E (II 5-10, 116-121) (Ex. 3a,b). Besides, this theme is developed from the cello and viola lines, containing

Example 4

2nd & 3rd movements

138

Example 5

cont'd.

139

Ex. 5, *cont'd.*

Example 6

Allegretto ma non troppo

140

the second theme of the first movement, by transposition of a minor ninth from D♭ to D♮ (cf. I 22-24, 24-26) (Ex. 7). This cello figure, in turn, is derived from the counterpoint in the first violin to the transposed main theme in the cello (I 6-8) (Ex. 2).

The fugato theme of the second movement likewise has the range of a ninth from D down to C and from A down to G♯ in the answer (II 35-38, 39-42) (Ex. 6). In the third movement the major ninth appears as the melodic contour in the first violin from D to C (III 1-8) and is answered by the rising minor ninth C-D♭ in the viola (at that moment the highest voice! III 9) (Ex. 4). In the Trio theme in the second violin we have the range of the major ninth G♭ to A♭ (III 40-48) (Ex. 8). Obviously, this theme is related to the cello figure in I 22-24 and thus to the main theme of the second movement (Exx. 7 and 3). In the fourth movement the contrast of minor and major ninth can also be found, e.g., in IV 123-128 (Ex. 9).

While the sixths and ninths are of the greatest importance melodically, we must emphasize the fifth (or fourth) as the principal structural and harmonic element. The pillars of the main themes of the first, third, and fourth movements are F and C; in the second movement these pillars are D and A since it is in D major. In the coda runs F and C are emphasized by being placed on heavy beats, ornamented or repeated (e.g. in IV 141-145, 151-154) (Ex. 1).

Upon closer investigation one realizes that the notes D, C, and B with various accidentals also play a significant role. This has already been recognized by D. G. Mason but not pursued systematically through the whole quartet.[4] A few brief references must suffice here to illustrate the various uses of those pitches: in the first movement mm. 8 and 9 in the first violin if C♭ is read as B♮ (Ex. 2), mm. 12-17 in the first violin (Ex. 2); in the second movement the first three notes of the cello introduction (Ex. 3a), the head of the fugato theme D-C♯-C♮ -B (II 35-37) (Ex. 6); in the third movement the first four notes in the cello and first violin (Ex. 4); and in the fourth movement the rondo theme (IV 11-13 et al.,) (Ex. 5). Finally, in the coda, the figure B♭ -C-D-C-(A)-B♭ appears as the first high point in IV 136 (Ex. 1). The wavering between B♮ and B♭, which is especially apparent in the second movement, also belongs to this idea of generating several musical inventions from the use of D-C-B in various combinations and with various accidentals. In the coda it appears in the run from high F to low E via B♮ followed by a run from low E to high F this time via B♭ (IV 145-150) (Ex. 1)!

Each of these runs contains a tritone, the first F-B♮ on the accented eighth-notes in m. 146, the second E-B♭ in m. 147f. This tritone is also an important component of the entire quartet and always appears in pairs, either melodically (as in this instance) or harmonically as a diminished-seventh chord (as on the first beat of m. 133); other places where it appears in the coda are mm. 156, 158, 160, 162 (Ex. 1). In the first movement it appears in m. 9 and many other passages; in the second movement it is found prominently in m. 23f., in the central passage mm. 65-79 and in the final chord which leads directly to the third movement where the double tritone is immediately repeated melodically and harmonically. In the fourth movement we find it in the Larghetto introduction, in the chord in m. 22 (Ex. 5), in the episodes between the rondo themes and in the last measures of the F minor part, harmonically and melodically (IV 123-128) (Ex. 9).

[4]Mason, pp. 148 ff.

Example 7

Example 8
3rd movement

142

Example 9
4th movement
Allegro agitato

143

However, the real key to the understanding of the coda is to be found in the fact that this coda belongs to the whole quartet and not to the fourth movement, which, by the way, has its own F minor coda beginning in IV 110 on a D♭ major chord (Ex. 9) just as that of the first movement in I 129. This coda to the fourth movement actually extends from IV 110 to IV 132. That the F major coda (IV 132-175) (Ex. 1) belongs to the whole quartet is evident also for aesthetic reasons.

While the mood of the whole quartet is serious, often even oppressive, melancholic, agitated and, at times, defiant, the coda is serene, gay, light, and airy. Only once during the whole quartet do we get, very briefly, a similar impression, and that is toward the end of the second movement in the D major arpeggio with a following trill, both features being a symbol of joy in Beethoven's musical language (II 180-183) (Ex. 4). In the coda all violent tensions, accumulated in the course of the quartet, are relaxed. During the quartet none of the closing figures gave us real satisfaction, no thematic line came to a complete repose; nor were the rests points of repose, but rather they interrupted all musical thoughts abruptly, or these thoughts lost themselves in groping uncertainty. Up to the coda Beethoven avoids the perfect authentic cadence except in a few places in the third movement. The tonic was often veiled, dissonances were accumulated, and the tritone seemed to grow in importance. Compact scale runs with strong chromatic flavor came to an abrupt end that was felt as a concentration of ever-increasing tension; frequent syncopations gave the impression of an oppressive restlessness. In the coda the light breaks through. The dissonances, expecially the tritones, gradually recede; syncopation is de-emphasized and vanishes at last when the coda ends on the strong beat of a strong measure; the runs are now smooth and expansive and communicate the feeling of soaring joy; the tonic F major is now unequivocally established by frequent perfect cadences. Wide range and divergent contrary motion in the last scale runs contrast with the other closing sections that ended in dry, often gasping, falling unison fifths after convergent scale runs. This falling fifth has been smoothly embedded in the final, joyous scale runs of the coda: high C to high F in the first violin (IV 170 and 175) (Ex. 1). Thus the listener is now completely relaxed and satisfied and cannot help but agree with the noted composer, Randall Thompson, that "no bottle of champagne was ever uncorked at a better time."[5]

[5]Quoted in Mason, p. 159, and Radcliffe, p. 97.

A FRENCH POLYPHONIC HYMNAL OF THE 16TH CENTURY: CAMBRAI, BIBLIOTHÈQUE MUNICIPALE, MS 17

by Craig Wright and Robert Ford

As one of the principal musical institutions in northern Europe during the late Middle Ages and Renaissance, the cathedral of Cambrai saw the compilation of a number of polyphonic music manuscripts. More than fifty such sources are mentioned at various times in the many capitulary acts of the church that come from the 15th and 16th centuries.[1] Yet regrettably only a small portion of this once rich collection still survives, a tiny corpus of manuscripts today preserved in the Bibliothèque municipale of Cambrai.[2] These include Cambrai 6 and 11, an apparent pair of choirbooks from the Dufay period fraught with important implications for the history of performance practices; Cambrai 3, 4, and 18, three volumes of polyphonic Masses by Josquin and his near contemporaries; Cambrai 17, an assemblage principally of hymns and Magnificats from roughly this same period; and Cambrai 5 and 7, two later collections of Masses, the former preserving mainly works of Lupus Hellinck. Besides these polyphonic sources, there are volumes such as Cambrai 29 (*olim* 32) and 32 which were initially conceived as repositories of monophonic chant but which contain numerous polyphonic insertions. None of these collections has been the subject of a thorough musicological investigation. The following analysis of the hymnal Cambrai 17 is an initial step toward a more complete understanding of the extant polyphonic manuscripts that were compiled at this important musical center.

Cambrai 17 is a paper manuscript presently measuring 395 x 275 mm. It is thus not as large as most of the other choirbooks coming from the cathedral, some of which— Cambrai 3, 4, and 5, for example—extend to exactly twice its compass. The smaller size may be a reflection of the fact that Cambrai 17 was originally compiled for a singer's private use and not as a choirbook for the church. A single watermark is found throughout the volume. It is the hand-star, a mark common in northern French and Flemish paper of the period, the five fingers representing the five territories that Duke

[1] For references to many of these manuscripts, see Craig Wright, "Performance Practices at the Cathedral of Cambrai, 1475-1550," to appear in *The Musical Quarterly*, 1978.

[2] For descriptions of these volumes, see Edmond de Coussemaker, *Notice sur les collections musicales de la bibliothèque de Cambrai et des autres villes du département du Nord* (Paris, 1834), pp. 24-63; and Auguste Molinier, *Catalogue général des manuscrits des bibliothèques publiques de France: Cambrai* (Paris, 1891), pp. 1-5.

Philip the Good of Burgundy acquired through marriage and alliance.[3] Although the mark is not identical to any of those reproduced in Briquet's *Les Filigranes,* it is most similar to his numbers 11462 (1518-23) and 11463 (1524-27) that emanated from Cologne, Bar-le-Duc, Brussels, and Antwerp, among other places.[4] Yet no matter where the paper was fabricated, it most likely was bought for the cathedral in Antwerp, for it was to this city that the chapter of Cambrai sent its purchasers when in need of paper and parchment.[5]

It is clear from an inscription at the top of the title page of Cambrai 17 that the manuscript was originally owned by one Jean de Cornuaille, and that after his death it was to be given to the singers of the left side of the choir (see Figure 1):

> Johannes de Cornuaille perpetuus vicarius ecclesie cameracensis me possidet donatque post decessum suum prefate ecclesie pro sinistra parte chori orate pro eo et pro cunctis fidelibus defunctis.

The remainder of the page consists of Latin verses drawn from Horace, Juvenal, Ovid, and Virgil—excerpts which bespeak Cornuaille's activity as a pedagogue of classical Latin—and a distich by Cornuaille himself.

Jean de Cornuaille was a factotum at the cathedral of Cambrai for almost twenty-five years. He was first received as a clerk of the vestry on 10 February 1507 and is mentioned as being the son of Balthasar Cornuaille.[6] Undoubtedly he was a competent musician because during the years 1516-18 he sang in the choir as a *petit vicaire.*[7] Similarly, he must have had religious training since by 1514 he had attained the priesthood and by 1519 had been appointed a *grand vicaire.*[8] His vow of celibacy, however, was apparently not inviolate, and in 1524 his mistress became a source of embarrassment to the chapter,

[3]Samuel L. Sotheby, *Principia Typographica,* vol. III, *Paper Marks* (London, 1858), pp. 8 and 54. This same design is present in the first portion (folios 1-40) of Cambrai 3 and in a single folio of London, Royal College of Music, 1070, a collection apparently once owned by Anne Boleyn but probably compiled in France. See Edward E. Lowinsky, "MS 1070 of the Royal College of Music in London," *Proceedings of the Royal Musical Association,* XCVI(1969-70), pp. 1-28; *ibidem,* "A Music Book for Anne Boleyn," *Florilegium Historiale: Essays Presented to Wallace K. Ferguson* (Toronto, 1971), pp. 161-235; James R. Braithwaite, "The Introduction of Franco-Netherlandish Manuscripts to Early Tudor England: The Motet Repertory" (Ph.D. diss., Boston University, 1967), I, pp. 40-50; and Jeremy Noble's review of Edward E. Lowinsky, ed., *The Medici Codex of 1518* (vols. 3-5 of *Monuments of Renaissance Music*), *The Musical Times,* CXIII (1972), p. 75.

[4]C. M. Briquet, *Les Filigranes: Dictionnaire historique des marques du papier des leur apparition vers 1282 jusqu'en 1600,* ed. Allan Stevenson (Amsterdam, 1968), nos. 11462 and 11463.

[5]Lille, Archives départementales du Nord (hereafter cited as LAN), 4 G 4702, fol. 32v; and LAN, 4 G 4703, fol. 37v.

[6]Cambrai, Bibliothèque municipale (hereafter cited as CBM), 1065, fol. 203.

[7]LAN, 4 G 6794 (1516-17), fol. 10v; and LAN, 4 G 6794(1517-18), fol. 6v.

[8]CBM, 1066, fol. 239v; and LAN, 4 G 4709, fol. 37.

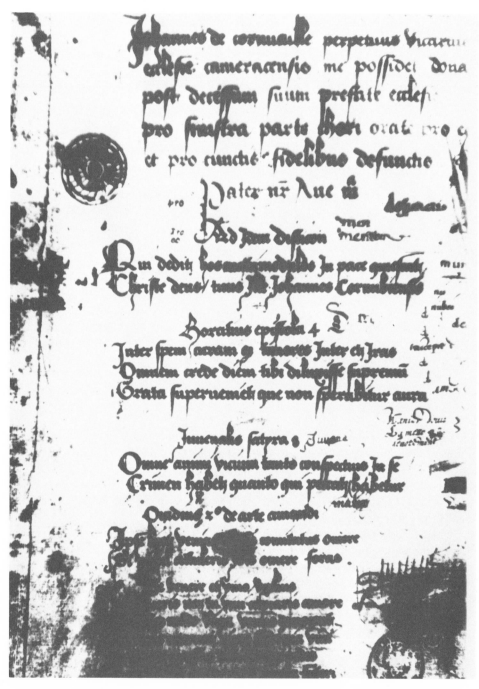

Figure 1: Cambrai, Bibliothèque municipale, MS 17, title page.

requiring her incarceration in the tower of the cathedral.[9] Besides serving as one of the nine *grands vicaires* of the church, a position that demanded his daily attendance at Mass and the canonical hours, Cornuaille acted as master of grammar to the choirboys (1522-30),[10] copied the accounts of the singers of the church (1524-30),[11] and occasionally corrected and augmented manuscripts for the chapter, as can be seen in the following order of payment:[12]

> 1518-19. Item, a maistre Jehan de Cornuaille, grant vicaire, pour avoir corrigie et poinctie l'evangelier semblable et y escripte et mis pluseurs evangilles que n'estoient audit livre a este paye, xliiij s. vj d.

Cornuaille died on 18 July 1531 and was buried in the cathedral.[13]

Not only was Jean de Cornuaille the owner of Cambrai 17, he was also its principal scribe—his record of activity as the copyist of the accounts of the *petits vicaires* during the 1520's makes this apparent. The accounts for the years 1524-30 are unquestionably in Cornuaille's hand inasmuch as an introduction to each says that they were "factus per manus Jo. de Cornuaille." The initial inscription for the ledger of 1528-29 reads as follows (see Figure 2):

> Compotus dominj Vincentij Mizonne ecclesie cameracensis canonicj de officio parvorum vicariorum eiusdem ecclesie a sabbato ante festum nativitatj Johannis baptiste annj xv^c vigesimj octavj inclusive usque ad idem sabbatum annj subsequentis quingentesimj [vigesimj] nonj exclusive factus per manus Jo. de Cornuaille presbyterj magnj vicarij in prefata ecclesia.

A comparison of the principal hand of Cambrai 17 as seen in the title page (Figure 1) or the soprano voice of the Lupi *Te deum* (Figure 3) with the hand of Cornuaille as found in the accounts of the lesser vicars of 1528-29 (Figure 2) will demonstrate the identity of script. Moreover, given the careful integration of text and music on the page in Cambrai 17 and the fact that Cornuaille served at the cathedral as both scribe and musician, it seems probable that this vicar copied the music as well as the text for that portion of the manuscript which he executed.

Cornuaille designed the nucleus of his collection to be an assemblage of thirty-five hymns and eight Magnificats, one for each of the eight church modes. The volume extended through 140 folios which he rubricated, initialed, and foliated, and for which he provided an alphabetical index at the beginning. For whatever reason, the vicar did not inscribe all the compositions that he originally planned to include and that he listed

---

[9]CBM, 1068, fol. 209v.

[10]LAN, 4 G 6794 (1522-23), fol. 9v; and LAN, 4 G 6797 (1529-30), fol. 8v.

[11]LAN, 4 G 6797 (1524-25), fol. 1; and LAN, 4 G 6797 (1529-30), fol. 1.

[12]LAN, 4 G 4709, fol. 37.

[13]CBM, 1069, fols. 286v and 287; CBM, 1070, fol. 14v.

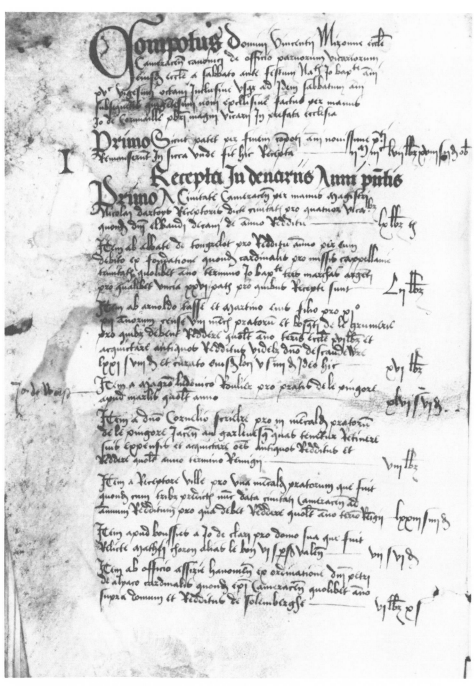

Figure 2: Lille, Archives départementales du Nord, 4 G 6797 (1528-29), fol. 1.

149

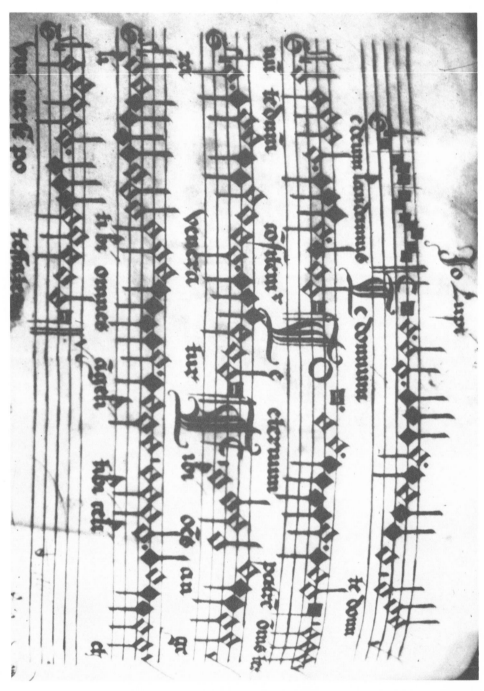

Figure 3: Cambrai, Bibliothèque municipale, MS 17 [fol. aᵛ]; beginning of the superius of Jean Lupi's *Te deum*.

in his index. Two hymns for Corpus Christi, one for the Dedication of a Church, and one for the Purification of the Virgin as well as the fourth through eighth Magnificats were not entered in their allotted spaces. Only later were these blank folios filled in by other scribes, and not always with a composition that agreed with the rubric that the vicar had left. Thus where Cornuaille had intended *Sacris solemniis,* a hymn for the feast of Corpus Christi, we now find in a later hand [*Gaudeamus*] *omnes in domino,* an introit for Marian Masses. To this volume of hymns and Magnificats Cornuaille joined two smaller fascicle manuscripts, each of ten folios: one, which contains the *Te deum* by Jean Lupi, was added at the beginning of the manuscript, before the index; a second, which preserves the Missa *Va-t'en regretz* by Simonet Censier, was appended to the end, after the Magnificats. Cornuaille then noted the presence of these two additional gatherings in his index: "In principio huius codicis habetur Te deum In fine vero missa Vaten regretz." In the course of the 16th and 17th centuries other folios were affixed to the manuscript, two before the *Te deum* and three after Mass. And blank openings at the conjunction of the *Te deum* and index, index and hymnal, and hymnal and Mass were also filled with music. The Appendix offers a detailed conspectus of Cambrai 17 as it presently rests and distinguishes that portion of the manuscript executed by Jean de Cornuaille from these later additions.[14]

THE HYMNS AND MAGNIFICATS

The bulk of Cambrai 17 is composed of hymns, and these are grouped according to their appropriate liturgical position, beginning with the *Proprium de tempore* and continuing through the *Commune sanctorum* and *Proprium sanctorum.* Surprising is the paucity of works for the *Proprium sanctorum,* for here only the feasts of the Virgin receive polyphonic settings. One would additionally expect to find, for example, compositions for St. John the Evangelist (the second patron of the cathedral after the Virgin) or for St. Aubert or any of the other local saints who are so generously represented in the monophonic hymnals surviving from Cambrai.[15] But the modest size of the *Proprium sanctorum* is more than compensated for by the richness of the *Proprium de tempore* which includes not only eleven hymns for Vespers but an almost equal number for Compline, as well as a few for Matins and the lesser hours. Thus Cambrai 17 contrasts markedly with other polyphonic hymnals of the 15th and early 16th centuries, which typically provide compositions only for Vespers—and offers further testimony to the diffusion of polyphony throughout the entire liturgy at Cambrai, at least on feasts of duplex rank.

Of special interest is the irregular fashion in which the polyphony is assigned to the text of the hymns. In the 15th and early 16th centuries a hymn was normally supplied with polyphonic music only in alternate verses; the remaining strophes were sung in

---

[14]Two folios of the Censier Mass, which contained portions of the *Credo* and *Sanctus,* have been torn away, and the last four folios have been bound in incorrect order. The foilios of the Mass are listed in the Appendix in their original sequence.

[15]See Cambrai MSS 28,29,30, and 32.

monophonic chant (presumably by an opposing side of the choir) or played on the organ. In Italy the even-numbered stanzas usually received the polyphony; this was likewise true in Germany, though much less rigidly so. In some musical centers, notably Ferrara, all strophes of a hymn were set, and the two sides of the choir sang alternately in polyphony.[16] At Cambrai, however, an inflexible tradition of *alternatim* performance does not seem to have been firmly established. The dozen or so hymns scattered about Cambrai 6, 28, and 29—the only sources of polyphonic hymns from the cathedral before Cambrai 17—almost invariably have the first verse set to the music and all the remaining strophes written out in full at the end of the polyphony. There is no implication of alternation. And the absence of an organ in the church precluded an instrumental alternative. The capitulary acts, moreover, suggest that those manuscripts copied in duplicate for the church were in fact facsimiles and did not provide alternate verses of the hymns, psalms, or canticles to be sung in turn by the opposing sides of the choir. In Cambrai 17 the assignation of polyphony to the various stanzas of the hymns results in an impressive variety of arrangements. Some of these patterns can be seen below (the numbers represent stanzas, the asterisks polyphonic settings):

*1, 2, *3, 4, *5
*1, 2, 3, 4
*1, 2, 3, *4, 5, 6
*1, 2, 3, *4, 5, *6, 7, 8
*1, 2, *3, 4, *5, 6,
*1, 2, *3, 4, 5, *6, 7
*1, *2, 3

No one scheme enjoys a majority here. Furthermore, the original format of some hymns has been modified by later additions that provide polyphonic settings for verses that did not have polyphony, or alternative versions for verses that did.[17] And in at least three instances a later hand has taken a residual verse (one without polyphony) and copied it beneath the existing music and text of that opening.[18]

Thus a number of possibilities exist as to how these hymns may have been performed. Perhaps there was an alternation of polyphony and monophony between the left and right sides of the choir (in which case the left side sang the polyphony as given in the manuscript, and the right side sang the chant from a monophonic hymnal) or between polyphony and polyphony (in which case another polyphonic manuscript, now lost, must have once existed). An equally cogent interpretation is that the members of the left side of the choir sang all the verses in polyphony, probably simultaneously with the right side; in so doing they would have been required simply to transpose mentally the residual verses to a position beneath the music that was present on each opening—a not impossible task for professional singers who, as clerics, undoubtedly had the complete

---

[16]See Modena, Biblioteca Estense, MSS ∝ M.1.11 (*olim* lat. 454) and ∝ M.1.12 (*olim* lat. 455).

[17]See the Appendix under "Later Additions."

[18]Fols. XIIIIv, XXv, and XXIIv.

text well within their memory. In view of the later polyphonic additions, the later text underlaying, and the lack of a uniform application of polyphony to the text, it seems reasonable to assume that the singers were given a measure of freedom in choosing which verses were to be sung polyphonically and which polyphony was to be heard; likely no one format remained constant over the years. All of the compositions in Cambrai 17 were sung in all parts, each voice being fully texted. The total absence of musical instruments in the cathedral assures, moreover, that they were always performed *a cappella*.

With the Magnificats in Cambrai 17 we need not suppose, but can be certain that there was no alternation during performance: all verses are set in all Magnificats. Because the complete texts are supplied with polyphony here, and because the tradition at Cambrai was to provide both sides of the choir with polyphonic sources for this Marian canticle; we can likewise be confident that the Magnificat was sung simultaneously by both sides. The following record of payment to a scribe of polyphony, Louis de Teraiche, establishes the presence of duplicate choirbooks, each containing twenty-one Magnificats, at Cambrai in 1512:[19]

> Primier, paie a sire Loys Terrache, chappellain, le ix[e] jour d'octobre pour avoyr nottetz xxj magnificat en double dont on en a fait deux livres par l'ordonnance de chapitre et luy fut octroye v florins . . . viij lbz. vj s. viij d.

Since Cambrai 17 presumably was visible only to the singers of the left side of the choir, there likely were also duplicate copies of these Magnificats accessible to the singers of the right side.

As can be seen by the Appendix, Cornuaille entered only the Magnificats for the first, second, and third tones, though he left space for and rubricated the pages of all eight. Into these interstices a later hand inserted settings of the fourth through eighth tones as composed by Cristóbal de Morales.[20] The scribe of these later additions can be tentatively identified as Julien de Ligne who served at the cathedral as *petit vicaire* (1555), master of the choirboys (1571), and *grand vicaire* (1575), and died at Cambrai in 1615.[21] Significantly, Cornuaille and de Ligne each wrote his name inside a colored initial found within the final section of the last Magnificat each copied (at the end of the third and eighth Magnificats, respectively). Besides his name de Ligne also inscribed the date 1561, presumably the year in which he added the five Magnificats by Morales. Sometime in the succeeding centuries more than twenty folios were riven from this section, so that at present the Magnificats on the sixth and seventh tones are lacking, and those on the fifth and eighth tones are incomplete.

The three anonymous Magnificats copied by Cornuaille are characterized by large-scale sectional repetitions, long sequential descents, and textures of varying density. The

---

[19]LAN, 4 G 4706 (1512-13), fol. 32v.

[20]Printed in Cristóbal de Morales, *Opera Omnia: XVI Magnificat*, ed. Higinio Anglès, vol. 17 of *Monumentos de la Música Española* (Barcelona, 1956).

[21]A. Le Glay, *Recherches sur l'église métropolitaine de Cambrai* (Paris, 1825), p. 137.

settings of Morales are stylistically more uniform and of a consistently higher artistic quality—a not unexpected disclosure, given Morales' excellence as a composer and the fact that his were arguably the most widely circulated Magnificats of the mid-16th century.

The musical style of the hymns of Cambrai 17 is typical of early 16th-century sacred polyphony with respect to structure, but idiosyncratic in regard to detail. As is normally the case with the polyphonic hymn of this period, the successive phrases of the monophonic melody are extracted, embellished, and made to serve in turn as the primary thematic material in an imitative, polyphonic complex. The usual complement is four voices, although sometimes this is reduced to three or augmented to five or six as sonorous variety is needed. The tenor and soprano generally transmit the melody of the hymn in its least embellished form; if a counter-theme or free counterpoint is present, it usually is to be found in the alto or bass. Four of the hymns draw upon more than one pre-existing melody. In *Magno salutis,* the Compline hymn for Palm Sunday, the antiphon *Pueri hebreorum* is sung in long notes by an added fifth voice (second tenor), while the remaining parts interweave an ornamented version of the *Magno salutis* melody into an accompanying imitative texture. Similarly, in *Vexilla regis* the antiphon *Adoremus crucis* is sung together with the melody of the hymn in the seventh strophe ("Fundis armona"). A secular song, the popular *La rousée du moys de may,* is combined in the second strophe ("Precamur sancte") of *Christe qui lux* with the melody of that Advent hymn.[22] And three *cantus firmi* are employed simultaneously in the six-voice Marian hymn *Quem terra ponthus—O quam glorifica—Ave maris stella*; the soprano and second tenor sing *Quem terra ponthus,* the first and third tenors carry *O quam glorifica,* and the contratenor and bass add *Ave maris stella,* each pair paraphrasing its respective chant. By this use of multiple *cantus firmi* Cambrai 17 appears to evince an affinity to the German polyphonic hymn tradition, inasmuch as more than twenty pieces incorporating this procedure can be identified in coeval German manuscripts and prints:[23]

A detailed examination of the part-writing in the Cambrai hymns reveals a unique or very special approach to musical composition at best, a deficiency of contrapuntal skill at worst. Voices are kept constantly on the move, often with merely mechanical phrases whose function is seemingly more to produce a fuller texture than to advance the melodic line. Parallel fifths and octaves abound, caused perhaps in part by this predilection for full sonority. Unprepared dissonances, harsh appogiaturas, and cross relations appear freely and generate sometimes archaic, sometimes awkward effects. The frequent absence of purposeful melodic movement and long-term harmonic planning suggests a lack of technical fluency. Perhaps some of these compositions represent the better works of a few of the older choirboys of the cathedral, or of young men who had

---

[22]On *La rousée du moys de may,* see Howard M. Brown, *Music in the French Secular Theater, 1400-1550* (Cambridge, Mass., 1963), pp.198-99.

[23]Tom R. Ward, "The Polyphonic Office Hymn from the late Fourteenth Century until the early Sixteenth Century" (Ph.D. diss., University of Pittsburgh, 1969), pp. 144-46; and Rudolf Gerber, ed., *Georg Rhau Sacrorum Hymnorum Liber Primus,* vols. 21 and 25 of *Das Erbe deutscher Musik* (Lippstadt, 1961), nos. 6, 55, 56, and 106.

only recently been choirboys. This conjecture fits well with our knowledge that Jean de Cornuaille was master of grammar to the boys in the 1520's, and it is not inconsistent with the biography of the most prominent composer in the original portion of the manuscript, Jean Lupi.

All of the compositions copied by Cornuaille in the section of hymns and Magnificats of Cambrai 17 are anonymous, and no concordances for them have been found in other sources. In the index, however, a later scribe has named "Lupi" as the author of the *Quem terra ponthus—O quam glorifica—Ave maris stella* found on fol. LXXIIIv and "Ceneau" as the composer of the *O quam glorifica* added on fol. LXXVIIv. This identification was apparently made to distinguish these settings by Jean Lupi and Robin Ceneau from yet a third version of the *O quam glorifica* hymn, this one copied by Cornuaille on fol. IIIIxxIIv. Lupi, the scion of a family that had been established in Cambrai since at least the early 15th century, was born in the city about 1506.[24] He was admitted to the cathedral as a choirboy in June 1514 and served in this capacity for more than seven years. Sometime during this interval he found the opportunity to inscribe his name on the guardleaf at the back of Cambrai 6: "Johannes Lupus enfant de ♥ ." In May 1522 he was sent to the University of Louvain to study philosophy; then four years later he returned to Cambrai to be installed, on 18 June 1526, as a *petit vicaire* of the choir. On 21 March 1527 he was made master of the choirboys, and it was in this position that he served, with varying degrees of success and periods of absence, until his premature death on 20 December 1539. Thus during the years 1527-30 Jean Lupi was master of music to the choirboys while his colleague and fellow vicar Jean de Cornuaille was their master of grammar; the two were in daily communication, both teaching in the house of the choirboys situated next to the cathedral on the south side. It is therefore not surprising that at least two compositions in Cambrai 17, the *Te deum* and the hymn with triple *cantus firmus,* as well as possibly several of the many anonymous hymns, come from the pen of master Lupi. Because most of Cambrai 17 was copied no later than July 1531, the month of Cornuaille's death, the works of Jean Lupi preserved herein must all be youthful compositions, pieces written before his twenty-fifth year.

The composer "Ceneau" identified in the index as the author of the *O quam glorifica* added by a later scribe was also a choirboy at Cambrai. Like Lupi, he too entered his name on the guardleaf at the back of Cambray 6: "Robin Chenneau Enfant de ♥ de nostre dame de Cambray L'an mille vc et xxviij."[25] His *O quam glorifica* is a skillful piece unencumbered with the harsh dissonances and disjunct part-writing found in many of the earlier hymns of Cambrai 17. Besides this one work, no compositions by Ceneau are known, and no additional biographical information has yet come to light.

---

[24]The information on Lupi is drawn from Bonnie J. Blackburn, "Johannes Lupi and Lupus Hellinck: A Double Portrait," *The Musical Quarterly,* LIX (1973), pp. 547-83.

[25]*Ibid.*, Plate 1, bottom right corner.

LUPI'S *TE DEUM* AND CENSIER'S
MISSA *VA-T'EN REGRETZ*

Jean Lupi's *Te deum* shares several characteristics with the anonymous Magnificats of Cambrai 17. As in the settings of the Marian canticle, the plainchant is paraphrased in the soprano or tenor voice, sometimes in both, and polyphony is provided for the entire text, except the intonation. Musically the *Te deum* is not a superior work, falling short of the artistic level reached in the collection of Lupi's motets published posthumously by Pierre Attaingnant.[26] Of special interest is his setting of the verse "Et laudamus," here for three voices. The bass and tenor are written out in full (the latter bearing the *cantus firmus*), but the contratenor must be derived by the performers of that part; they are to sing in parallel fourths above the tenor according to the canon "Quere cum tenore dyatessaron." Thus a short composition in *fauxbourdon* is created. Though incongruent with the musical style of the other sections of the *Te deum*, the verse "Et laudamus" is nonetheless a further manifestation of the long tradition of singing in *fauxbourdon* and *falsobordone* at Cambrai.[27]

Nothing is known of Simonet Censier, the composer of the incompletely preserved Missa *Va-t'en regretz*. Yet the inclusion of his work in a manuscript entirely local in repertory (excluding the later additions) suggests that he, too, may have been a musician at Cambrai perhaps, like Lupi and Ceneau, an *enfant de choeur*. His Mass is fully as unusual as he is obscure. The tenor voice throughout consists of strictly controlled repetitions of all or part of the tenor of Compère's famous chanson of this name.[28] In the five-voice *Credo,* for example, the chanson is divided into fragments of one or more notes, and each of these units is then immediately repeated. Censier's preoccupation with the linear, constructional aspects of his borrowed melody is somewhat of an archaism, since most Masses in manuscripts contemporary with Cambrai 17—Cambrai 3 and 4, for example—are of the newer, free parody sort. Similarly, his refusal to allow the melody-bearing tenor to take part in the many imitations found in the other voices is a vestige of the older, *cantus-firmus* style Mass of the era of Dufay and his contemporaries.

One final observation about Lupi's *Te deum* and Censier's Mass need be made: the soprano voice here is regularly a third higher than it is in the hymns and Magnificats. Perhaps the soprano of these two works was sung partly or wholly by choirboys, whereas the soprano of the hymns and Magnificats may have been executed only by adult males in falsetto, the upper-most range of the choirboys being roughly a third higher than that of the adult falsettists. We know that as a rule the choirboys did not participate in the singing of the psalms and hymns at the canonical hours at Cambrai. They did, however, frequently join in the performance of polyphonic Masses and ceremonial motets; the *Te deum,* which often served at Cambrai, as elsewhere, as a paraliturgical hymn of joy or welcome, fell into this latter category.

---

[26]*Jo. Lupi, Chori Sacre Virginis Marie Cameracensis Magistri, Musice Cantiones* (Paris, 1542).

[27]For more on *fauxbourdon* at Cambrai, see Wright, "Performance Practices."

[28]The chanson is printed in Loyset Compère, *Opera Omnia,* ed. Ludwig Finscher, vol. 15 of *Corpus Mensurabilis Musicae,* (American Institute of Musicology [Rome], 1972), V, p. 58.

DATE AND PROVENANCE

Unlike many manuscripts of Renaissance music, the date and place of origin of Cambrai 17 can be determined with precision. We may reasonably conclude that the volume was not begun before the spring of 1526, for it was at this time that the twenty-year-old Jean Lupi returned to Cambrai from the University of Louvain; even if the youthful Lupi had acquired the skill to create the lengthy *Te deum* and the hymn incorporating three *cantus firmi*, it seems improbable that Cornuaille would have had access to them before the composer's return to Cambrai. Obviously the original portion of the manuscript must have been completed before July 1531, the month of Cornuaille's death. Thus the years 1526-31 stand as the broad temporal parameters for all but the later additions. Within these limits it may be possible to circumscribe the date of the manuscript even more narrowly. On fols. LIII and CVv are found two coats of arms: the first, three fleurs-de-lis on a shield surmounted by a crown, are those of the king of France, at this time King Francis I; the second, a double-headed eagle with crown, are those of the Holy Roman Emperor, specifically Emperor Charles V since his device, "Plus oultre," is inscribed here. The appearance of the arms of Francis I and Charles V in a manuscript from Cambrai immediately calls to mind an important political event that transpired in that city in 1529: the signing of the so-called *Paix des dames.* It was during August of that year that Louise of Savoy, the mother of Francis, and Margaret of Austria, the aunt of Charles, negotiated an end to the hostilities between the Most Christian King and his enemy the Holy Roman Emperor.[29] The relationship between the contents of manuscripts Cambrai 3 and 4 and the conference of 1529 has already been the subject of fruitful speculation.[30] It appears that the principal scribe of Cambrai 17 was also not oblivious to the political events that swirled around his church in the summer of 1529 and made symbolic reference to them by including the arms of the rival factions in his manuscript. If the blazons are in fact a product of the *Paix des dames,* then the bulk of Cambrai 17 was executed between August 1529 and July 1531.

As for the later additions, we may presume that the Magnificats of Morales were copied early in the second half of the 16th century, since the scribe, Julien de Ligne, affixed the date 1561 to one of these. The interpolated strophes of the hymns *Signum cruce* and *Christe qui lux* as well as the introit [*Gaudeamus*] *omnes in domino* were likely inserted about this same time, judging from the similar appearance of the hands. Only Censier's setting of *O quam glorifica,* with its earlier calligraphic style, is roughly contemporary with the hymns copied by Cornuaille. Two other additional pieces, one, "Sex ante pasche" (strophe two of *Magno salutis*) inserted between the *Te deum* and index, and the other, "Nardi Maria" (strophe three of the same hymn) appended to the very end of the manuscript, carry the dates 1601 and 1560, respectively. Taken in sum, these later musical insertions and the added textual marginalia—the latter being in most

---

[29]See A. Durieux, "Les logements de la paix des dames," *Mémoires de la Société d'émulation de Cambrai,* XXXIV (1878), pp. 223-62.

[30]Herbert Kellman, "Musical Links between France and the Empire, 1500-1530," paper read at the Annual Meeting of the American Musicological Society, Toronto, Canada, 5-8, November 1970.

cases the scribbling of restless choirboys—attest to the continual presence of this manuscript within the choir of the church; Cambrai 17 was apparently in use at the cathedral as late as the end of the 17th century. It thus stands as further testimony to the generally conservative nature of the polyphonic repertory of many ecclesiastical centers of music.

The presence of Cambrai 17 within the choir of the cathedral, the biographies of Cornuaille, de Ligne, Lupi, and Ceneau, and the absence of concordances for all pieces except the Morales Magnificats strongly suggest that this manuscript is of local origin—that it emanated from the cathedral itself. Any lingering doubt as to its provenance is dispelled by a consideration of liturgical traditions. Cambrai 17 provides settings for the hymns *Eterne rex* for Vespers of Ascension and *Beata nobis* for Vespers of Pentecost. Neither of these hymns is usually included in Italian or German sources where *Jesu nostra redemptio* or *Festum nunc celebre* is traditionally employed for Ascension and *Veni creator spiritus* for Pentecost.[31] Both, however, are found without exception in the monophonic hymnals of Cambrai, hymnals such as Cambrai 28, 29, 30, and 32. Yet none of these 13th- and 14th-century monophonic sources can be identified as the one manuscript from which the *cantus firmi* of Cambrai 17 were drawn.[32] Undoubtedly there were other, later hymnals in use in the choir of the cathedral which have not survived. Two payments recorded in the accounts of the *fabrique* of the church suggest the existence of such manuscripts:

> 1506. A Symon Miellet pour avoir escript et note plusieurs hymnes et les suffrages communes de toute l'annee en les deux psaultiers du coeur pour les petis vicaires . . .[33]

> 1517-18. Item, a messire Julien de Freumont, alias Cruppedoziere, vicaire de St. Gery, pour avoir escript six cayers en velin du volume des grandz psaultiers qui sont noeufs ou sont toutes les hymnes notees de toutes les heures du jour, selon le change de toute l'annee avec les rubriques, ossy aulcunes hymnes de Complie en discant et le Te deum . . . x 1b.[34]

In sum, the liturgical, calligraphical, armorial, and biographical evidence leads ineluctably to Cambrai as the place of origin of our manuscript. And herein lies the significance of this source: there are no extant polyphonic hymnals from French-

---

[31]Ward, "Polyphonic Office Hymn," pp. 85 and 158.

[32]The great number of melodic variants revealed by a comparison of these monophonic sources forcefully demonstrates that there were different melodic traditions not only within a single region or diocese, but also within a particular church, and, as in the case of Cambrai 29, sometimes even within one and the same manuscript.

[33]Jules Houdoy, *Histoire artistique de la cathédral de Cambrai, ancienne église métropolitaine Notre-Dame: Comptes, inventaires et documents inédits* (Mémoires de la Société des sciences, de l'agriculture et des arts de Lille, 4th series, vol. VII [1880]), p. 206.

[34]LAN, 4 G 4708 (1517-18), fol. 40; and Houdoy, *Histoire*, p. 209.

speaking lands that pre-date this volume. Only the Apt manuscript, a collection compiled at the end of the 14th century under the influence of the papal court at Avignon, is an earlier French cycle;[35] but the ten hymns contained therein occupy only three folios of the manuscript, and, even if the source is French in origin, the liturgical usage these hymns represent is decidedly Italian.[36] The long span between Apt and Cambrai 17 is nearly void of French musical sources: there are virtually no surviving manuscripts of sacred polyphony of French origin for the 15th century. Thus Cambrai 17, despite its relatively late date, emerges as the first extant French polyphonic hymnal.

---

[35]Printed in *Le manuscrit du trésor d'Apt* (*XIVe-XVe siècles*), ed. Amédée Gastoué, vol. 10 of *Publications de la Société francaise de musicologie* (Paris, 1936), pp.56-64.

[36]Ward, ''Polyphonic Office Hymn,'' p. 11.

ORIGINAL FORMAT OF CAMBRAI 17 AS CONCEIVED BY JEAN DE CORNUAILLE	LATER ADDITIONS

fol. 1: *

fol. 1v-2:

fol. 2v:

fol. a: (Title page)

fol. av-j: Jo. Lupi: *Te deum*

fol. jv-0:

fol. 0v: (Index)

fol. I:

fol. Iv-V: *Conditor alme: dominica prima adventus ad vesperas hymnus*

fol. Vv-VIII: *Criste qui lux: ad completorium*

fol. VIIIv-X: *Verbum supernum: dominica prima ad matutinas*

fol. Xv-XII: *A solis ortus: in nativitate domini ad vesperas hymnus*

fol. XIIv-XV: *Agnoscat omne: in nativitate domini ad completorium et ad horas hymnus*

fol. XVv-XVII: *Corde natus: in nativitate domini ad matutinas*

fol. XVIIv-XVIII: *Hostis herodes: in epyphania domini ad vesperas hymnus*

fol. XVIIIv-XX: *Nuncium vobis: ad completorium et ad matutinas inepyphania domini*

fol. XXv-XXIII: *Jhesu salvator: a septuagesima usque ad quadragesimam ad completorium*

fol. XXIIIv-XXV: *Audi benigne: dominica prima et secunda in quadragesima ad vesperas*

fol. XXVv-XXVIII: *Cultor dei memento: ad completorium hymnus in quadragesima per quatuor ebdomadas*

LATER ADDITIONS:

''Amen;'' scribbles; date 1607

Hymn *Verbum supernum;* scribbles; date 1638.

Scribbles; dates 1660 & 1663.

''Sex ante pasche,'' strophe two of hymn *Magno salutis,* dated 1601

''Amen primj toni''

*The Arabic and alphabetical foliations are not present in the manuscript; they have been added here by the authors for clarity of presentation.

fol. XXVIIIv-XXX: *Clarum decus: dominica tercia in quadragesima ad vesperas hymnus*

fol. XXXv-XXXII: *Jhesu quadragenarie: dominica quarta in quadragesima ad vesperas.*

fol. XXXIIv-XXXV: *Vexilla regis: dominica in passione ad vesperas hymnus*

fol. XXXVv-XXXVII: *Jam ter quaternis: dominica in passione ad completorium*

fol. XXXVIIv-XXXIX: *Magno salutis-Pueri hebreorum: dominica in ramis palmarum sabbato precedente ad completorium et per totam diem*

fol. XXXIXv-XLII: *Ad cenam agni: ab octavis pasce usque ad ascensionem ad vesperas hymnus*

fol. XLIIv-XLV: *Jhesu nostra redemptio: ab octavis pasche usque ad penthecostes ad completorium hymnus*

fol. XLVv-XLVIII: *Eterne rex: in ascensione domini ad vesperas hymnus*

fol. XLVIIIv-L: *Beata nobis: in festo penthecostes ad vesperas hymnus*

fol. Lv-LII: *Illuminator omnium: in festo penthecostes ad completorium hymnus*

fol. LIIv-LIIII: *Nunc sancte nobis: in festo penthecostes ad horas diei*

fol. LIIIIv-LVI: *Pange lingua: in solemnitate sacramenti altaris ad vesperas*

fol. LVIv-LVII: [Verbum supernum sacramenti: in solemnitate sacramenti altaris ad completorium hymnus]

"Ut ore tibi," strophe four of hymn *Signum cruce* sung at Cambrai *in exaltatione crucis ad vesperas*

fol. LVIIv-LX: [Sacris solemniis: in solemnitate sacramenti ad matutinas]

[*Gaudeamus*] *omnes in domino,* introit for Marian Masses

fol. LXv-LXIII: [Urbs beata: in dedicatione ecclesie ad vesperas hymnus]

"Oculi somnum," "Memento nostri" and "Precamur sancte," strophes four, six and two of hymn *Christe qui lux* (see fol. Vv)

fol. LXIIIv-LXV: *Te lucis: ad completorium post trinitatem*

fol.LXVv-LXVII: *Exultet celum: unius vel plurimum apostolorum ad vesperas hymnus*

fol. LXVIIv-LXIX: *Martir dei: unius martiris ad vesperas hymnus*

161

fol. LXIXv-LXXI: *Sanctorum meritis: plurimorum martirum ad vesperas hymnus*

fol. LXXIv-LXXIII: *Iste confessor: unius confessoris ad vesperas*

fol. LXXIIIv-LXXIIII: [Jo. Lupi]: *Quem terra-O quam glorifica-Ave maris stella* (Vespers hymn for Marian feasts)

fol. LXXIIIIv-LXXVII: *Quem terra: in festo conceptionis et nativitatis beate marie ad vesperas hymnus*

fol. LXXVIIv-LXXIX: [Quod chorus vatem: in festo purificationis beate marie ad vesperas]

"Amen" in a later hand [Robin Ceneau]: *O quam glorifica: in festo assumptionis beate marie ad vesperas*

fol. LXXIXv-IIIIxxII: *Ave maris stella: in festo anunciationis beate marie ad vesperas hymnus*

fol. IIIIxxIIv-IIIIxxIIII: *O quam glorifica: in festo assumptionis beate marie virginis ad vesperas*

fol. IIIIxxIIIIv-IIIIxxV: (blank)

fol. IIIIxxVv-IIIIxxXII: *Magnificat: primi toni*

fol. IIIIxxXIIv-IIIIxxXVIII: *Magnificat: secundi toni*

fol. IIIIxxXVIIIv-CV: *Magnificat: tercii toni*

fol. CVv-CXI: [Magnificat: quarti toni]

[Morales]: *Magnificat: quarti toni*

fol. CXIv-[CXVIII]: [Magnificat: quinti toni]

[Morales]: *Magnificat: quinti toni* (incomplete)

fol. [CXVIIIv-CXXVI]: [Magnificat: sexti toni]

[Morales: Magnificat: sexti toni]

fol. [CXXVIv-CXXXIII]: [Magnificat: septi toni]

[Morales: Magnificat: septi toni]

fol. [CXXXIIIv]-CXL: [Magnificat: octavi toni]

[Morales]: *Magnificat: octavi toni* (incomplete)

fol. CXLv-A:

Hymn *Jesu quadragenarie*

fol. Av-B: Simonet Censier: *Missa Vaten regretz*, "Kyrie"

fol. Bv-C: "Et in terra"

fol. Cv-D: "Patrem omnipotentem"

fol. Dv-E: "Crucifixus"

fol. Ev-[F]: "Et unam sanctam"

fol. [Fv-G]: ["Sanctus"]

162

fol. [Gv]-H: "Osanna"

fol. Hv-I: "Agnus dei" (I & II)

fol. Iv-J: "Agnus dei" (III)

fol. Jv: Hymn *O quam glorifica*

fol. 3:   "Ut dum grani," strophe four of
                                                hymn *Jhesu salvator*

fol. 3v: Scribbles

fol. 4:   "Te deprecamur," strophe three of
                                                hymn *Jhesu salvator*

fol. 4v: Scribbles

fol. 5:   "Nardi Maris," strophe three of
                                                hymn *Magno salutis,* dated 1560

fol. 5v: Scribbles; dates 1666 & 1681

PROGRESSIVE CONCEPTS OF PITCH RELATIONSHIPS AS OBSERVED IN THE SYMPHONIES OF BRAHMS

by Louise E. Cuyler

Almost a century has passed since Brahms' four symphonies, all completed within a span of nine years between 1876 and 1885, were heard for the first time. These works were widely played during Brahms' lifetime and remain an important part of the standard symphonic repertoire. But even today writers tend to discuss them romantically and subjectively. In general, they follow the lead of such enthusiasts as Clara Schumann and Theodor Billroth;[1] or they are only slightly less contemptuous than G. B. Shaw and Hugo Wolf, dismissing the symphonies as derivative or wanting in substance.

The purpose of this brief article is to depart from such personal views of Brahms' music to survey a particular aspect of his compositional technique—pitch organization—in serious analytical fashion. As will be shown presently, Brahms was indeed progressive in his concepts, often anticipating such innovative composers of the next generation as Stravinsky and Darius Milhaud. A number of passages that have baffled aspirant critics (along with many conductors who read them in murky fashion) become plausible, bold, and musically sound when realized as early instances of bitonality, progressive tonality, or stratified texture.

Bitonality

Although the four symphonies were products of Brahms' middle years (the first movement of the First Symphony was written intermittently during some fifteen years before 1876), a youthful orchestral work, the First Piano Concerto (1854-61) is really their prototype, since it was conceived first as a symphony. Brahms was never bolder in his comprehension of advanced pitch relationships than in the first movement of this concerto. Its opening statement presents convincing instances of both principal types of bitonality:

1) *Linear bitonality,* which is sometimes called *progressive tonality.* In its typical context, two keys are adjacent within a palpable unit such as a principal thematic member, which commences at a different tonal level than that confirmed by the terminal (or other determinative) cadence. The key at this cadence point is most often that prescribed by Classical tradition. For

[1]Who wrote of the Second Syphony when first he played it (1877): "It is all rippling streams, blue sky, sunshine and cool green shadows." (Quoted in Karl Geiringer, *Brahms, His Life and Work* [New York, 1961], p. 119.)

example, a movement in F major with a first theme in that key might have a second theme commencing in D minor but cadencing in C major, the traditional dominant key. This is actually the case in the second movement of Mozart's C major Piano Concerto K. 467, which might well have been one of Brahms' models.

2) *Vertical bitonality*, which employs two key levels simultaneously, most effectively within *stratified texture* to keep the two levels well delineated. Obviously this type is much more overt than linear bitonality; and it is most convincing when projected in an ensemble medium, or by harpsichord or organ, instruments offering a variety of timbres.

Example 1

Brahms, *First Piano Concerto*, Opening (mm. 1–13)

As seen in Example 1, the principal key of D minor (confirmed by key signature) is implied by the opening unison on the note *D* which is prolonged into a ten-measure pedal point. A second, simultaneous stratum of this opening texture (Violin 1 and Cello) superposes the broken B-flat triad (VI of D minor) to the *D* pedal; the linear development of this stratum adds the note *A* flat recurrently with a strong suggestion of V^7-of-IV of the key of B flat. The result in this clearly stratified texture is a strong sense of bitonality: D minor and B flat major. The next vital harmony is achieved when the bass line moves to the pitch *C* sharp (m. 11) set as the first inversion note of V^7 of the key of D minor; since the superposed melodic stratum overlays a sequence of the opening motive (the broken A major triad) to this, D minor emerges as the essential key. This passage presents one of Brahms' earliest experiments with both linear (in the melodic stratum, B flat-E flat) and vertical (D minor-B flat) bitonality. The reprise of this passage at the beginning of the Recapitulation section of this sonata-type design (see Ex. 2) overlays the E major triad in solo piano to the D minor pedal point; this serves at once to project the piano over the orchestra, and to deny the repose characteristic of the Classic Recapitulation. While it has the immediate effect of vertical bitonality, the composite

Example 2
Brahms, *First Piano Concerto*, Recapitulation (mm. 310 – 322)

harmonic result is that of V^7-of-V (E-G♯-B-D) of D minor, confirmed with the arrival of dominant harmony at measures 320-21.

Two conditions present in these early bitonal examples should be pointed out. First, the tension is the less great because the implication of one of the keys—D minor—is carried by a single note, the pedal point. Second, the most abrasive note in the second stratum of bitonality is enharmonically equivalent in the two instances: the A flat in the opening statement equals G sharp in the Recapitulation. The A flat in the former suggests E flat, a key totally foreign to D minor; but its enharmonic equivalent, G sharp, as third of V^7-of-V, seems less alien and is easily realized within the environment of the key of D minor.

As contrasted with their probable prototypes in the First Piano Concerto, most of the instances of bitonal texture in the symphonies are less complex, hence clearer. Their primary purpose, however, is similar: the creation of tension and, often, of propulsion.

In the First Symphony

The single instance of bitonality in the First Symphony is reserved for the final movement, and its placement is unique since it occurs during a passage of transition. Interestingly, the situation in the thematic areas of the first movement provides the very kind of stratified texture so often employed by Brahms to project bitonality. In this case, however, the composer used it to delineate another type of contrast, which might be described as ''The Diatonic'' versus ''The Chromatic.''(See Ex. 3). The principal theme is comprised of two superposed melodic strata: the higher, diatonic (triadic) one carried by first violins, and the lower, chromatic one by bassoons and cellos. (Both motives had been introduced in elemental form during the introductory *Un poco sostenuto*.)

Example 3
Brahms, *Symphony I/1* (mm. 42 – 46)[2]

[2]Reference to specific movements in the text and examples may be as follows: I/1 (= First Symphony, first movement), III/4 (= Third Symphony, fourth movement), and so on.

Turning to the finale of the First Symphony, it might be recalled that this movement is cast in a large sonata design which is unusual because it lacks a genuine Midsection (Development). Instead, the second tonal area of the Exposition veers away from its conventional tonal axis, G major, around measure 148 where the key of E minor is confirmed. After a brief return to G (meas. 164-67), the texture becomes definitely bitonal: E minor is asserted by the triplet-bearing parts, whereas C major is suggested simultaneously by all parts carrying the iambic (= ♩. ♪) rhythm. This bitonal mixture persists until a brief passage of transient modulation intervenes, which but leads to a strong confirmation of E minor at measure 182-83. The V⁷ of C is then interjected suddenly, and the first principal theme appears immediately in that key to confirm Recapitulation. In this passage, Brahms apparently intends that the bitonal joust between E minor and C major provide the tension and propulsion for retransition, more conventionally supplied by a prolonged dominant passage (see Ex. 4).

Example 4
Brahms, *Symphony I/4*, Retransition (mm. 168–87)

cont'd.

Ex. 4, cont'd.

In the Second Symphony

During the first movement of the Second Symphony, the second principal theme offers a fine example of Brahms' characteristic tonal coyness. While this quality is achieved by a kind of linear bitonality, "progressive tonality" is perhaps a more suitable term here, since successive cadence points suggest at least two different tonal levels, neither of them that of the key implicit during the entire, prolonged thematic area. In fact, the very avoidance of determinative key establishment is the principal means of prolongation. As will be observed in Example 5, a modulation to F-sharp minor, the mediant key of the opening D major, is prepared in measure 81, and the new theme enters in the next measure (violas and cellos). Despite the clear F-sharp minor of its opening, the traditional dominant key, A major, is probably implicit during the long linear expansion of this theme: measure 85 has a light cadence (I $^6_4$ -V) in that key but without pause; and measures 88-9 have an instance of extreme tonal coyness since the cadential bass (E to A) strongly suggests the key of A, while the overlying parts provide another dominant (I $^6_4$ -V) cadence, this time in D major. The ensuing measures are tonally ambiguous, especially the cadence group (measures 96-100) where the keys of D, then F-sharp minor are implied although without confirmation by any dominant-to-tonic succession. An immediate reprise of the thematic group (measure 102 ff.) again commences in F sharp minor and is extended, with more tonal ambivalence, until a unison outcome on the dominant note (*E*) of the key of A, which has been implicit though largely unexpressed throughout the statement. The proof of this lies in the embellished restatement of this second principal theme that occurs thirty-eight measures later, as the result of a massive dominant pedal point. This time the theme is

Example 5
Brahms, *Symphony II /1*, Second Theme (mm. 80 – 118)

cont'd.

170

Ex. 5, *cont'd.*

cont'd.

171

Ex. 5, *cont'd.*

cont'd.

Ex. 5, cont'd.

etc.

set unequivocally in A major and leads quickly to the traditional cadence in that key at the close of the Exposition section.

The third movement of the Second Symphony has a very simple example of vertical bitonality in its opening subject. Here the arpeggiated figure of the cello implies G major, whereas the melodic part (oboe) is strongly suggestive of E minor (see Ex. 6).

Example 6
Brahms, *Symphony II /3*, Opening (mm. 1 – 6)

173

The single example of bitonality in the Third Symphony occurs in the second movement, and it is the boldest, least equivocal of all. After an opening subject in a singularly uncomplicated key of C major, the second subject, by Classic tradition in G major, is approached, at first directly through introduction of the note *F* sharp. But soon this traditional preparation is circumvented by the incursion of one of Brahms' most devious non-tonal passages which will be discussed presently under a separate heading. The close of this passage, however, returns to the climate of the expected G major when the chord A-C#-E-G, V^7-of-V of G major, is taken (m. 40 in Ex. 7). The second principal subject commences immediately, and is unmistakably bitonal in texture. The strings fulfill the G major preparation in highly tonal harmonies (mm. 41-5):

Harmonies:	V^7	II^7	V^7	vii^7 of II	II^7	I	vii^7 of V
Measures as in Ex. 7:	41	42	43	44			45

Example 7

Brahms, *Symphony III / 2* (mm. 27 – 47)

cont'd.

174

Ex. 7, *cont'd.*

Above this passage is projected a melodic member (clarinet and bassoon) which constitutes the second principal theme. The theme is organized on purely linear precepts
and implies the key of A minor, unmistakably signalled by the succession F-sharp, G-
sharp, A (mm. 43-4) from the so-called "melodic" minor of A. With the cadence of

175

measure 45, the two strata of activity concur for the first time in the strong "half" cadence of G major. The ensuing phrase is in nearly exact sequence a fourth higher, and superposes a melodic member in D minor to supportive harmony in C major.

In the Fourth Symphony

Like so many of his peer composers of the later nineteenth century, Brahms often sought refreshment for the undeniably tired harmonic language of his day in sounds that were current in earlier times, especially in the ecclesiastical modes. In the second and fourth movements of the Fourth Symphony, the exemplar is clearly the Phrygian, the most distinctive of the modes through its characteristic semitone between the first and second degrees. Even in a sixteenth-century contrapuntal context, the Phrygian mode often emerged as a bitonal entity through conflict between its *finalis E,* and its typical cadence taken on an *A*-based sonority. At a definitive cadence point, the lowest voice in a setting of a Phrygian tune often vacillated between the notes *E* and *A* as a point of final closure. Moreover, when the final sonority was *E*-based, the triadic third, if present, was generally inflected *G* sharp for the "tierce de Picardie." The effect of this, to modern, tonally-oriented ears is that the closure is taken on V of A minor.

The opening motto of the second movement of the Fourth Symphony is clear in its Phrygian derivation, for the unison linear passage of the first three measures is entirely of the "white keys" but has its outcome (m. 4) in the E major triad, the first harmony heard (Ex. 8).

The theme itself enters in the next measure and is inherently in E major; however, the notes *D* natural and *C* natural (violas, then other parts) link the passage to the "white key" environment of the opening motto. Furthermore, the alternation of bass notes between *E* and *A* heightens the Phrygian reference. This is often cited as one of Brahms' most "exotic" movements. However, the supposed exotic sound is typically Phrygian-derived.

The well-known Passacaglia-Chaconne subject of the finale of the Fourth Symphony also shows Phrygian influences (see Ex. 9).

The principal Phrygian link is perceived in a beginning-to-end view of the structure: the opening establishes an A minor harmony whereas the close is the E major triad. Thus the immediate effect is a pause on V of A minor, creating automatic propulsion toward the A minor start of the variation which follows. Between these two points, however, the ordinary key of E minor is clearly inherent (also indicated by the signature), and the harmony of measures 2 through 6 is a typical progression for that key. At the penultimate chord (measure 7), the Phrygian mode is again suggested when the dominant-seventh chord of E minor is inflected with *F* natural (B-D♯-F♮ -A), the second inversion providing the typical semitonal progression to the note *E* in the bass in measure 8.

Many other works, composed at various times throughout Brahms' life, show how consistent was his bitonal thinking. From the viewpoint of the performer, comprehension of the essentially ambivalent nature of passages such as those cited above can lead to intelligent readings that stress the tension and conflict inherent in them.

176

Example 8
Brahms, *Symphony IV/2*, Opening (mm. 1 – 8)

177

Example 9
Brahms, *Symphony IV/4*, Passacaglia Theme

Non-tonal Pitch Organization

For his large-scale works Brahms preferred strongly tonal themes (occasionally bitonal ones, as seen above). The reason is that Brahms' chosen designs—almost always a sonata type or a simple partite structure—required projection of a strong tonal dualism for their delineation. Hence, examples of non-tonal pitch organization are found exclusively during passages of extension or transition. Certainly Brahms never achieved true duodecuplism, and even his freest passages have a tonal outcome. But some of Brahms' characteristic and adroit means of maintaining cohesiveness during temporary suspension of key bear examination.

The long pedal point was, of course, the anchor used by all nineteenth century composers to secure long passages of nebulous organization, and Brahms made full use of the pedal point—the simple, as well as the so-called "inverted" or "internal" ones. An interesting variant is the recurrent note that is a centripetal point during prolonged, active figuration; in ensemble pieces, this note is likely to occur in various octaves and various instruments. A few examples are cited below but without musical illustrations.

Symphony I/4, measures 23-25. The note *C* is probably implicit all during this discursive passage which leads to the great C major horn subject of the Introduction.

Symphony III/1, measures 116-123. The note *F* is implicit during this entire passage, which is the immediate retransition to the Recapitulation of the sonata design, although *F* is not expressed until the third measure of the passage. Here, Brahms devises an interesting substitute for the traditional dominant as a retransitional means. *F* of this passage actually anticipates the point of arrival, the reprise of the first principal theme in F major (mm. 124 ff.). All during the passage of approach (mm.116-123), the *F* is complicated by conflicting lines and inflections foreign to F major. The relaxation traditional at the Recapitulation is achieved when all conflicting elements

178

disappear and the first principal theme sounds a strong, uncomplicated *F* major.

Symphony IV/1, measures 9-15. This passage is an extension of the opening statement of the first principal subject. The note *C* is centripetal during the entire passage, mostly in upper parts; the outcome, however, is the bass *C* of measure 15, which commences a "circle-of-fifths" bass movement (C-F♯-B-E) leading to restatement of the subject.

A second anchoring device favored by Brahms is the chromatic bass, descending or ascending, which is often comprised of the notes of the upper tetrachord of the "melodic" minor mode. This is another anachronistic figure, one used routinely by seventeenth- and eighteenth-century composers (see, for example, Dido's "Lament" of Purcell, or the "Qui tollis" of the Great C minor Mass of Mozart). The Fourth Symphony with its Phrygian-influenced second and fourth movements shows, not surprisingly, this additional archaism. At measures 9 through 14 of the first movement (just discussed in the paragraph above), the bass note *D* sharp initiates a chromatic ascent to *A*; this is an additional factor in organizing this essentially non-tonal passage. The counterpart of this passage occurs at measures 27 through 31: here the note *D* sharp initiates a chromatic descent to *B* (m. 31), the notes of the passage comprising the members of the chromatic upper tetrachord of the E minor scale.

A third means of cohesiveness employed by Brahms during non-tonal passages is sequence—melodic, harmonic, perhaps both, and sometimes carried out to remarkable length. In this, Mozart may again have been his model, for Mozart devised some spectacular sequential passages, especially during retransition to Recapitulation in his sonata designs. The retransition areas in the first movements of his G minor Symphony (K. 550) and his D major "Hunt" Sonata (K. 576) have fine examples. The boldest of all Brahms' passages of similar intent occurs in the second movement of the Third Symphony. As can be seen in Example 7, the direct approach to the bitonal second theme is taken in a passage of strikingly non-tonal content. However, close scrutiny reveals that this passage is organized from a four-note melodic figure treated sequentially, supported by a series of major-minor seventh chords on the roots B, A, G, A, connected by passing harmonies. The portion of Ex. 7 devoted to this passage is rearranged in Example 10 to show the sequences:

Example 10

Brahms, *Symphony III/2*, Reduction of mm. 33–40 to show sequences

As was pointed out earlier, this non-tonal passage has its outcome in measure 40 on the chord A-C♯-E-G, V^7-of-V for the approaching key of G major, which is implicit all during the second thematic area.

The transitional passage just discussed sounds unconvincing in nearly all readings of this movement, and the fault lies not entirely with the conductor. The composer himself probably erred in approaching a bitonal subject through a passage that is itself abstruse. In the musical language of the late nineteenth century, non-tonal and polytonal passages are most effective when they stand in clear juxtaposition to their opposites: passages of clear, uncomplicated tonal organization. For the most part, Brahms appears to have recognized this. His recourse to the oldest and perhaps most successful of bitonal entities, the Phrygian mode, makes his Fourth Symphony singularly effective in projecting its tonal ambivalence. As in so many instances, the sixteenth-century masters were the best models!

AMERICAN AWARENESS OF THE OTHER AMERICAS TO 1900

by Robert Stevenson

During the 19th century, American interest in Latin American political events stimulated a constant stream of sheet music publications. The two decades during which Latin America was most to the fore were of course the 1840's and the 1890's. However, as early as 1810 the New York-based Peter Weldon published there a *Brazilian Waltz* for flute, clarinet, or violin and piano, welcoming King John VI of Portugal to the New World.[1] In an article tracing musical relations between Brazil and the United States, Carleton Sprague Smith began with Weldon's waltz, the Portuguese title of which was *Favorita Waltz Brazilense Para Piano Forte com Accompanhamento de Flauta Clarinete ò Violin.*[2] The engraving on Weldon's cover shows the royal disembarkation at Rio de Janeiro in January of 1808.

According to Smith, a change from major to minor would infuse a more Brazilian character into the perky waltz theme. Weldon's piano part glistens with brilliant sixteenth-note arpeggiated figuration in the treble supported by a close-position waltz bass. The opening strains of the melody for flute, clarinet, or violin read thus:

Example 1
Brazilian Waltz (1810)

[1] Peter Weldon's New York City addresses from 1800 through 1808 are listed in Virginia Larkin Redway, *Music Directory of Early New York City* (New York,1941), p. 24. Musicians with French and Italian surnames frequently turn up in the pre-1850 New York City directories indexed by her, but not those with Spanish surnames. As an exception, she found Antonio C. Martínez variously listed as "professor of music" or "musician" from 1844 through 1875. Only in the 1850's and 1860's did New York begin receiving Spanish surname musicians such as Jaime Nunó and the Carreños.

[2] "Relañoes musicais entre o Brasil e os Estados Unidos de Norte America," *Boletín Latino-Americano de Música,* VI (Rio de Janeiro, 1946), pp. 140-141. See also his remarks on Weldon's Brazilian Waltz in Richard J. Wolfe, *Secular Music in America 1801-1825: A Bibliography* (New York, 1964), I, pp. xv-xvi.

Whether in any true sense Brazilian or not, Weldon's waltz did catch the American public's fancy. Richard J. Wolfe listed ten further issues at New York, Boston, and Philadelphia, all presumably antedating 1825.[3]

Among other sheet music antedating 1825, Carleton Sprague Smith signaled a song and two marches paying tribute to Simón Bolívar (1783-1830), a set of five waltzes dedicated to Bernardo O'Higgins (1778-1842), and two marches dedicated to Jean Pierre Boyer (1776-1850), the ruler of Haiti from 1818 to 1843.[4] The second of the marches honoring Haiti's longest ruler is additionally significant because Francis Johnson (1792-1844), who wrote it, was in his epoch by all odds the most-published composer of African descent. Around 1823 President Boyer had begun offering free passage and a small settlement allowance to attract free Blacks from the United States. By 1825 enough Blacks from the North had arrived at Port-au-Prince to start an African Methodist Episcopal church there.[5] Johnson's *Recognition March* not only called attention to the guaranteed safety of Haiti's coasts, now that France had (for a promised indemnity) relinquished all claims to what was formerly her richest New World colony, but the march also cast a glow on President Boyer's immigration offers. Decisively his most elaborate published work, Johnson's tribute to the ruler of Haiti presents some Beethovenish motives, modulates effectively, and contains a few bars in which melody and accompaniment answer each other imitatively.[6] Boyer, who had in his youth visited Paris and who died there, presumably had sufficient musical taste to appreciate these gestures.

---

[3]Wolfe, *Secular Music In America*, III, pp. 949-950.

[4]*Bolivar. A Peruvian Battle Song. As sung by Mr. Howard with unbounded applause at the Chatham Theatre. Written by G. P. Morris, Esqr. Arranged by T. W. H. B. B.* Philadelphia, Published and sold by Geo. Willig, 171 Chestnut St. Price 38 cts. (Wolfe, item 384); *General Bolivar's Grand March.* New York, Published by N. Thurston, and *General Bolivar's March Dedicated to the Columbians by the Publishers.* New York, Published by A. & W. Geib, 23 Maiden lane (Wolfe, 2938, 2939; both marches are by George Geib).

Five South American waltzes. Dedicated to Don Bernardo O'Higgins, Supreme Dictator of Chili. New York, Engraved, printed & sold by E. Riley, 29 Chatham street. In numerical order the five waltzes are entitled: "O'Higgins waltz," "Buenos Ayres waltz," "Constellation waltz," "The Siege of Callao," "Gen. San Martin's waltz" (Wolfe, 8458). These waltzes were copyrighted August 29, 1823.

The President of Hayti's march. Composed for & respectfully dedicated to His Excellency Jean Pierre Boyar by E. C. Riley. New York, Engraved, printed & sold by E. Riley, 29 Chatham street (Wolfe, 7487 [1825]).

Recognition march on the Independence of Hayti. For the piano forte & flute. Composed expressly for the occasion and dedicated to President J. P. Boyer by his humble servant with every sentiment of respect, Francis Johnson. Philadelphia, Published & sold by G. Willig, No. 171 Chestnut St. (Wolfe, 4662; Haitian independence was recognized by France on April 17, 1825, conditional on the payment of an indemnity).

[5]Mark Baker Bird, *The Black Man; or Haytian Independence* (New York, 1869), pp. 152-153. As originally conceived in 1823, Boyer's plan envisaged attracting to Haiti 20,000 free American Blacks.

[6]In 1976 Arthur La Brew concluded *Selected Works of Francis Johnson, A Study in Military and Terpsichorean History* with facsimile reproductions of the *Recognition March*, original imprint, and of a 1976 orchestration by Joseph Hayes, pp. 189-210. See also his perceptive comments on the *Recognition March* and incipient Pan-Americanism, p. 5.

Sometime within the years 1824 through 1826, Carl Meineke (1782-1850),[7] who is still represented in most Protestant hymnals with a Gloria Patri,[8] published at Baltimore *The Mexican Waltz for the piano Forte*. For whatever the two contrasting strains in this fast 3/8 waltz tell, they are shown here. The left hand plays a repetitious bass (C-E-G twice, G-D-G four times, C-E-G, C-C for the first strain; C-C-C four times, G-G-G twice, C-E-G, C for the second strain). If neither strain sounds idiomatically Mexican, neither was there anything identifiably Moorish in the *Moorish March* intruded as a bit of local color in *The Siege of Tripoli* published in 1804 or 1805 by Benjamin Carr,[9] or Turkish in *Commodore Decatur's Turkish March* published around 1817 by Philip Trajetta, or Spanish in the *Spanish Waltz* published between 1818 and 1821 by Julius Metz (Wolfe, 1653, 9401, 5849).

Example 2
The Mexican Waltz (ca. 1825)

To honor the memory of Bolívar, more profound music than this was needed. Accordingly, the second movement of Beethoven's "Eroica" was fitted in 1831 to Samuel Woodworth's poetic translation of Bolívar's proclamation dated December 10, 1830, only a week before his death.[10] The "Beethoven of America," as Anthony Philip Heinrich began being called in the Boston *Euterpeiad* of April 13, 1822, gave one of his nine symphonies a South American cachet when he entitled it *The Ornithological Combat of Kings; or, The Condor of the Andes, and the Eagle of the Cordilleras.* He

[7]His first name is alternately given as Christopher. John Cole, the Baltimore publisher listed on the cover of *The Mexican Waltz* with No. 123 Market Street as his location, did business there in 1824, 1825, and 1826. George Willig published the same waltz at Philadelphia.

[8]Robert G. McCutchan, *Our Hymnody; A Manual of the Methodist Hymnal* (New York, 1937), pp. 538-539. Meineke's Gloria Patri dates from 1844. Earlier he published a *Railroad March For the Fourth of July* (Baltimore: G. Willig, junr., 1828) that counts as another historic first.

[9]Carr attributed the Moorish in *The Siege of Tripoli* to Storace. Samuel Arnold's Moorish March in *The Mountaineers* (London: Preston & Son, 1795, p. 19) appeared at Boston in *The Musical Magazine*, I, (1802-1803), p. 15 (Wolfe, 268).

[10]"*I pity and forgive*" *The Last Words of Gen.* Simon Bolivar Sung by Mr. Jones the Poetry by S. Woodworth Esq. Music from Beethoven Arranged with an Accompaniment for the Piano Forte by N. C. Bochsa Respectfully Dedicated to Silas E. Barrows Esq. (New York: Firth & Hall, 1831). The first stanza reads: "Just Heav'n, from each oppressor / Preserve my country's wealth; / And if my death can bless her, / Oh then I welcome death."

subtitled the four movements "The Conflict of the Condor in the Air," "The Repose of the Condor," "The Combat of the Condor on the Land," and "Victory of the Condor."[11] It was the first movement of this symphony which the longtime guardian of Schubert's "Unfinished" Symphony, Anselm von Hüttenbrenner, rehearsed with the Styrian Musik-Verein at Graz on May 25 and June 7, 1836, and performed on June 9.[12] The printed program specified the movement as a "characteristically American tone-painting" by a composer "of Kentucky" Whether or not any of its themes was characteristically American, at least Heinrich chose the right year for a "combat" symphony. On March 6, 1836, Santa Anna captured the Alamo and slew the 183-man garrison, only to be himself captured on April 22, after his forces were defeated at the battle of San Jacinto on April 21. A decade later the long-brewing war between the United States and Mexico broke out, simultaneously loosing a flood-tide of sheet music. Among the first publications to acclaim Zachary Taylor (1784-1850) for occupying a base in disputed territory at Corpus Christi was *General Taylor's Encampment Quick Step, as performed by The Bands of the United States Army (in Texas)* (New York: Jacques & Brother, 1846 [25¢]). The opening strain went thus:

Example 3
General Taylor's Encampment Quick Step (1846)

Zachary Taylor's arrival on March 28, 1846, at the north bank of the Rio Grande opposite Matamoras, followed by its occupation May 18, was immediately commemorated with *The Matamoras Grand March, As performed by the Brass Bands, Arranged & partly Composed for the Piano Forte, And most Respectfully Dedicated to Major Gen.¹ Z. Taylor by W. C. Peters* (Louisville: W. C. Peters, 1846 [5 pp.,25¢]). Next off the press in rapid succession were *The Rio Grande Quick March dedicated to Gen.¹ Z. Taylor Commander of the Army of Occupation* by John C. Andrews (New York: Firth, Hall, 1846) and *The Rio Grande Funeral March Composed and Dedicated to the Philadelphia Greys* by A. R. Breiter (Philadelphia: A. Fiot, 1846). The Battle of Palo Alto, fought on May 8, 1846, was at once commemorated by a *Palo Alto Grand Military Waltz dedicated to General Z. Taylor and his gallant associates by a Lady* who declared her breeding by elegant turns in 3/8, C Major (New York: Firth & Hall, 1846). Each battle had its

[11]William Treat Upton, *Anthony Philip Heinrich: A Nineteenth-Century Composer in America* (New York, 1939), pp. 286-287.

[12]Wilbur Richard Maust, "The Symphonies of Anthony Philip Heinrich based on American Themes" (Ph.D. diss., Indiana University, 1973), pp. 281-321, includes a facsimile of the Library of Congress manuscript of this first movement. According to the printed program, the Sunday evening concert began with the *Erster Satz der Simfonie, The Combat of the Condor (Der Kampf des Condor), amerikanisch charakteristisches Tongemählde von Anton Philipp Heinrich, of Kentucky.* See Upton, p. 141.

heroes. The martyr of Palo Alto was an artillery major, Samuel Ringgold, who, as he lay mortally wounded, was reported to have urged his fellow combatants on to the fray with these words: "Leave me to my fate, there's work for every man to do."[13] These dying words were used by John Hill Hewitt (1801-1890)[14] as the motto for his song sung in Baltimore at Ringgold's burial with highest civic and military honors on December 22, 1846, *On to the Charge! Inscribed to the memory of Major Ringgold Late of the U.S. Light Artillery* (Baltimore: F. D. Benteen, 1846). Further to enshrine Ringgold's name, T. H. Chambers composed a *Palo Alto Triumphant Grand March The Music arranged & inscribed to the Memory of the late Major Ringgold* (New York: J. F. Atwill, 1847).

After Palo Alto, Taylor advanced on Monterrey. With 6,000 men he invested the city on September 19, 1846, capturing it five days later. To celebrate this victory Francis Buck of Richmond published before the year's end the *Storming of Monterey September 21st 22d & 23d 1846 A Descriptive Military Waltz Composed and dedicated to Genl Z. Taylor and Officers of the American Army in Mexico* (Baltimore: F. D. Benteen, 1846), the strains of which bear such captions as "General Worth successfully storms the forts by the Saltillo Road," "The gallant Texans cut their way from house to house," "Attack of the Mexican lancers," "An armistice proposed by Gen. Ampudia," and "Rejoicing of the conquering troops." In 1847 Karl W. Petersilie published *Monterey: Co.l Campbell's March dedicated to the Officers & Members of the 1st Regt. Tennessee Volunteers* (Philadelphia: George Willig; Lexington, Ky.: Bodley & Curd). Austin Phillips published in 1847 *Monterey A National Song The Words by F. W. Watson* (New York: Wm. Vanderbeek). On the other hand, sorrow over the American death toll inspired *The Field of Monterey Ballad Affectionately dedicated to Mrs. Virginia Q. S. (of Virginia)* by M. Dix Sullivan (Boston: Oliver Ditson, 1846). This lament for a son lost in the battle begins: "The sweet church bells are pealing out / A chorus wild and free."

None of the Mexican War publications mentioned so far professed to contain anything specifically Mexican. As if to compensate for the spread-eagleism of *On to the Charge!* John Hill Hewitt did return in 1848 to the subject of Monterrey with an entirely different sort of song entitled *The Maid of Monterey from "Illustrations of the Mexican War" Written and adapted to a Mexican Melody* (Baltimore: F. D. Benteen; New Orleans: W. T. Mayo, 1848). The four stanzas tell the story of a Mexican Florence Nightingale who succored the American wounded and dying. The purportedly Mexican melody runs thus:

---

[13]For his biography, see *National Cyclopaedia of American Biography* (New York, 1897), VII, 69. He died three days after the battle. Lieutenant Slover, who tried to help him, reported his words as: "Never mind, you have work to do; go ahead with your men; all are wanted in front."

[14]Concerning Hewitt, see Richard B. Harwell, *Confederate Music* (Chapel Hill, 1950), pp. 28-40; and Coy E. Huggins, "John Hill Hewitt: Bard of the Confederacy" (Ph.D. diss., Florida State University, 1964).

Example 4
The Maid of Monterey (1848)

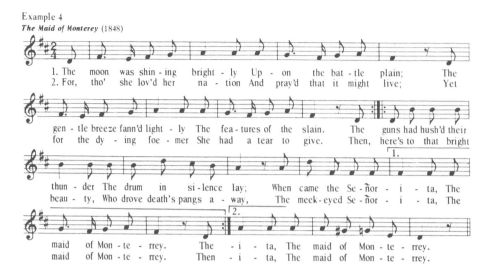

1. The moon was shin-ing bright-ly Up-on the bat-tle plain; The
2. For, tho' she lov'd her na-tion And pray'd that it might live; Yet

gen-tle breeze fann'd light-ly The fea-tures of the slain. The guns had hush'd their
for the dy-ing foe-mer She had a tear to give. Then, here's to that bright

thun-der The drum in si-lence lay; When came the Se-ñor-i-ta, The
beau-ty, Who drove death's pangs a-way, The meek-eyed Se-ñor-i-ta, The

maid of Mon-te-rrey. The -i-ta, The maid of Mon-te-rrey.
maid of Mon-te-rrey. Then -i-ta, The maid of Mon-te-rrey.

After securing Monterrey, Taylor's forces occupied Saltillo November 16, 1846, and on February 22-23, 1847, prevailed against Santa Anna's 20,000 troops at the Battle of Buena Vista. Charles Grobe, the most prolific and most published composer in American history,[15] had already in 1846 rushed into the Mexican War market with a jaunty C Major piece in 6/8, *General Taylor's Grand March arranged for the Piano . . . Most respectfully dedicated to General Taylor by the Publishers* (Philadelphia: Lee & Walker) and *Old Rough and Ready. Quick Step dedicated to General Zac. Taylor* (Philadelphia: George Willig) — the latter an Allegro molto 2/4 piece in E flat, heavily laden with touch and expression signs. His *pièce de résistance* among war compositions came out, however, in 1847 with the title *Veni, Vidi, Vici. The Battle of Buena Vista A Descriptive Fantasie for the Piano, Composed and most respectfully inscribed to Gen.[1] Z. Taylor The Hero who never lost a battle by Ch.[1] Grobe. Opus 101. Price 75 cts. net* (Baltimore: G. Willig, J.[r]). Grobe's *Buena Vista* was yet another in the long procession of the Willigs's expensive battle compositions that by 1815 and 1816 had already included Philippe Laroque's 15-page *Battle of the memorable 8th of January 1815*, selling for $1.50, presumably because it gave battle descriptions in both French and English, Ricksecker's *The Battle of New Orleans* that contained a British March on page 4, followed by various American generals' marches on pages 3 and 9.[16] What was

[15]H. Wiley Hitchcock, *Music in the United States: A Historical Introduction,* 2nd ed. (Englewood Cliffs, 1974), pp. 75-77. Eventually Grobe garnered almost 2,000 published opuses.

[16]Peter Weldon's 15-page *La Battalla de Baylen y rendicion de el General Dupont al exercito Español patriotico al mando de los Generales Castaños y Reding. Pieza historica y militar para el piano forte Dedicada a la Junta Supreme de Sevilla* (New York, 1809) sold for $2; James Hewitt's 15-page *The Battle of Tenton. A favorite historical military sonata* (Philadelphia: G. E. Blake, 1812-1814), sold for $1.25. Denis-Germain Etienne's 20-page *Battle of New Orleans* (Boston: For the Author by G. Graupner, 1816) was sold by subscription. See Wolfe, items 9730A, 3683, and 2718.

unquestionably new about Grobe's 13-page *Buena Vista* was the Mexican march at page 4. The incidents immediately preceding its introduction are labeled as follows (page.3): "Gen. Taylor apprized of the Mexican approach, breaks up his camp at Agua Nueva and takes post in a strong position at Buena Vista." Next comes: "The Mexicans appear immediately in front of the American forces, their bands playing their favorite march 'Perico.'" Grobe accompanied the 6/8 *Perico* C Major tune first with an Alberti bass, next with galloping chords marked *crescendo* to suggest the Mexican band's approach.

Example 5

Perico (1847)

The rest of the battle events,[17] all portrayed with the usual literalness of this class of music, terminate in a Burial of the Dead (pages 9 and 10) closely echoing the strains of the funeral march in Beethoven's "Eroica." The coda on the last two pages contains the customary apotheosis of the battle heroes. Two more pieces of sheet music published in 1847 purported to contain authentic Mexican strains. The first was *Santa Anna's March As played by the Bands of the Mexican Army On the field of Buena Vista the night previous to the battle Arranged for the Piano Forte by William Ratel. NB This beautiful air was brought on by some Kentucky Volunteers having heard it played by the Mexican Bands at Buena Vista while on sentry duty* (Philadelphia: George Willig; Lexington, Ky.: Bodley & Curd). The wistful C Major Santa Anna March tune brought back by Kentuckians goes thus (compare it with *The Maid of Monterey*):

[17]The following incidents lead up to the most famous phrase coined during the war. P. 4: "Flag of truce from Santa Anna who demands an unconditional surrender; 'Gen. Taylor never surrenders [German augmented-6th chord]; The American army gives one-two-three cheers. The enemy attempts to turn the American left flank." P. 5: "Sherman's and Bragg's batteries order'd to the left. Col. Bissell takes position between them and the Kentuckians, under Col. McKee, move from the right to the centre. The artillery of both armies opens fire." P. 6: "The Mexican infantry opens a tremendous fire on the entire American line which is returned with fatal effect by the Kentuckians under Clay and Fry, Gen. Taylor in the thickest of the Battle encourages his troops. The battle rages with greatest fury. Washington's Battery opens a fire and repulses a body of lancers." P. 7: "Col. [Jefferson] Davis throws his troops into the form of a [wedge] the opening towards the enemy and is reinforced by a body of cavalry under Col. Lane. Gen. Taylor advises Capt. Bragg to supply the enemy with a 'little more grape.'"

Example 6
Santa Anna's March (1847)

Transposed from C to G Major, this same optimistic Santa Anna tune reappeared later in that same year (1847) — now with the explanatory title: *Santa Anna's March to which is added a Popular Melody composed on the Battle Field of Buena Vista by an American Officer Arrang'd for the Piano Forte And Inscribed to Miss* [Mary-Ann] *Fitzgerald by W. C. Peters* (Louisville: W. C. Peter; Cincinnati: Peters & Field). Copyrighted in Ohio, this arrangement sold as either a piano duet or solo for 25¢. A few bars of the C Major trio section "composed on the Battle field of Buena Vista by an American Officer" deserve reprinting here, if only because this is the first published example of Mexican-American musical collaboration:

Example 7

Taylor's success at Buena Vista inspired more sheet music tributes than any other engagement of the war. The majority were instrumental pieces.[18] Even Stephen Collins Foster, not usually thought of as an instrumental composer, published *Santa Anna's Retreat from Buena Vista Quick Step As performed by the Military Bands* (Louisville:

[18]*General Taylor's Quick March at Buena Vista Dedicated to him by Louis Reimer* (Philadelphia: Lee & Walker, 1847); *Buena Vista Grand Triumphal March Composed in Honor of Major General Taylor's Victory in Mexico February 23d 1847* [by F. Weiland] (Philadelphia: J. G. Osborn [1847]); *Buena Vista Quick Step Composed and Dedicated to Lieut John F. Reynolds Comp.y E. 3rd Artillery U.S.A. by John B. Müller*

188

W. C. Peters, 1848).[19] Among songs, William J. Lemon's *"A Little More Grape Captain Flagg"* (Philadelphia: Lee & Walker; New Orleans: W. T. Mayo, 1847), selling for 50 cents, capitalized on Taylor's famous phrase. Musically, it swashbuckles with the bravado of Figaro's entry song in *Il Barbiere di Siviglia.* Edward O. Eaton's *To the boy defender of Kentucky's honor* (Vicksburg, Mississippi: Blackmar & Brother, 1860) told in six stanzas how "at the Battle of Buena Vista, Sergeant William F. Goines, then a boy of sixteen years, twice rescued the colors of the 2nd Regiment, Kentucky, from Mexicans." The fate of Americans who fell was mourned in *The Dying Soldier of Buena Vista The Music Composed and most respectfully dedicated to his Honor Charles J. M. McCurdy Lieutenant Governor of the State of Connecticut by Orramel Whittlesey, of Salem Conn. Words by Col. Henry Petrikin* (with a lachrymose lithograph on tbe cover by William Endicott of New York, but no date or publisher).

In comparison with Taylor, Winfield Scott (1786-1866) surrounded himself with much less of a musical penumbra. The only programmatic piece celebrating events in his ascent to Mexico City was composed by the same Francis Buck of Richmond who in 1846 had celebrated Taylor's storming of Monterrey with *A Descriptive Military Waltz.* Buck's 1847 nine-page sequel honoring Scott came out with the title *Fall of Vera Cruz And Surrender of the City & Castle of S.¹ Juan D'Ulloa* [San Juan de Ulùa] *To the American Forces under Major Gen.¹ Scott (29. March 1847) A Descriptive Piece Composed & respectfully Dedicated to the Officers & Men of the U.S. Army & Navy Engaged in that Glorius Achievement* (Baltimore: Frederick D. Benteen, 1847).[20] Scott's capture of Cerro Gordo on April 18 inspired T. Bricher's *Cerro Gordo Quick Step* (Boston: Martin & Beals, 1847). The victory at Contreras on August 20 evoked a tribute not to Scott but to one of his generals — *Smith's March Composed and dedicated to Gen. Persifor F. Smith the Hero of Contreras by J. T. Martin* (Baltimore: Miller & Beacham, Successors to F. D. Benteen, 1848).[21] Unlike other music related to

(Philadelphia: George Willig, 1847); *Buena Vista Grand March Respectfully Dedicated to Major Gen.¹ Zachary Taylor. Subject from Mercadante Arranged for the Piano Forte, by E. Nathan* (New York: Pond & Co., 1847); *The Buena Vista Polka, Composed & dedicated to Brigadier General Wool, by a Lady of Virginia* (New York: F. Riley & Co., 1848). Other instrumental pieces possibly tied to Buena Vista include A. G. Pickens, *General Taylor's Quick Step* (Boston: Oliver Ditson) and Matthias Keller, *General Taylor's Quick Step* (Philadelphia: Lee & Walker).

[19]Vera Brodsky Lawrence, *Music for Patriots, Politicians, and Presidents* (New York, 1975), p. 317, shows in facsimile the first page of this galloping 6/8 *con spirito* G Major effusion.

[20]A synopsis of the events depicted by Buck: p. 3: Two o'clock. Gen. Scott addressed at two o'clock P.M. a summons to the Governor of Vera Cruz &c.; p. 4: Seven mortars in battery open upon the City. Part of Commodore Perry's squadron firing towards the Castle; p. 5. Gallant Capt. John R. Vinton shot; p. 6: Funeral of Capt. J. R. Vinton. Three guns fired over his grave. A heavy Norther then set in; p. 7: Attack on the 24th of March. At page 9 the American flag waves over the Castle.

[21]Concerning Smith (1798-1858), see T. F. McNeill, "Smith, Persifor Frazer," *Dictionary of American ᴌiography*, XVII, 331-332. "His arrival on the field of Contreras was welcomed by the soldiers with cries of 'Here he is!' and 'Now we'll have them'." His surprise attack in the early morning of August 20, 1847, "resulted in the destruction of Valencia's army."

189

Scott's campaign *Smith's March* or *Smith's Grand March,* as it was titled in Oliver Ditson and National Music Company of Chicago reissues, continued enjoying popularity to the end of the century. *Gen.¹ Scott's Mexican Quick Step: Composed for the Piano Forte, and Respectfully dedicated to Gen.¹ Scott and Officers and men of the American Army in Commemoration of the Capture of the City of Mexico* by Ludwig Hagemann (New York: C. Holt, 1847) was on the other hand a puerile four-page C Major piece ending on a second-inversion chord. The rest of the Scott repertoire, from *Gen. Scott's Quick Step arranged for the Piano Forte from the celebrated Sturm March Gallop* (Boston: Oliver Ditson, 1852) and *Festival March* by J. Pychowski (New York: William Hall & Son, 1852) with Scott's lithographed portrait on the cover, to *Lieutenant General Scott's Grand Funeral March* by E. Mack (Philadelphia: Lee & Walker, 1866), tried to keep alive the memory of his Mexican exploits but contained nothing remotely savoring of Mexican music.

Once the successful outcome was assured, all apostolic fervor was drained from the Mexican cause and American songsters could turn somewhat cynical. The crusading zeal of *"Tis a Nation's Jubilee A Patriotic Song dedicated to General Zach. Taylor by Thomas Power adapted to a favorite melody* (Boston: Oliver Ditson, 1846) gave way two years later to the arrogance of *We're the boys from Mexico* "sung to the tune of Yankee Doodle" in *The Rough and Ready Songster: Embellished with Twenty-Five Splendid Engravings, illustrative of the American victories in Mexico* (New York: Napis & Cornish, 1848). The other tunes specified in this same 1848 songster containing poetry by William Cullen Bryant and William Gilmore Simns echoed anything but Mexico: Boatman's Song, Bruce's Address, Campbells are coming, Dan Tucker, Draw the sword Scotland, Fine old English Gentleman, Gray Goose, Green Mountain Boys, Hail to the Chief, Lucy Neale, Rose of Alabama, Scots wha' hae' wi' Wallace bled.

In 1856 Nicaragua became the scene of another Latin American adventure but one that ended less happily for the invaders. William Walker (1824-1860) having proclaimed himself president, music at once appeared to signal the event, *Gen.¹ Walker's Nicaraguan Grand March composed by E. Haskell* (Baltimore: Miller & Beacham, successor to F. O. Benteen, 1856 [plate 2994]). One of the few "Latin American" works of the century unconnected with any military incursion was *The Andes Marche di Bravura. Homage to Church's Picture "The Heart of the Andes"* by George William Warren (New York: William A. Pond & C.°, 1863). This 17-page exercise in Thalbergian runs, arpeggios, and other virtuostic figuration, paid tribute to a canvas by Frederick Edwin Church (1826-1900), who had spent 1853 in South America.[22]

After the Mexican Cession and the Gadsen Purchase, American sentiment did sanctimoniously deplore any further incursions on Mexican territory. In 1865 mounting opposition to the Emperor Maximilian was typically vented in a song burlesquing his foreign accent, *"Oh! I vants to go home"* or *Maximilian's Lament Song & Chorus Music by T. M. Brown Words by Bob Barkis* (Saint Louis: Endres & Compton). On the cover is

---

[22]Church's *The Falls of Niagara* (1857) hangs at the Corcoran Gallery. His *Heart of the Andes* (1855) was the first of his panoramas that eventually "made him rich as well as world famous." Warren (1828-1902) was the American-born organist who wrote the tune to which *God of Our Fathers* is sung.

a lithograph lampooning him as a big overgrown crybaby. Advertised as "Sung by Harry Pell at Morris & Wilson's Opera House," the song begins: " 'Oh, I vants to go home' was the doleful cry / That came mournfully over the sea / To the ears of the Emperor of the French / From his Austrian protégé. / 'Oh, I vants to go home vare de sauerkraut grows / And de lager bier flows like de streams. / Oh goot leber vurst; mit pretzels and bier, / Are the themes of my midnight dreams.' "

Scenting Yankee profit, but ostensibly to show solidarity with the first widespread revolt in Cuban history, Rosaline V. Murden in 1869 dedicated *The Cuban Patriots Grand March* (Philadelphia; Lee & Walker) to Carlos Manuel de Céspedes (1819-1874), the leader of the rebels who before defeat in 1878 controlled half the island. Typical of the many musical encouragements to Cuban revolt in the 1890's were Arthur M. Cohen's *Belle of Cuba Quickstep,* Opus 284 (Philadelphia: The Current Publishing Co., 1895) and George H. Hayes' five-page *Cuban March "Viva Cuba Libre"* (Boston: G. W. Setchell, 1896) dedicated to Gonzalo de Quesada. With insouciance born of remoteness from the action Hayes' text began: "To combat advance, Bayameses, / Fear not death when the death will be glorious / For to die for the land is to live / And in bondage to live, is to live in disgrace / Hark the trumpet!"

However, these "Cuban" pieces were all as devoid of anything authentically Latin American as had been the bulk of the Mexican War repertory. For piquant Mexican flavor in mid-century publication, the sheet music enthusiast can best turn to *La pasadita A Satirical Mexican Song as sung with rapturous applause by Madame Anna Bishop* [1814-1884] *in the Cities of Mexico* (Philadelphia: J. E. Gould, Successor to A. Fiot, 1850). This is labeled on the cover "A Mexican National Air" with her harpist husband, the scandal-ridden Nicolas Bochsa (1789-1856) cited as arranger. The Spanish text of the song racily recounts how only the ladies of Mexico had found ways to subdue the Yankees (the bowdlerized English translation softens the sense considerably).

Example 8
La pasadita (1850)

Ay a-mi-gos mi-os Les voy a con-tar Lo que he pa-sa-do en es-ta ciu-dad

The 1850's was the decade during which Gottschalk began distilling Antilles flavor in *El Cocoyé, Ojos criollos, Escenas campestres cubanas,* and numerous other Caribbean classics that deserve a chapter apart. A growing awareness of the West Indies imparted something of the same authentic local flavor to the *Cuba Plantation Dance* by Charles H. Walker (Philadelphia: Edward L. Walker, 1855). His cover shows Blacks dancing. The opening melodic strain, typical of the rest of this C-minor piece, goes thus:

Example 9

Cuban Plantation Dance (1855)

At San Francisco in 1871 Matthias Gray, the Steinway West Coast representative, published a Spanish-text song, *La Chacha Canción Española Regalada por M. Gray Almacen de Steinway No. 117 Calle Post,* as a souvenir to give Spanish-speaking customers who entered his showrooms. Not San Francisco but New Orleans and Chicago became, however, the two cities in which were published, during the rest of the century, most songs and instrumental pieces by Cuban and Mexican composers. Because these frequently appeared with no indication of copyright, they resist easy dating. *A la sombra de un sauce* by Angela Peralta (1845-1863), the greatest Mexican operatic diva of the century, was, for instance, published at New Orleans by Junius Hart for 50 cents, in a series of 76 items of "Mexican Music," none of which bears a copyright date. From Mexican sheet music catalogues of the 1890's the composers represented in the series can usually be identified as salon writers, singers, orchestral musicans, or band leaders active in mid-Porfirian Mexico. A closer study would probably reveal A. Wagner y Levien[23] at Mexico City as the chief publisher from whose files Hart of New Orleans borrowed with or without authorization the repertory attributed on his covers to Leonardo F. Bolado, J. H. Cuevas, J. Dávila, P. M. Fuentes, N. Martínez, F. J. Navarro, J. Olague, G. Oritz, Miguel Ríos Toledano, R. Susano Robles, and others. However, only one of the composers' names turns up among the 391 pieces of Mexican sheet music assembled in 1883 for the Bolívar centennial celebration at Caracas — Miguel Ríos Toledano.[24] Hart did publish with copyright date of 1885 a piece called *El Nopal* (*The Cactus*) *Mazurka* by the fifth composer in his list, Narciso Martínez. The copy gives Hart's address as 191 Canal Street, New Orleans. Both Mexican and American flags in color grace the cover and the pianist D. Delacroix is named as the dedicatee. (Inside, Mrs. Frank D. Hamilton is listed as the dedicatee.)

The first known issue anywhere of the music of *La Golondrina*[25] by Narciso Serradell (1843-1910) was not in Mexico but in September 1883 at Chicago, engraved by Poole Brothers Printers and Engravers for the General Passenger Department of the Mexican

[23]The other Mexican sheet music publishers named in the official inventory list prepared in 1883 for Caracas were H. Nagel Sucesores, Rivera hijo y Cía, and D. Carlos Godard. See the next footnote.

[24]Gerónimo Baqueiro Fóster, "Aportación musical de México para la formación de la Biblioteca Americana de Caracas, 1882-1883," *Revista Musical Mexicana,* II/2 (July 21, 1942), p. 31. Complete list alphabetized by composer at pp. 28-32. Next to Melesio Morales and Ignacio Tejeda, Miguel Píos Toledano is the composer most voluminously present in this list signed May 22, 1883, by the director of the Conservatorio Nacional Alfredo Bablot.

[25]James J. Fuld, *The Book of World-Famous Music,* rev. ed. (New York, 1971), p. 254. The reissue of January 1885 contains only Westrup's English translation, not Francisco Martínez de la Rosa's Spanish text set by Sarradell.

National Railway to pass out as a tourist inducement. On the front cover appear the two republics' flags in color, on page 4 a railway map by "Poole Map Engravers." The English translation, credited to "Rev. Thos. M. Westrup,"[26] a pioneer missionary in Monterrey, still widely known as a hymn translator, bears the title "An Exile to a Swallow." An accompanying note calls *La Golondrina* "next to the national anthem the most popular song in Mexico." The tune, as published at Chicago in 1883 and 1885 differs in small details from the present-day *textus receptus,* and is therefore worth repeating here.

Example 10

The chief Chicago houses specializing in Mexican music throughout the 1890's were the National Music Company and McKinley Music Company. In 1892 National at 215 to 220 Wabash Avenue issued a *Choice Collection of Mexican Music* consisting of 15 pieces denominated either schottische, waltz, or mazurka. Luis de Aranjo, Julio Ituarte, Tomás León, Francisco J. Navarro, Juventino Rosas, and Ignacio Tejada were the composers. In 1893 National copyrighted Rosas' *Amelia* Waltzes (50 cents) and *Josefina*

[26]Although of English birth and an Anglican, Westrup greatly aided in the establishment of the first Baptist church at Monterrey January 30, 1864. In 1866 he became Mexican agent for the American Bible Society. See Gonzalo Baez Camargo and Kenneth G. Grubb, *Religion in the Republic of Mexico* (New York, 1935), pp.88, 117, 122.

Waltz (60 cents). His *Ensueño Seductor*[27] was advertised on the National Music cover as "nearest to *Over the Waves* in popularity."[28] Other National copyrights in 1893, the year of the World's Columbian Exposition at Chicago, included *La Serenata de la luna* by José Alvarado (dedicated to Juventino Rosas), three schottisches, *Adora y tenete quedo, Casada de perlas,* and *Mexico Adios,* by Alvarado, Ortiz, and Tejada, a *Polka de los Toreros* by Navarro, and much similar ephemera designed for quick sale. In 1897 National published something more substantial, Rosas' 11-page tribute to Mexico's First Lady, *Carmen Valse pour piano A la digna Señora Carmen Romero Rubio de Díaz.* Short parlor waltzes continued however as National's favorites when around the same year this firm published Damián López Sánchez's *Dolores Waltz,* Genaro Codina's[29] *Culto a lo bello Valse* dedicated "to the studious young ladies in the Zacatecan regional orchestra directed by Professor Primitivo Calero,"[30] and Casimiro Alvarado's *En Medio del Mar* ("Upon the Sea Waltz").

Since no such stream of Mexican waltzes and other dance pieces would have continued flowing from Chicago presses unless they had proved commercially viable, their publication showed no great altruism. Nor can any yearning to "glorify Mexico" be imputed to McKinley Music Company, publisher of Narciso Martínez' *Victorioso March,* Armstrong and Bacon, publisher of Genaro Codina's *Zacatecas March,* or National with numerous like-minded regional titles. What did show loftier musical ideals at Chicago in the late 19th century, so far as Mexico goes, was a work of entirely different cast — *Montezuma*, a three-act opera by Chicago's finest composer of the epoch, Frederic Grant Gleason (1848-1903; in Chicago from 1877 to his death). Begun in October of 1878 only a year after arriving in Chicago, and finished August 30, 1884 (except for some scoring), *Montezuma*, Opus 16, was his second opera. *Otho Visconti*, Opus 7, completed in 1877 while he was organist at New Britain, Connecticut, was his first. According to Edward E. Hipsher's parochial and unreliable *American Opera and its Composers* (Philadelphia: Theodore Presser, 1927), pages 216-217, Gleason left instructions that neither *Otho Visconti* nor *Montezuma*[31] was to be performed or even

[27]M. D. Swisher of Philadelphia (115 South Tenth Street) copyrighted this in 1892 with the alternate English title "Impassioned Dream Waltz," publishing in the same year what was titled Rosa' *Carmela Polka,* Opus 13; *Cantar llorando* and *Rumor de Brisas* by T. Moreno; *Te volví a ver* (set of waltzes) by Manuel Estrada; and *Eterno amor* by Francisco J. Navarro.

[28]*Sobre las olas,* according to Fuld, was copyrighted by A. Wagner y Levien "about August 1888."

[29]Concerning Genaro Codina (1852-1901), see Jesús C. Romero, *La música en Zacatecas y los músicos zacatecanos* (Mexico City, 1963), pp. 38-39. He composed his *Marcha Zacatecas* in 1891 (premiered October, 1893). The Orquesta Típica Zacatecana of 19 players (7 *bandalones,* 2 violins, 1 viola, 1 flute, 2 psalteries, 2 cellos, 1 harp, 1 piano, 2 basses) left for their United States tour February 24, 1893. See Romero, *op. cit.,* p. 144, for further details.

[30]Dedicated *A las estudiosas Señoritas que forman la Orquesta Típica Zacatecana bajo la dirección del Profesor Primitivo Calero,* this set of five waltzes starts with an Andante religioso introduction, but, after thus invoking the Blessed Virgin, soon gets down to business.

[31]Gleason left fragments of another three-act opera, *Galahad,* from which came the "Processional to the Holy Grail" played by the Exposition orchestra under Theodore Thomas July 7, 1893. During the next decade he

examined until fifty years after his death. This report was proved false immediately by *Otho Visconti*, which was performed four times at the new College Theatre of DePaul University, Chicago, under Walter Keller's baton June 4, 6, and 8 (twice), 1907, with Joseph F. Sheehan (1869-1936) in the title tole. As a result of the cavalier treatment of most things American by most musicologists, Franz Stieger's *Opernlexikon* (Tutzing, 1975) got everything wrong about both *Otho Visconti* and *Montezuma*.[32] Gleason himself wrote the librettos for both operas. *Montezuma*, after having been a favorite subject for mid-18th-century Italian three-act operas from Vivaldi at Venice in the autumn of 1733 to Zingarelli in 1781,[33] fell out of favor in the 19th century. Before Gleason, nothing like it had ever been attempted by an American. Nor was it to be quickly followed with a *Montezuma* by any other American. At Mexico City, only Aniceto Ortega[34] had composed an *episodio musical* in nine sections entitled *Guatimotzín* (= Montezuma's nephew). Premiered at the Gran Teatro Nacional by the Angela Peralta company September 13, 1871,[35] Ortega's score included a *Danza Tlaxcalteca* reminiscent of the third movement in Beethoven's Symphony, Opus 92.

On April 19, 1964, eighty years after Gleason put the finishing touches on his *Montezuma*,[36] was at last premiered Roger Sessions' *Montezuma*—the only subsequent

worked on a one-act *Benedicta* set in a convent in Germany, and a three-act-with-prologue (or four-act) *Luciferos* based on *Paradise Lost*. He died while pushing himself unmercifully to compose the latter. See Aileen M. Peters, "Analysis of Frederic Grant Gleason Collections of Music, Songbooks and Diaries" (M. Ed. thesis, Department of Library Science; Chicago Teachers College South, August 1964), p. 45. Concerning the Gleason materials bequeathed to the Newberry Library by Mrs. Robert Perez of Poughkeepsie, Gleason's niece, see Thomas Willis, "Newberry Library Acquires Manuscripts and Diaries of Tribune Critic of 1880's," *Chicago Tribune*, September 8, 1963 (Gleason served as *Tribune* critic from 1884 to 1889).

[32]Umberto Manferrari, *Dizionario universale delle opere melodrammatiche* (Florence, 1955) does not admit that he existed. Only Alfred Loewenberg, *Annals of Opera 1597-1940* (Geneva, 1943; 2d ed., 1955), I, p. 1280, includes *Otho Visconti*.

[33]Majo (1765), Paisiello (1772), Galuppi (1772), Sacchini (1775), Anfossi (1776), and Insanguine (1780), composed operas entitled *Montezuma* or *Motezuma*. At Berlin Graun's *Montezuma* was given in 1765 and 1771. To 1771 belongs also Mysliweczek's three-act *Montezuma*. The first opera introducing Aztecs playing their own idomatic instruments (ayacachtlis) was Spontini's *Fernand Cortez*, 1809. Prior operas with Cortez as the named protagonist were mounted in 1787, 1789, and 1798. See O. G. T. Sonneck, *Catalogue of Opera Librettos printed before 1800* (Washington, 1914), I, pp. 490-491.

[34]Ortega wrote his own libretto. The tenor Enrico Tamberlick who sang the role of Cuauhtémoc-Guatimozín was largely responsible for the success of *Guatimozín*. However, Ortega's one-act opera never reached the boards again. See Armando de María y Campos, *Angela Peralta El Ruiseñor mexicano* (Mexico City, 1944), pp. 112-114.

[35]Gerónimo Baqueiro Fóster, *Historia de la Música en México. III. La música en el período independiente* (Mexico City, 1964), pp. 221-231, with thematic analysis.

[36]Although not performed in its entirety in Gleason's lifetime, his *Montezuma* was heard in excerpts. Theodore Thomas programmed the Priests' March from Act I at his last summer concert in 1882, the Introduction to Act II August 11, 1883, the Introduction, Processional, and Storm from Act III August 5, 1885. Among events for the National Music Teachers Convention, Gleason conducted the New York City premiere of the Introduction to Act II at the Academy of Music July 2, 1885.

opera with that title by an American. Premiered at the Deutsche Oper, Berlin, Sessions'
three-act *Montezuma* calls for an enormous singing cast of nine sopranos, a mezzo
soprano, ten tenors, eight baritones, and four basses, plus four choruses on and off
stage. The scenes shift from the Gulf Coast in March 1519 to Tenochititlan (= Mexico
City) in June 1520. Because of the exigencies of the libretto, Sessions' opera unfolds
more as a historical pageant framed within the backward glances of the old Bernal Díaz
del Castillo than as any straightforward march of events. Montezuma himself, although
the title character, does not even begin singing until page 201 of the extremely elaborate
score. By the time pages 456-458 are reached, he praises Malinche for "being a builder
of a new race of men," and to exculpate her defection to the Spaniards, equates her with
Mary Magdalene. At page 463-464 he foresees the day when Spaniard and Indian will
live in harmony "for this land is roomy, of bounteous lap, fit to be happy under the
custody of all gods." For all these conciliatory gestures, Cuauhtémoc at pages 465-466
brands him who has now become a Christian a traitor to the ancestral deities. Not the
Spaniards but Aztec warriors shoot Montezuma blind and stone him to death.

Among other exotica, Sessions' huge orchestra includes two-toned Mexican
teponaxtlis and huehuetli. To emphasize diversities, his is the first opera in history to
mix passages in Latin with dialogue in Nahuatl, language of the Aztecs. All these
disparate elements swirl about in a harmonic cauldron where every morsel is a relent-
lessly urged minor 9th, major 7th, or augmented 4th.[37] In reward for all the com-
plexities, one German critic lauded him, another lashed him. What all the critics agreed
upon was its being a "message" opera exalting Montezuma's noble spirit of forgiveness
while at the same time deploring the fanatic partisanship of his underling Cuauhtémoc.

Gleason's opera was also message-laden. But his message differed radically. His told
the redeeming power of a woman's love—a love untinctured by sexual passion. Yeteva is
a vestal priestess who loves Montezuma with such intensity that to save his kingdom
from the war-god's threatened revenge she spontaneously offers herself as a human
sacrifice to Huitzilopochtli. Instead of being a fiery Aztec zealot, Cuauhtémoc—or as his
is called in this opera, Guatemozin—blesses the coming of the White God, Quetzalcóatl. It is the White God who promises to liberate the Mexican people from the
loathsome eternal round of human sacrifices demanded by Huitzilopochtli. Upon being
falsely accused of treasonable designs against Montezuma, Guatemozin in Scene ii of
Act I is summarily banished. But he creeps back in minstrel's disguise. In Scene iii he
sings a long narrative telling how at divine command the Aztec nation journeyed south
to found their capital of Tenochtitlan. As a sample of Gleason's melos, 36 measures
from pages 60-63 of the piano score are here shown:

---

[37]Heinz Joachim, "Montezuma and the Messiah," *Musical America*, 84 (May 1964), p. 20: "The harsh and
austere sound of the score surprisingly complements the exotic coloration and the sacerdotal rigidity of the
scenery;" Werner Oehlmann, " 'Montezumas' Untergang; Roger-Sessions-Uraufführung in der Deutschen
Oper," *Neue Zeitschrift für Musik*, 125/6 (1964), p. 266: "Der Komponist braucht viele Noten, um wenig
damit zu sagen." H. H. Stuckenschmidt, "Sessions' 'Montezuma'," *Opera*, 15 (June 1964), pp.401-402,
remarked that Sessions had begun it 23 years earlier, that the libretto by Giuseppe Antonio Borgese (Thomas
Mann's son-in-law) had been shortened by Sessions himself to bring it within a three-hour span, and that the
high intellectual and ethical level had in a measure redeemed it.

Example 11

A - zat - lan's sons in splen - dor dwelt in their nor - thern home.

Now at the god's com - mand, their on - ward march be - gins.

South - ward they turn their fa - ces towards lakes__ and flow - 'ry vales. Like

moun - tain tor - rents rush - ing on__ in their re - sist - less course. The

na - tions fled af - fright - ed or felt their con - q'ring sword. O-ver moun-tains, plains, and

tor - rents Naught stayed their swift ap - proach,_ to earth's most love - ly vale.

Here, on this spot the o - men, Sent by the gods was seen.

Here, build - ed they the ci - ty, Here rose a tem - ple fair.

Guatemozin the minstrel continues by contrasting the former golden age with the present bloody and degenerate epoch of Huitzilopochtli. Just as he is about to have his heart torn out for blasphemy, a messenger rushes in to announce that the White God has indeed arrived. Now that his prophecy has been so soon vindicated the populace demands that the minstrel be spared. Huitzilopochtli through his priests agrees only on condition that some other human victim be found who will absolve the guilt of blasphemy by willingly taking the blasphemer's place on the sacrificial altar. Faced with so impossible a demand the assembled worshippers give vent to despair and horror in the chorus closing Act I. As the curtain opens on Act II, Montezuma's daughter Tula is seen reclining on a couch of jaguar skins while her attendant does feather work. Guatemozin, to whom Tula was affianced before his banishment, sneaks in, whereupon they sing a love duet. They are no sooner done than Montezuma walks in unannounced, unarmed, and unattended. Guatemozin convinces Montezuma of his loyalty, inasmuch as he could easily have killed him at that very moment if he so desired. They are reconciled and exit together to fight the Spanish invaders as Act II closes. When the

197

curtain draws for Act III, Yeteva is alone in the garden of the Great Temple. Montezuma, whose plight has now become desperate, joins her with an offer to escape through enemy lines—she at his side—so that he can continue fighting elsewhere. She renounces such a plan and convinces him that duty requires his remaining in the capital with his people. He is slain immediately upon leaving her, whereupon she mounts the pyre in a last vain effort to regain Huitzilopochtli's favor. But the war god will have none of his formerly darling Aztecs. Guatemozin and Tula try to restrain her from what they now conceive as useless self-immolation. But she herself lights the pyre so that she may join Montezuma in The Great Yonder.

As for influences, Gleason could not escape Wagner who by 1880 was so much an American fad that for a cool million he was considering locating in the United States.[38] Gleason therefore unified *Montezuma* with 28 motives variously labeled Festival, Adoration, Fate, Quetzalcóatl, Peace, Huitzilopochtli, Human Sacrifice, Montezuma, Guatemozin, Banishment, Vale of Mexico, Migration, Tula's sorrow, Tula's love, Separation of Montezuma and Yeteva, Fire Motive of Yeteva's Sacrifice, and the like. The latter two motives (shown here) illustrate the lushly chromatic character of Gleason's harmonies. In extenuation, he could look only to the perfect Wagnerite Theodore Thomas for performances of so much as excerpts. Not yet the epoch when Carlos Chávez in his *Xochipilli-Macuilxóchitl* (1940)[39] and Candelario Huízar in his *Oxpaniztli* (1936) succeeded in imposing upon the international public their concepts of "reconstructed" Aztecan, Gleason's *Montezuma* deserves no more to be faulted for lack of authenticity than does Sessions' *Montezuma*.

Example 12
Separation motive

Fire motive of Yeteva's sacrifice

[38]The literature on Wagner's American settlement plans that came to a head in 1880 is summarized (with bibliographical footnotes) in Curt von Westernhagen, "Wagner und das Reich," *Neue Wagner-Forschungen*, Erste Folge (Karlsruhe i. B., 1943), pp. 70-72.

[39]Published with the title *Xochipilli: An Imagined Aztec Music* (New York, 1964). Chávez's two-page literary introduction covers Instruments, Technical Aspect, and Stylistic Aspect of Aztec music; and the piece itself is for piccolo, flute, E flat clarinet, trombone, and six percussionists.

While writing it Gleason was himself passing through the crisis of being deserted by his first wife, the soprano Grace Hiltz, who in December of 1881 sailed for Europe, ostensibly to study with Sbriglia.[40] Around the same time he was co-editing with Mrs. Sara Hershey-Eddy (wife of Clarence Eddy) the *Musical Bulletin* published by The Hershey School of Music and Art in three volumes (from December 1879 through November 1882). With considerable foresight, Gleason, through the columns of this periodical, was during the very years of composing *Montezuma* voicing his misgivings for the future of his opera. His forebodings in "American Opera" (I/2 [January 1880]), "Native Composers" (II/10 [September 1881]), and "The Future of Opera in America" (III/5 and 10 [April and September 1882]), took such shape as these: "The Americans are the only people who take no pride in the works of native writers, and extend to them no sympathy or encouragement;" "Mr. [Theodore] Thomas is the only orchestral conductor who has always shown himself ready and willing to place worthy works of American composers before the public;" "America promises no future for operas more ambitious than imitation Pinafores."

In the American musical climate of the 1880's, all the more remarkably, *Montezuma* excerpts did enjoy some success. Charles A. Brittan, the supercilious critic who preceded Gleason on the *Chicago Tribune*, sniffed at the portions premiered at Thomas' summer concerts in 1882, 1883, and 1885. Nevertheless when Gleason himself conducted a symphonic portion of Act II at the New York Academy of Music July 2, 1885, William M. Thoms responded with a lengthy encomium in the *American Art Journal*, XLIV/3 (November 7, 1885), pages 33-34. Although lengthy, Thoms' review merits more than casual attention.

> Judging from this fragment, the opera must be one of great musical value. The harmony is rich, flowing and melodious, while possessing a certain unique tone that we would charactertize as typical of the nation of which Montezuma was the heroic representative. The possibilities of such a subject as the gifted composer has chosen are very great, and as the ability of the composer, rich in imagination, individuality and musical erudition and enthusiasm is undisputed, we should be glad when the opportunity offers to present the entire opera in a fitting manner before the public. The instrumentation to the introduction is free and vigorous, the motives are fresh and particularly that which is most prominent and which vividly depicts the sombre depths of the nation's despondency is original and impressive. Mr. Gleason conducted his work with an easy grace and showed familiarity with the post. The entire effect of his work excited both astonishment and admiration—[amazement] that such a magnificent orchestral composition should be so long unkown in New York [combined with] admiration as the great talent and genius of Mr. Gleason displayed in this particular field of work. Mr. Thomas has played the following selections from *Montezuma*, namely "Introduction and March of the Priests [of Huitzilopochtli]," Act I;

[40]G. L. Howe and W. S. B. Mathews, *A Hundred Years of Music in America* (Chicago, 1889), pp. 220-221; *Musical Bulletin* (Chicago), III/8 (July 1882), p. 116.

"Introduction" to Act II; "Introduction," "Death Song," "Yeteva's Processional," and the "Storm Finale" to Scene ii, the latter being four selections from Act III.[41]

Continuing in like encomiastic vein, Thoms commended Gleason for not hoarding his gift, instead rearing up worthy pupils. At Chicago John A. West, five years his pupil, had conducted two original large choral works with orchestra, and Eleanor Smith had conducted an original cantata for soloists and chorus.

Despite whatever solace such hearty praise brought him, *Montezuma* not only during his lifetime but even yet remains unmounted. The fact that only excerpts were performed at Chicago in the 1880's foreshadows the fate of António Carlos Gomes (Campinas, July 11, 1836; Pará, September 16, 1896), Latin America's leading 19th-century opera composer, brought to Chicago in 1893 three years before his death, as the stellar musical attraction during the World's Columbian Exposition. Gomes' first experiences with a major United States exposition dated from 1876. To coincide with the first centennial, Dom Pedro II (1825-1891), Emperor of Brazil, paid the United States a state visit that lasted from April 15 to June 12.[42] On April 20, Gomes replied to Salvador de Mendonça, the librettist of his opera *Joanna de Flandres* (1863). This very opera had won him the emperor's patronage for European studies that culminated in the triumph of *Il Guarany* at La Scala March 19, 1870. Mendonça, only recently appointed Brazilian Consul General at New York, began in 1875 a 23-year diplomatic sojourn in the United States. Despite their intimate friendship, Gomes in a letter dated April 20 declined Mendonça's invitation to write a work to be sung at Philadelphia during the Dom Pedro's visit. "Last year I was invited to write a Cantata for the Chile Exposition but had to refuse; however, I will write any musical piece that my own native

---

[41]For all the excerpts played by Thomas, the Gleason bequest to the Newberry Library includes scores and corrected sets of parts with the printed program notes written for the respective Chicago concerts by G. M. McConnel.

[42]Dom Pedro II was the first reigning monarch ever to visit the United States. During his three months' stay he travelled to San Francisco and back, everywhere enthusiastically received. For details of his historic American tour, see Heitor Lyra, *Dom Pedro II 1825-1891* (Sao Paulo, 1938-1940), II (1939), pp. 371-379. In footnote 8, page 146, of Smith's article, *Boletín Latino-Americano de Música*, VI (April 1946), Francisco Curt Lange itemized three pieces of sheet music published in the United States to welcome Dom Pedro II: P. J. Boris, *Dom Pedro Grand March In honor of His Imperial Majesty's visit to the United States* (*Centennial Year, 1876*) (Boston: John F. Perry & Co.); H. May Lath, *Brazilian Grand March Dedicated to Dom Pedro II Emperor of Brazil* (Boston: Oliver Ditson & Co.); E. de Barry, *Columbia's Flag is waving a Welcome to All Centenial Song and Chorus A.S.I.M. O Imperador do Brazil com os mais humildes respeitos da autora. N. York. Junho 29, 1876* (New York, J. L. Peters). A fourth piece dedicated to him was August Buechel's *We mourn our Country's loss* (New York: P. A. Wundermann). The copies in the Seçao de Música of the Biblioteca Nacional, Rio de Janeiro, are catalogued IV, 103, 6, 5/4; IV, 103, 6, 5/5; IV, 103, 6, 13/4; and IV, 103, 6, 5/6.

land desires, which I love more than all the Chiles and Philadelphias of this world!"[43]
But no sooner was the letter to Mendonça dispatched when there arrived at his Milan
residence a telegram from the Brazilian minister at Rome, Barão de Javary, informing
Gomes that is was the Emperor himself who wished the hymn for performance at
Philadelphia July 4, 1876. By return telegram, Gomes asked what kind of hymn was
desired. For large orchestra, something majestic but without voices, was the reply.
Gomes set to work at once and within a week had it sketched. In his letter of May 2 to
Mendonça he now wrote: "My most important message for the Emperor is that the
orchestra must absolutely have at least eight harps, let me repeat, *eight harps*. I rely on
the cabled promise of a perfect performance. If performed exactly according to my
written indications, it will make a good effect, otherwise not." He also insisted that the
orchestra be large enough that it would be capable of making a huge crescendo, little by
little, from pianissimo to a formidable fortissimo.[44]

Forwarded from Rome, nine rolls of Gomes' hymn reached the Brazilian legation at
Paris on June 1 and two days later were sent from Havre on a steamship destined to
arrive at New York June 12 or 13. In a letter dated June 4, the Brazilian minister at
Rome complimented Gomes extravagantly. "I greatly like your ppp introduction with
the gradual tremolo crescendo over the E in the horns resolving to A at the moment the
tutti motive is introduced. Your work will enjoy resounding success. It is colorful,
contains fine contrasts of forte and piano, the harps play wonderful chordal sweeps, and
the chief theme is given out with great pomp."[45] That Javary rightly foresaw its success
is proved by the Emperor's letter of July 10, 1876, from New York, written in his own
hand, congratulating and thanking Gomes in the warmest terms.[46]

Gomes' contribution to the World's Columbian Exposition at Chicago 17 years later
loomed much larger. Already in Volume I of the first edition of *Grove's Dictionary*,
1880, Grove himself wrote an article on Gomes in which he mentioned the successful

[43]Itala Gomes Vaz de Carvalho, *A vida de Carlos Gomes,* 2nd ed. (Rio de Janeiro, 1937), pp. 124-125; "Meu
Poeta e Amigo; Estou desolado mas falta-me tempo material para isto; estou abarbado com o remodelamento
da *Fosca,* e com minha nova opera *Maria Tudor,* que, por contracto, devo entregar ao Editor Ricordi no mez de
Setembro deste anno, senão . . . multa (e multa formidavel). O anno passado fui convidad para escrever uma
Cantata para a Exposiçao do Chile. Recusei . . . mas não recusarei quando fôr convidado para escrever uma
peça qualquer de musica para a minha terra, que amo mais que todos os Chiles e as Philadelphias do mundo!"

[44]*Ibid.,* pp. 127-128: "Infelizmente não posso ir até lá mas tu vaes me substituir para obter uma orchestra que
seja mesmo grande e que saiba fazer os pianissimos, os crescendos pouco a pouco, até o "calmo" e "fortissimo," que dere ser formidavel! O mais importante, que dirás de minha parte ao Imperador, é que eu faço
absoluta questão de ter pelo menos oito harpas na orchestra: torno a dizer, *Oito Harpas* . . . Eu sou forte da
promessa do Imperador que me garante por telegrapho a execuação perfeita do meu Hymno. Se a execução fôr
conforme às indicações que eu escrevi na partitura, fará bom effeito, do contrario farei má figura!"

[45]*Ibid.,* pp. 130-131. So much overnight musical analysis of a large orchestral work would have exceeded the
powers of any American diplomat of the epoch but A. W. Thayer, consul at Trieste from 1865.

[46]*Ibid.,* p. 132. After having heard the string parts rehearsed Dom Pedro heard the premiere July 9. For in-
formation on the other Centennial music, see Abram Loft, "Richard Wagner, Theodore Thomas and the
American Centennial," *Musical Quarterly,* XXXVII/2 (April 1951), pp. 184-202, and Robert A. Gerson,
Music in Philadelphia (Philadelphia, 1940), pp. 134-141.

premiere of *Il Guarany* at Covent Garden July 13, 1872, and called his music "full or spirit and picturesque effect." Having been admitted to Grove and to Fétis (*Supplément,* I, 399),[47] Gomes had entered every American encyclopedia from John Denison Champlin and William Foster Apthorp (1889) onward.

It was Columbus' discovery that inspired the Chicago exposition — all the more reason for Latin America to be represented copiously. Not only Brazil but also Argentina, Guatemala, Mexico, and Uruguay were therefore all invited to send compositions for display. Argentina was represented by Hilda Fortunato with *A Salute to Chicago Symphony for grand orchestra,* Eduardo García Mansilla (1866-1930) with an *Oración Dominical* for solo voice, piano, and cello, and a *Chicago Waltz,* Francisco A. Hargreaves (1849-1900) with a *Chicago March,* and Vicente Mazzacco with an orchestral ode, *Glory to Columbus (Gloria a Colón).* Argentina also sent an item coyly identified in the Exposition catalogue[48] as a "treatise on modern music" by Saturnino Beron "of Buenos Ayres." Apart from Gomes, whose *Cóndor* (1891) and *Colombo* (1892) were advertised as having been especially composed with the thought of performance at the World's Columbian Exposition in mind, Brazil was represented by José Gomes de Araujo (1846-1943, quartets), Francisco Braga (1868-1945, piano and orchestral works), Henrique Braga (dance music), F. de Carvalho (piano compositions), Alexandre Levy (1864-1892, orchestral and piano compositions), A. Cardosa de Menezes (orchestral and piano compositions), Carlos de Mesquita (1864-1953, *Esmeralda,* opera), Henrique Alves de Mesquita (1838-1906, serious and bouffe opera scores), Leopold Miguéz (1850-1902, symphony), and Arthur Napoleão (1843-1925). Two Rio de Janeiro publishers of sheet music sent displays, Izidoro Bevilacqua and Bushman & Guimäraes.[49]

Guatemala, in addition to sending for display a five-octave marimba "made entirely of native woods," sent Benedicto Sáenz's *Missa solemnis,* the only mass from any Latin American country, and a symphony by Yndalecio Castro. With both works came complete sets of orchestral parts — proof that the Chicago authorities had advertised for large compositions with an eye to possible performance. Five other Guatemalans sent band music, Julián Paniagua (of Quezaltenango), Lucas Paniagua, Manuel Montúfar, Lorenzo Morales, and Salvador Yriarte. Band music also loomed large among Mexican works on exhibition at Chicago.[50]

---

[47]The *Supplément et complément,* ed. by Arthur Pougin (Paris, 1878-1880), I, p. 154, also put Teresa Carreço in all subsequent foreign and American encyclopedias.

[48]Frank D. Abbott, ed., *Musical Instruments at the World's Columbian Exposition* (Chicago, 1895), p. 258. All Abbott's other information concerning Argentine representation is at his page 256. Argentine composers listed above without dates are those not mentioned in the second volume of Vicente Gesualdo, *Historia de la música en la Argentina* (Buenos Aires, 1961). Brazilian composers without dates are those not included in Luiz Heitor Correa de Azevedo, *150 Anos de Música no Brasil* (Rio de Janeiro, 1956).

[49]Abbott, *op. cit.,* p. 257.

[50]*Ibid.,* p. 258.

As a sample of the provincial Mexican composers' biographies submitted with their works, Marciano Morales sent this *curriculum vitae:*[51] Born at Oaxaca, November 2, 1861, he was at 12 flautist there of the First Regiment Infantry Band directed by Francisco Zacar, with whom he studied. At 15 he transferred to Puebla Battalion but lost his post during the revolution of Tuxtepec. After several months of self-study he became in 1878 a sergeant and First musician of the 17th Battalion. In 1881 he left the Army to reside at Jalapa and to direct the Jalapa Seguridad Pública Band (police band). His works composed for Chicago were: *Don Carlos, Hasta el Cielo,* and *La Tempestad.* Another Mexican provincial composer who sent a similarly lengthy biography was Francisco Villalpando of Zacatecas. To add zest to her displays, Mexico was the only Latin American nation represented by women: among them María Galicia de Charro of Mexico City, composer of a march, and Adela Rodríguez of Durango, responsible for *Por claro de luna,* "full of the grace and fire of the Southland," according to the Exposition catalogue.[52] Under Group 158, Class 937, the catalogue listed a "collection of 40 books & pieces of music for bands, orchestras, the piano, violin, and other instruments, representing the national music of Mexico" — without, however, giving the titles of individual works. The same failure to itemize obscures the contents of "a book containing several classical pieces by Félix M. Alcerreca of Mexico."

Uruguay was represented by Antonio Metallo of Montevideo with a *Protector Waltz,* and Damiro Costa, composer of some un-itemized piano pieces awarded a prize "for sweetness of melody." The works by all of these other Latin Americans served, however, but as the base of a pyramid at the top of which dwelt Gomes. As the catalogue stated:[53] "In some respects he was distinguished above all others in the host of famous foreign musicians." The concert of fifteen numbers, all of them his own works, given September 7, 1893, under auspices of the Brazilian Commission, glowed with "marvelous energy and nervous force," thanks not only to the genius that wrought the music but also his "firm control over the Exposition orchestra."[54]

As befitted what was intended as a transcendental event Gomes' concert made prime news copy the next day. *The Chicago Record* of Friday, September 8 (XIII/215,4-5) carried a long review under the caption "All Roads lead to the World's Fair." Illustrated with a drawing of the handsome Brazilian Building at the Exposition, the review read:

> Maestro Carlos Gomes is the Brazilian master of music. He has a bronzed countenance, a pair of flashing eyes, a thin and whitening mustache and iron-gray hair falling nearly to his shoulders. It was only natural that having come all the way from Brazil to conduct the concert on the day of Brazilian independence, he should be given a great welcome. Music Hall held several hundred invited guests. The entire Brazilian colony was there . . . Every true Brazilian wore a bow made of the national colors. Very few people knew,

[51]*Ibid.,* p. 269.

[52]*Ibid.,* p. 258.

[53]*Ibid.,* p. 269.

[54]*Ibid.,* p. 270.

perhaps, that 200 Brazilians are at the Columbian Exposition . . . The Exposition Orchestra played, the great Brazilian master waved the baton and the whole programme was punctuated with rousing cheers, bravos and floral offerings. When Maestro Carlos Gomes first came on the stage his countrymen rose to their feet and greeted him with waving hats and fluttering handkerchiefs. The first orchestral number of the programme was the dashing symphony of the opera *Il Guarany*. At the conclusion the happy Brazilians cheered for the maestro, who in turn applauded the orchestra. Mr. Al. Boetti, the tenor, sang the romance of the opera *Salvator Rosa* and Miss Kate Bensberg, the soprano, gave a ballad from the opera *Il Guarany*. Both singers were applauded to the echo and another outbreak of enthusiasm awaited Mr. Orne Darval, the basso, who appeared later in the program. All the music was selected from the operas of *Côndor*, *Il Guarany*, *Salvator Rosa*, *Fosca*, and *Schiavo*.

The concert was the main incident of the day's celebration. On September 7, 1822, Brazil secured independence, so that yesterday was the Fourth of July for the Estados Unidos do Brasil. On the programmes and invitations appeared another date, November 15, 1889, for it was then that Brazil became a republic.

The remainder of the account gives the number of musicians in the Festival Orchestra as 160, states that Gomes conducted at 3 in the afternoon, and gives the total paid attendance at the Fair on September 7 as 172,765. After the concert, Gomes went with his countrymen to the Brazilian building for coffee, Francisco Manuel de Silva's national anthem music was several times repeated by a Fair band, and then Gomes and the soloists adjourned to a dinner at which they were honored guests.

The Chicago Herald reviewing the same concert gloried in the enormous orchestra (''far larger than Wagner's 114''), compared Gomes' waving hair with Paderewski's and claimed that his ovation equaled Paderewski's best, continued with further rapturous details concerning his reception, declared that this event was the loudest and longest homage ever paid Brazil in any foreign land, and concluded by giving the entire itemized program.[55]

Recalling Gomes' Chicago triumphs 42 years later, his son added however some less sanguine details. The program consisted of excerpts because the stingy republican government of Brazil refused to appropriate matching funds for the stage presentation of *Côndor*, premiered at La Scala February 21, 1891, *O Esravo*, first heard of the Theatro Lyrico in Rio September 27, 1889, and *Il Guarany*.[56] The root of the problem was a change of regimes. Gomes had been a favorite of the emperor who in 1888 was forced into exile. In requital, the new ministers of state treated him coldly and would have denied him any funds whatsoever, had not the Columbian Exposition authorities so widely advertised him that his absence would have caused scandal. Even so, the Brazilian government representative at Chicago, a certain ''cidadão Maurity'' had the

[55]Gomes Vaz de Carvalho, *op. cit.*, pp. 249-250.

[56]*Ibid.*, p. 244. For details of his *Via crucis* in getting funds for the trip, see pp. 233-244.

gall to present Gomes with a bill for $1,114 after the one September 7 concert of excerpts,[57] on the pretext that he had overspent the budgeted amount.[58]

Gomes was the most renowned Latin American composer to visit the United States before 1900. The most renowned executant, Teresa Carreño, was born at Caracas December 22, 1853, spent August 1862 to April 1866 chiefly at New York and Boston, and returned from Europe to spend 1874 to October of 1885 and May 1887 to July 1889 again in the United States — the rest of her life being that of a world touring artist recognized everywhere as the finest living woman pianist. On the same ship with her and her father (the deposed Venezuelan minister of finance) when in 1862 they voyaged to the United States, was Juan Buitrago, a Colombian violinist and pianist who gave Edward A. MacDowell his first lessons,[59] before handing the youth over to Pablo Desvernine[60] (a Cuban expatriate pianist teaching in New York after 1869).

Carreño's championing of MacDowell crucially established his worldwide reputation. While European-born celebrities such as Anton Rubinstein, Josef Hofmann, Paderewski, Joseffy, Backhaus, Rosenthal, Godowsky, and their ilk did nothing for any native-born Americans, only she among worldwide celebrities committed herself time and again at her most glittering appearances in Europe as well as the United States to large works by MacDowell, not miniatures.[61] In earlier life, she also played William Mason and especially Gottschalk,[62] who briefly taught her. Her resplendent career, properly studied by anyone taking the true measure of Latin American contributions to United States music, entitles her name to be capitalized in large golden letters. Indeed it may fairly be argued that no paramount foreign-born executant anytime thus far in history has so placed any United States composers in her debt as did wonderful, beautiful Teresa Carreño of Venezuela.

[57]Although not the place to discuss the excerpts, a study of the program with the opera scores in hand shows that Gomes made some extremely judicious choices. For instance, the Nocturno from *Condor* (item 4) foreshadows thematically the Serenata from Act III of that opera (item 5).

[58]*Ibid.*, p. 260.

[59]See Marta Milinowski, *Teresa Carreço "by the grace of God"* (New Haven, 1940), p. 121. See also pp. 122, 146, 308.

[60]Pablo Desvernine, born at Havana in 1823, toured the United States in 1848 (New York, Philadelphia, Cincinnati, St. Louis, New Orleans, Mobile) as piano accompanist to Arditi and Bottesini. After twenty years of teaching at Havana he settled at New York, his mother's native city, to begin there in 1869 a 22-year teaching career. He died in 1910, two years after MacDowell. See Serafín Ramírez, *La Habana artística* (Havana, 1891), pp. 75-79.

[61]*Ibid.*, indexed entries under MacDowell, Edward. Up until at least 1900 Carreço was "the only great artist who had the courage and the will to actually play his music" (p. 308).

[62]*Ibid.*, p. 52. She was the first to play for Liszt any of Gottschalk's music. See pp. 69-70. She played variations on Richard Milburn's *Listen to the Mocking Bird* for Lincoln, p. 62.

THE RIOT AT THE RITE: NOT SO SURPRISING AFTER ALL

by Truman Bullard

The first performance in Paris of Igor Stravinsky's *Sacre du Printemps* on May 29, 1913 is universally acknowledged to be a decisive moment in the history of music, of the dance, and of the cultural life of Europe and the world. This judgment has been restated countless times in written history ever since that historic premiere turned a fashionable Parisian audience into a mob of shouting, whistling, stamping, and even fist-fighting partisans. Whether this work itself represents a culmination of the Romantic era or the dawn of the modern age has been debated for years, and from the musical standpoint there is much to be said on both sides. In all these discussions and reassessments of *Le Sacre*, however, the significance of the premiere as a battle over artistic principles has never been forgotten. In less than one hour's time the patrons of the Ballets Russes de Serge de Diaghilev took up their positions and performed a ritual of public conflict while the dancers on the stage and the musicians in the pit were playing out their own "jeux des cités rivales."

In the years following that tumultuous evening the story of the riot has been told and retold both by members of that elite assembly who were present and by biographers and historians of the age. And it is not surprising to observe that within a few decades the tale acquired all those characteristics of exaggeration, contradiction, obsurity, and even untruth that tend to accrue to all those unique moments in human history to which man returns again and again to learn from his past. It must also be observed that as the story of the riot has been embroidered through time and repetition, it has also lost many details of fact and opinion that were never recorded at the moment, and have since receded from human memory.

Several of the protagonists in this drama at the new Théâtre des Champs-Elysées have written about their memories of the event.[1] These memoirs have unique value and authenticity for any systematic study of the circumstances surrounding the premiere of *Le Sacre*, and yet they are also the sources of much of the misunderstanding that is still to be found in second and third-generation renditions of the story.

One myth connected with the premiere which shows remarkable vitality is what might be called the "spontaneous combustion" theory: the audience rose up in a unanimous and momentarily inspired expression of either repudiation or defense of the new work.

---

[1]Of particular importance are the reminiscences of Gabriel Astruc, manager of the Théâtre des Champs-Elysées, *Le Pavillon des Fantômes* (Paris, 1929); of the conductor Pierre Monteux, "The *Sacre* and Pierre Monteux," in *Boston Symphony Orchestra Programmes 1950-1951*; of Diaghilev as recounted to Serge Lifar in *Serge Diaghilev: His Life, His Work, His Legend* (New York, 1940); and of Stravinsky as recorded in the autobiography (published in French with Walter Nouvel as *Chroniques de ma Vie*, 2 vols. (Paris, 1935) and in English (New York, 1936).

This interpretation would logically follow from Stravinsky's remark in the *Autobiography* of 1935.

> Oddly enough, at the dress rehearsal, to which we had as usual invited a number of actors, painters, musicians, writers, and the most cultured representatives of society, everything had gone off peacefully, and I was far from expecting such an outburst [at the public premiere on the following evening].[2]

An examination of the sources and documents from the time of the premiere reveals that a violent reception was, in fact, both anticipated and stimulated by the management of the Ballets Russes, and there can be little doubt that the master strategist behind the campaign was that genius of the theater, Sergei Diaghilev. It was he who sought every opportunity to dramatize in the press every aspect of the life and work of his company through the cleverest use of secrecy, news leaks, and planted "ghost-written" articles and interviews.

Of particular interest at present is the "sneak preview" technique referred to by Stavinsky which Diaghilev utilized to generate passionate interest in new productions. An excellent description of this ploy and its effect has been recorded by Serge Grigoriev, Diaghilev's *regisseur*, in his invaluable book, *The Diaghilev Ballet: 1909-1929*. The new ballet in this instance was *L'Après-midi d'un Faune* of 1912 in which the great dancer Nijinsky made his debut as a choreographer.

> It remained for us to show the public *L''Après-midi d'un Faune*. From the day of our arrival Diaghilev began preparing opinion for its reception. Friends of his would be brought to all Nijinsky's rehearsals and invited to admire his original choreography, after which they would broadcast news of it all over Paris. The result was that everyone was soon talking about it. Parisians are always eager for what is new and unusual, and were now all agog to see this sensational work for which an unprecedented success was freely predicted. At the rehearsals attended by Diaghilev's friends, Nijinsky never did more than walk through his own part. It was not, consequently, until just before the dress rehearsal, when he first played it in detail, that anyone had a chance to see what it consisted of; and everyone was then astounded at his final pose, when the faun is left with the nymph's scarf, pointing out to Diaghilev that it was highly indecent, and warning him that it would create a scandal . . . This dress rehearsal was followed by a reception in the foyer; and no effort was neglected to nurse opinion and encourage a favorable reaction to *L'Après-midi*.[3]

---

[2] Stravinsky, *An Autobiography* (republished New York: 1962), p. 47. Among those reviewers known to have attended the invitational rehearsal were Adolphe Boschot of *l'Echo de Paris,* Jean Chantavoine of *Excelsior,* Gustave Linor of *Comoedia*, Georges Pioch of *Gil Blas,* and Gaston Carraud of *La Liberté.*

[3] S. L. Grigoriev, *The Diaghilev Ballet: 1909-1929*, trans. and ed. Vera Brown (London, 1953), pp. 78-79.

The calculated outcome of such rehearsals was the earliest possible beating of the publicity drum in the Parisian press.[4] The unanticipated result of Diaghilev's previews was growing suspicion and hostility from the very reviewers he sought to use. Gaston Carraud, critic of *La Liberté* was only one of at least four early reviewers of *Le Sacre*, who described and deplored this "unique" treatment:

> I have no idea how the audience received the music and the production of this new ballet yesterday. I should love to have known it. But the administration of the *Saisons russes* has always maintained its own unique idea about the treatment of the press services which is subsumed under the category of "special tickets" . . . We need not concern ourselves with how wrongly this practice treats the *critics*. What is important is that this makes impossible the exercise of *criticism*. Will all these directors never understand that free criticism—even though it be at times unfavorable to them—is the primary agent of their prosperity and the ultimate safeguard of their dignity? Now we are forced to express an opinion based upon a rehearsal, wherein many things may not yet be polished and the work itself does not occur clothed in the atmosphere of a true performance. It is all the more annoying when the work is touted to be from every standpoint the point of departure of a new art . . .[5]

Thus, the dress rehearsal which Stravinsky described as uneventful was attended by critics ready to bare their knives in the morning edition. And if the stimulation of discussion and debate were the object of Diaghilev in his invitational "rehearsals," he seems to have succeeded brilliantly, for the critic Louis Vuillemin, who wrote regularly for the lavish arts magazine *Comoedia,* confirms our hypothesis in his review of *Le Sacre:*

> Some people, invited to a few final rehearsals went back out into the streets of Paris wild-looking and convinced they had reason to be. There were two kinds: both wild and both convinced. "Marvelous! Magnificent! Splendid! Definitive!" cried some to everyone who would listen. "Abominable! Hateful! Ridiculous! Pretentious!" screamed the others even to those who did not, or would not, listen. It spread through the entire public like wild-fire thirty six hours before the curtain rose. "Just you wait," those convinced said, "We are about to witness the great musical revolution. This evening is the appointed time for the symphony of the future!" "Watch out!" warned the skeptics, "they are about to make fools of us. They take us for idiots. We must defend ourselves!" Result: the

[4]Typically a lapse of one day was found between the presentation of an evening event and its first reviews. It was therefore impossible for reviews based upon the dress rehearsal to appear in print on the day of the public premiere.

[5]Gaston Carraud, "Au Théâtre des Champs-Elysées: *Le Sacre du Printemps,*" *La Liberté,* XLVIII/17,255 (May 31, 1913), p. 3. See also Adolphe Boschot in *l'Echo de Paris,* XXX/10,518 (May 30, 1913), p. 6, Jean Chantavoine in *Excelsior,* IV/927 (May 30, 1913), p. 6, and Georges Pioch in *Gil Blas,* XXXV/13,348 (May 30, 1913), p. 3.

curtain goes up—I should say even before the curtain went up—you could hear, "Oh!" and then they all began to sing, to hiss, to whistle. Some clapped, some cried, "Bravo!", some shrieked, some cheered, some hooted, some extolled. And there you have the premiere of *Le Sacre du Printemps*.[6]

On the day of the premiere two momentous articles were published, one brief and artfully worded news release in every major newspaper and one attributed to the composer himself in the avant-garde magazine *Montjoie!* The formal announcement baits the hook at the very end in a manner which today appears rather obvious, but the "signature" of Diaghilev is to be found not in the final sentence but in the opening paragraph where the unity of artistic conception among Stravinsky, Nijinsky, and Nicholas Roerich (the scenic designer) is heavily stressed. This "triple vision" was the personal triumph and pride of the great catalytic figure who had drawn them together.

> *Le Sacre du Printemps*, which the Russian Ballet will perform for the first time this evening at the Théâtre des Champs Elysées, is the most amazing creation ever attempted by M. Serge de Diaghilev's marvelous company. It evokes the primitive gestures of pagan Russia as conceived by the triple vision of Stravinsky, poet and composer, of Nicholas Roerich, poet and painter, and of Nijinsky, poet and choreographer.
>
> Here we will see the characteristic attitudes of the Slavic race portrayed powerfully in its response to beauty in the prehistoric era.
>
> Only the wonderful Russian dancers could portray these first stammered gestures of a half-savage humanity; only they could represent these frenzied mobs of people who untiringly stamp out the most startling polyrhythms ever produced by the brain of a musician. Here is truly a new sensation which will undoubtedly provoke heated discussions, but will leave every spectator with an unforgettable memory of the artists.[7]

A far more controversial and intriguing history surrounds the article attributed to Stravinsky and entitled "Ce que j'ai voulu exprimer dans *Le Sacre du printemps*" which was published in *Montjoie!* by Ricciotto Canudo, its editor on May 29.[8] The composer states emphatically in his autobiography that the article was written by the editor after

[6]Louis Vuillemin, *"Le Sacre du Printemps,"* Comoedia, VVI/2068 (May 31, 1913), p. 2.

[7]*"Le Sacre du Printemps,"* Le Figaro, LIX, 3eme serie/149 (May 29, 1913), p. 6. This notice was printed identically in *l'Aurore, la France, Comoedia,* and *Le Gaulois.*

[8]Igor Stravinsky [?], "Ce que j'ai voulu exprimer dans *Le Sacre du Printemps*," Montjoie! *Organe de l'Impérialisme Artistique Francais,* I/8 (May 29, 1913), p. 1. A fascinating history of this short-lived journal and its editor has recently been written by Noëmi Blumenkranz-Onimus, "Montjoie! ou l'héroïque croisade pour une nouvelle culture," in *L'Année 1913,* ed. L. Brion Guerry, 2 vols. (Paris, 1971), Vol. II, pp. 1105-1106.

an interview and was dishonestly attributed to himself.[9] What he perhaps could not add was that this was done at the instruction of Diaghilev who wished to disarm in advance the criticism he fully anticipated regarding the suitability of Nijinsky's choreography to Stravinsky's score. It was just this charge which critics had levelled at Nijinsky's previous essays in choreography: Debussy's *L'Après-midi d'un Faune* in 1912, and two weeks earlier in 1913 in the new ballet *Jeux*.

The article begins with an almost patronizing address to the Parisian public:

> In the last few years the Parisian public has kindly tendered a warm welcome to my *Oiseau de Feu* and to *Petrouchka*. My friends have noticed the evolution of the animating conception which progresses from the fantastical fable in the first of these works to the fully human generalization in the second. I am afraid that *Le Sacre*, in which I make use neither of fairy tales nor of the themes of human sadness and joy, but in which I endeavor to portray a somewhat larger abstraction may mislead those who have, thus far, shown me such sympathetic appreciation.[10]

After a few awkwardly-stated remarks about the scoring techniques employed in the Prelude, the discussion turns to a plot synopsis which strongly suggests that it is a rewritten version of the printed program notes prepared for the premiere. But the concluding sentence of the article reveals its tactical purpose. The author states, "And I am happy to have found for this work of faith M. Nijinsky, the ideal choreographer, and M. Roerich, the creator of the pictorial atmosphere."[11] What critic could now accuse with impunity the hapless dancer-choreographer for having once betrayed the composer's intentions? Nevertheless, the scheme failed, for there were many who found the choreography to be the principally offensive element.

It is well known that Stravinsky himself began to criticize Nijinsky's work at the time of the 1920 revival of the ballet, with new choreography by Leonid Massine,[12] and he continued to speak and write in these terms to the end of his life. It is not generally known, however, that within days of the premiere, just before he fell ill with typhoid, the composer granted an interview to Henri Postel du Mas of the newspaper *Gil Blas*. On this occasion he forcefully defended his beleaguered collaborator:

> M. Nijinsky has been reproached for his production, and people have said that it seemed foreign to the music. They are wrong. M. Nijinsky is a

---

[9]*An Autobiography,* p. 49.

[10]*Op. cit.* This article in its original French and in English translation is included in the author's dissertation, *The First Performance of Igor Stravinsky's Sacre du Printemps* (The University of Rochester, Eastman School of Music, 1971), Vol. II, pp. 4-9 (English) and Vol. III, pp. 3-6 (French).

[11]*Ibid.*

[12]The first recorded remarks by Stravinsky critical of the Nijinsky realization are to be found in Michel Georges-Michel, "Les Deux *Sacres du Printemps*," *Comoedia Illustré* (December 11, 1920), reprinted in his book *Ballets Russes, Histoire Anecdotique* (Paris, 1923), pp. 47-50.

wonderful artist. He is capable of renewing the art of ballet. We have not ceased for one second to be in complete communion of thought. You will see what he will do someday. He is not only a marvelous dancer, he is able to create, to innovate, and his part in the collaboration for *Le Sacre du Primtemps* was most fruitful. All that is necessary is to educate the public so that it can recognize his success in these matters.[13]

M. du Mas describes in detail the time and place of this interview and characterizes the composer's mannerisms so vividly that there is no reason to believe that in this instance Stravinsky was being spoken for by his mentor. But it is fascinating to observe that the power of Diaghilev's artistic convictions had by this time extended from his company through the press, to the public, and it even held sway for the moment over the words of his most brilliant star, Igor Stravinsky. To the end of his life the great impresario looked upon the premiere of *Le Sacre du Printemps* as his greatest hour. *His* greatest hour? Yes, indeed.

[13]Henri Postel du Mas, ''Un Entretien avec M. Stravinsky,'' *Gil Blas,* XXXV/13,253 (June 4, 1913), p. 1. The same conversation was repeated by Edmond Stoullig in his *Annales du Théâtre et de la Musique,* XXXIX (January, 1914), pp. 327-330. Stoullig claims that the remarks were made directly to him by the composer, which suggests that he was present at the interview with du Mas.

RENAISSANCE DIALOGUE TECHNIQUES*

by Denis Stevens

"When I use a word," Humpty-Dumpty
said, in a rather scornful tone, "it means
just what I choose it to mean—neither
more nor less."
(*Alice through the Looking-Glass*)

All musicologists have, at one time or another, suffered from that peculiar kind of frustration which derives from an unsatisfied quest for factual knowledge in the great dictionaries and encyclopedias of our artistically inclined science. Look for a fact in six sources of information, and you get seven answers. This is certainly true if one attempts to trace the origin and development of the dialogue as a musical form or style, because each author appears to cherish an entirely individualistic outlook upon the actual meaning of the word. Dialogue is not infrequently misunderstood to be a conversation between two persons, whereas it really refers to a conversation between two or more interlocutors. Semantic considerations apart, however, the degree of divergence in coverage noticeable in half-a-dozen standard reference works must strike even the most casual of readers as remarkable.

Grove's Dictionary[1] damns the Dialogue with the faintest of praise. It mentions only one piece of music, and the entire article consists of only five lines. The *Harvard Dictionary*,[2] Riemann,[3] and *Larousse de la Musique*[4] offer relatively short articles of a general nature, dealing with the idea of dialogue in opera, oratorio, motet, chamber cantata, madrigal and various other relevant forms. *MGG*,[5] as we might expect, has a long and detailed article subdivided into six categories: General Remarks; Italian Sacred Dialogues in the Vernacular; Latin Dialogues in Italy; Motet Dialogues; Seventeenth-

---

*Many of the dialogues discussed in this paper have been recorded by the Accademia Monteverdiana on *Amorous Dialogues of the Renaissance* (Nonesuch H-71272), *The Music of Nicola Vicentino* (Vanguard HM 34 SD) and *Adrian Willaert* (Odyssey 32 1602 02). A collection of ten dialogues, in new performing editions by the writer, is published by Novello, London and New York.

[1]*Grove's Dictionary of Music and Musicians*, Fifth Edition (1954), II, p. 683 (unsigned).

[2]*Harvard Dictionary of Music*, Second Edition (1969), p. 230. By Willi Apel.

[3]*Riemann Musik Lexikon*, Twelfth Edition (1967), Sachteil p. 222. By Peter Schnaus.

[4]*Larousse de la Musique* (1957), I, p. 265. By Denise Launay.

[5]*Die Musik in Geschichte und Gegenwart* (1954), III, col. 391. By Elisabeth Noack.

Century Protestant Dialogues; Secular Dialogues in Italy, France, England, and Germany. At first glance, this seems to be very thorough, but when we seek information about the secular polyphonic dialogue of the Renaissance under the sixth and last of those headings in *MGG*, all that emerges is a bleak reference to the term *Madrigaldialoge*, a bare mention of Monteverdi's *Book VI* (published in 1614), and a brief bow in the direction of Theodore Kroyer, whose article on dialogue and echo compositions in early choral music is still the only reliable study, although it appeared as long ago as 1909.[6]

By a stroke of good musicological fortune, there is in the Ricordi *Enciclopedia*[7] a lengthy article, with music and text examples, dealing with that very aspect of the dialogue so hastily passed over in *MGG,* and indeed in all the other dictionaries—the polyphonic dialogue of the sixteenth century. The author, Egon Kenton, is so immersed in his topic that he hardly mentions any other kind of dialogue at all, so that if one were to use this article to trope the *MGG* essay by Elisabeth Noack, the result would be a very useful study of the dialogue in the round; and there would be no overlapping because the two articles are precisely complementary. It is worthy of note that a further account of madrigalesque dialogues, with copious examples, may be found in Kenton's book on Giovanni Gabrieli's life and works.[8]

If ever the dialogue becomes, as it surely will, the subject of a dissertation or a monograph, it is to be hoped that some mention will be made of its origins as a literary form, and the influence of that form on the didactic element in musical treatises throughout the ages. This influence is not, alas, discussed in any of the dictionary articles cited above. Plutarch wrote one of his famous dialogues on the subject of music, but we do not find another until Odo of Cluny's master-and-disciple discussion of musical theory in his *Enchiridion musices* of the early tenth century.[9] One of the most vivid and entertaining of all such works in Antonfrancesco Doni's *Dialogo della*

[6]*Jahrbuch der Musikbibliothek Peters,* XVI (1909), p. 13.

[7]*Enciclopedia della Musica,* (1964), II, p. 48. By Egon Kenton.

[8]*The Life and Works of Giovanni Gabrieli* (Zutphen, 1967), pp. 386-415. Among the works discussed and illustrated here are Donato's *Ahi, miserelle,* in which nymphs sing the upper trio and shepherds the lower quartet; Andrea Gabrieli's *Cantiam di Dio* for three choirs; Giovanni Gabrieli's *Addio, dolce mia vita,* for ten voices divided into two choirs; Striggio's *O passi sparsi,* for eleven voices in two choirs; and two dialogues by Vecchi calling for three choral groups—*Come al vago apparir,* and *Cantiamo ninfe* (which has a double echo). Kenton says of Bertani's *Tre gratiosi amanti* (p. 400) that "it is a narration, with the lady's words quoted. It is, therefore, not a dialogue at all, and the alternation of the choirs is not motivated." If we are forced to accept this attempt at categorization, a considerable number of works for alternating choirs, clearly referred to by their authors as dialogues, will have to be excluded from the canon. Among them will be all the settings of Guarini's *Tirsi morir volea* and Tasso's *Dormiva dolcemente,* both of which are narrations in which the lady's words are quoted. Perhaps it would be more reasonable to assume that the voice of the narrator could be construed as part of the dialogue, which (in a sense) it was, since the speaker is usually assumed to be the poet himself, and he is simply dialoguing with imaginary characters in the same way that Antonfrancesco Doni and Gioseffo Zarlino dialogue with real ones. Although no hard-and-fast definition of the dialogue is possible, Michel Brenet's epigrammatic statement in her *Dictionnaire de la Musique* offers food for thought: "Le dialogue sert en quelque sorte de trait d'union entre le madrigal et la cantate."

[9]Translation in Oliver Strunk, *Source Readings in Music History* (New York, 1950), p. 103.

musica,[10] which first saw the light in 1544. It goes far beyond the usual theoretical topics, bringing in ten or a dozen characters, some of whom were real musicians—Girolamo Parabosco and Perissone Cambio, for example—and it inspired several more Italian writers in subsequent decades.

In 1568, we have Vincenzo Galilei's *Fronimo,*[11] concerning the tuning and tablature of the lute, and in 1581 (by the same author), a polemical retort to Zarlino entitled *Dialogo della musica antica, e della moderna.*[12] In 1593, Girolamo Diruta published his dialogue-treatise on keyboard technique—*Il Transilvano,*[13] so called because its dedicatee was Sigismund Báthory, Prince of Transylvania. Ercole Bottrigari's *Il Desiderio*[14] followed in 1594, this being named for the inquisitive gentleman from Pavia who also took part in the dialogues of Zarlino's *Dimostrationi Harmoniche,*[15] published in Venice in 1571. The fashion then passes to England, causing Thomas Morley to set forth his *Plaine and Easie Introduction* (the first edition was in 1597) as a dialogue between the master and two pupils, whose characters are clearly differentiated, one being serious and the other argumentative.[16] The Bolognese canon, Giovanni Maria Artusi,[17] in his eponymous treatise of 1600 attacking Monteverdi's counterpoint, invented a conversation between two musical gentlemen of Ferrara. Among several later theoretical treatises in dialogue form are the *Gradus ad Parnassum*[18] of Fux (1725), and E.T.A. Hoffmann's *Die Serapions-Brüder,* a collection of short stories written between 1819 and 1821, about a group of musical and literary men much concerned with contemporary developments.[19]

To return to the polyphonic dialogue, it cannot have escaped the notice of those whose bedside reading includes Vogel's *Bibliothek der gedruckten weltlichen Vocalmusik Italiens* that an uncommonly high proportion of madrigal books issued in

[10]See G. F. Malipiero, *Antonfrancesco Doni* (Venice, 1946); *Collana di musiche veneziane inedite o rare* (Vol. 7, Vienna, 1965). Some of Doni's characters are real (Parabosco, Cambio, Landi, Domenichi) while others are apparently fictitious.

[11]Published by Scotto of Venice. Facsimile edition by Forni of Bologna.

[12]Facsimile with introduction by Fabio Fano in *Bolletino Bibliografico Musicale* (1934). Extracts are translated in Strunk, *op. cit.,* p. 302.

[13]Published originally in two parts: I (1612), II (1622). Facsimile edition by Forni of Bologna.

[14]Facsimile, with introduction by Kathi Meyer (Berlin, 1924); complete translation by Carol MacClintock ([Rome], 1962).

[15]Facsimile reprint by Gregg (London, 1966). The interlocutors are the author, Francesco Viola, Claudio Merulo, Adrian Willaert, and Desiderio da Pavia.

[16]Edition by R. Alec Harman (London, 1952).

[17]For translated extracts see Strunk, *op. cit.,* p. 393.

[18]Abbreviated translation by Alfred Mann, *Steps to Parnassus* (New York, 1943).

[19]Translated extracts in Strunk, *op. cit.,* p. 782.

the second half of the sixteenth century end with a dialogue for seven or eight voices, usually arranged in two choirs. At first a kind of culminating gesture, a means of involving all the singers who might turn up for an evening's music at one of the many *accademie* scattered throughout Italy, the dialogue eventually gained such a following that in 1590 it became necessary to issue a work entirely devoted to this form.[20] The partbooks contain 55 dialogues by some two dozen composers, scored for two or three choirs, and ranging from seven voices to twelve.

The diversity of types, techniques, forms and styles in the music alone of these dialogues (without taking into account their poetical texts) is amazing, especially when one considers the fact that most of them were produced within the same half-century and within the boundaries of continental Europe. Of course, they had predecessors, especially in Italy; and Einstein has shown that early examples of the secular dialogue existed as early as the first decade of the century. He twice attempted to pinpoint the first dialogue. In 1928, he singled out a frottola by Antonio Stringari, *Don don, al fuoco,*[21] first printed by Petrucci in 1514. In a subsequent article, however, he was able to push back this date by four years, citing Tromboncino's capitolo, *"Amor!" "Che vuoi?" "Ragion,"*[22] which appeared in Andrea Antico's *Canzoni nove* of 1510.

Recently Claudio Gallico[23] pointed out the existence of a dialogue which has so far escaped the attention of scholars, in Petrucci's *Frottole Libro Nono* published in 1509, the same year that saw the printed arrangement for lute and voice by Francis of Bosnia. This dialogue, *Aqua, aqua, aiuto, el foco*, reunites the poetry of Niccolò da Correggio and the music of Bartolomeo Tromboncino, but in spite of its literary and musical interest it brings back the date of the earliest dialogue by only one year, from 1510 to 1509. If we want to find an earlier example still, we must go to a manuscript source inventoried by Nanie Bridgman[24] in her study of the Italian anthology dated approximately 1502 in the Bibliothèque Nationale. This manuscript contains, among a wealth of four-part compositions of various types, a dialogue beginning with the words *"Morte!" "Che vuoi?" "Te bramo,"* which Fausto Torrefranca transcribed in his well-known study of fifteenth-century Italian music, *Il Segreto del Quattrocento.*[25] The similarity between this opening gambit and the first line of Tromboncino's *"Amor!" "Che vuoi?" "Ragion"* may well indicate a link between the poet and composer of both, or at least the influence of the earlier composition upon the later one.

Since all these works are frottole, we are dealing with only one vocal line and three

[20]*Dialoghi Musicali de Diversi Eccellentissimi Autori* (Venice, Gardano). Reprinted in 1592 and 1594.

[21]Einstein, "Das elfte Buch der Frottole," *Zeitschrift für Musikwissenschaft*, X (1928), p. 618.

[22]Einstein, "Andrea Antico's 'Canzoni nove' of 1510," *The Musical Quarterly*, XXXVII (1951), p. 330.

[23]"Un 'Dialogo d'Amore' di Niccolò da Correggio musicato da Bartolomeo Tromboncino," in *Studien zur Musikwissenschaft*, XXV (1962), p. 205.

[24]"Un manuscrit italien du début du XVIe s. à la Bibliothèque Nationale (Rés. Vm⁷ 676)," *Annales Musicologiques,* I (1953), p. 177.

[25](Milan, 1939), p. 497.

supporting instrumental parts. If the dialogue is to be performed dramatically, the vocal line must be divided between two singers, although this method is never expressly suggested by the early prints and manuscripts. This was entirely a matter for the performers, and it is quite possible that they shared the declamation between suitably contrasting voices, in spite of the relatively limited tessitura. In his *Aqua, aqua, aiuto, al foco* Tromboncino is careful to insert a rest between each melodic phrase corresponding to a statement or question by one of the interlocutors,[26] and he may therefore have counted on a performance by two singers, one representing *Amante,* the other *Amore.*

Example 1

When the frottola gave way to the madrigal, a new method had to be found for expressing a poetical question and answer in the form of polyphony.[27] In the case of a lengthy address and an equally lengthy reply, one madrigal could quite easily follow another, and this method of *proposta* and *risposta* was very frequently used as a means of contrast, though it is obvious that no dramatic differentiation of high and low parts

---

[26]Gallico does not suggest this possibility in his transcription of the music (*op. cit.*, p. 210), but he makes the identity of the speakers clear in his edition of the poem (p. 212).

[27]For an early example of this practice at the end of the frottola period see Ernst T. Ferand, "Two Unknown Frottole," *The Musical Quarterly,* XXVII (1941), p. 319.

was possible when both madrigals were scored for the same group of mixed voices.

It was surely as a way out of this artistic impasse that Adrian Willaert[28] invented the polyphonic dialogue. The use of the word "invented" in this context throws caution to the winds, especially in view of the abundant proof that Willaert did not invent the practice of *cori spezzati,*[29] those separated halves of a church choir whose special task it was to perform antiphonal psalmody, hymns, and canticles. The fact remains, however, that the earliest polyphonic dialogues to secular texts were undoubtedly those by Willaert, the group of four in his *Musica Nova* of 1559.[30] Admittedly Nicola Vicentino included a dialogue in his First Book of Madrigals, published in 1546; but he was a pupil of Willaert and a much younger man, and he employed a different kind of dialogue technique altogether. The point of vital importance here is that most if not all the madrigals and dialogues first published in *Musica Nova* were written in or before 1540.[31] They antedate Vicentino by at least six years, unless of course it can be proved that his own collection was written long before it went to press; and such proof is unlikely to appear at this stage.

If Willaert invented the secular polyphonic dialogue around the year 1540, a word should be coined to define and explain the way he went about his task. There is no clear separation of vocal groups to left and right, but rather a constantly changing pattern of vocal strands and textures within his seven-part ensemble, for seven is his maximum number. Yet from this ensemble he can extract now one kind of quartet, now another, by retaining one voice as common to both quartets. Mozart achieves a similar effect in his string quintets by playing off a trio of two violins and viola against a darker-toned trio of two violas and cello.[32] The first viola is part of both ensembles; and in the same way certain of Willaert's vocal lines perform double duty. Because of this constantly shifting tonal pattern, the word "kaleidophonic" might seem to be appropriate, because when we listen to Willaert's music we do indeed hear beautiful forms.

A superb example of a kaleidophonic dialogue, *Che fai, alma?* (based on a sonnet of Petrarch)[33] shows us many of the subtleties of Willaert's musical thought. The topic is unrequited love, and the poet sorrowfully interrogates his soul. Each side of the conversation is taken by four voices, but the make-up of these dialoguing quartets is constantly changing. The tone-color is generally dark, with a mezzo-soprano or alto on the top line, and a profusion below of tenors or baritones and basses. The following

[28]See the dissertation by Joan Long, *The Motets, Psalms and Hymns of Adrian Willaert—A Liturgico-Musical Study* (Columbia University, 1971).

[29]Giovanni d'Alessi, "Precursors of Adriano Willaert in the Practice of Coro Spezzato," *Journal of the American Musicological Society,* V (1952), p. 187.

[30]Edited by Walter Gerstenberg, *Collected Works of Adrian Willaert,* XIII.

[31]Einstein, *The Italian Madrigal* (Princeton, 1971), I, p. 335.

[32]See in particular the opening measures of the first movement of the G minor Quintet (K.516), and the second movement of the D major (K.593).

[33]Sonnet CL in vita di Madonna Laura.

pattern shows that Willaert employs four different kinds of vocal quartet before Poet and Soul unite in the final tercet:

	Poet	Soul	Poet	Soul	Poet	Soul	Poet	P&S
1 (alto)		1		1		1		1
2 (alto)	2		2		2		2	2
3 (tenor)	3		3	3	3		3	3
4 (tenor)		4	4		4	4	4	4
5 (baritone)	5	5		5		5		5
6 (bass)	6		6		6		6	6
7 (bass)		7		7		7		7
Pattern;	a	b	c	d	c	b	c	e

This particular technique of Willaert's has almost the effect of adding a metaphysical touch to the interchange of thoughts and ideas, and it may well have been intentional, because another of his dialogues exhibits a more straightforward scheme of interaction—his setting of the sonnet *Quando nascesti, Amor?* by Pamfilo Sasso. Although we are nearly at the stage of an audible juxtapositon of high trio (representing Cupid) and a darker-toned quartet (the Poet), the trio occasionally borrows a voice from the other group, so that the basic approach is still kaleidophonic (see Ex. 2).[34]

Vicentino followed the example of his revered master in setting the anonymous sonnet, *Amor, ecco ch'io moro,*[35] contained in his *First Book of Madrigals*[36] published in 1546. The same two characters, in the same costumes, flesh out the flimsy filigree of this well-worn Renaissance miniplot; and once again the darker hue of alto, two tenors, and bass lends a glow of dark despair to the words of the Poet, who is answered by the loftier tones of a Cupid shared between soprano, alto, and tenor. The separation between these two groups is perfectly clear-cut until we reach the climax of the poem, which corresponds to the answer given by Cupid to the Lover's question. ''Why,'' he says, ''do you make this girl disdain me and avoid me, when she ought to be so sweet and kind?'' And Cupid replies (borrowing for the first and last time an extra voice-part for emphasis) ''So that her charming and beloved countenance may be more dear to you than anything else, because happiness is indeed sweet when it is acquired through martyrdom.''

That particular method of maintaining, for the most part, a clear division between groups yet allowing the trio to borrow from the quartet is found also in the well-known

[34]Gustave Reese writes of this work: ''The effect approximates that of two choruses of contrasting timbre alternating with one another until they join together at the close.'' (Notes on *The Music of Adrian Willaert,* a stereo recording on Odyssey 32 16 0202.)

[35]Discussed in Henry W. Kaufmann, *The Life and Works of Nicola Vicentino* ([Rome], 1966), p. 53.

[36]Note that in the edition of Vicentino's *Omnia Opera* ([Rome], 1963), p. 61, the second stave from the top should appear as the fourth from the bottom, in order to make the dialogue texture clear.

Example 2

dialogue of Andrea Gabrieli, *Tirsi morir volea*.[37] Andrea's Venetian background, combined with his visit to Lassus at Munich, evidently induced him to experiment with dialogue techniques, as may be seen by comparing his compositions in the great anthology of *Dialoghi musicali* with those of his most eminent contemporaries.[38] Although his setting of *Tirsi morir volea* was not published until the *Concerti* of 1587, its style indicates a much earlier date of composition, possibly in the 1560's, for he is clearly indebted to both Willaert and Vicentino. What is particularly instructive in this connection is to compare Andrea's setting with that of Giaches de Wert, first printed in his Seventh Book in 1581.[39] Whereas Andrea indulges in the old practice of borrowing a voice, de Wert looks forward to the later ideal of complete separation between trio and quartet.

If we look over Andrea's shoulder, we find that he is actually doing more than borrowing just one voice, for his trio turns itself into a quartet on three occasions in order to repeat and emphasize a statement, borrowing first the altus, then septimus, and finally quintus. What is more, the quartet on one ocassion becomes a quintet by borrowing the tenor from aloft. The words of the girl are of course assigned to the higher tessitura of the trio, but since she speaks only twice, near the beginning and near the end of the poem, Andrea makes use of the trio at two further points in order to vary the texture. The first is at the words *"e mentre il guardo suo"* where the trio is answered immediately by the quartet, as if glances are being exchanged between the two lovers. The second point is at *"sentia i messi d'amore,"* giving the impression that this part of the narrative is as good as direct speech; in other words the girl is feeling love's messages, so the phrase is heard in the higher range. In its general outlook and style, this masterly dialogue lies somewhere between the kaleidophonic and the modern, and it is (as Einstein says) "a dramatically animated madrigal but still a madrigal."[40]

Giaches de Wert sets the same poem as a miniature drama.[41] The trio and the quartet are kept strictly separate, so much so that they could almost be placed in opposite corners of a room. There is no borrowing of voices, and the trio only sings when the girl's actual words appear in the poem. Basically homophonic, the texture allows the narrative to be heard with the utmost clarity, and there is little or no repetition of words for emphasis until the superimposition, near the climax, of the words of boy and girl: *"Mori, cor mio, ch'io moro"* and *"Et io, mia vita, moro"* (see Ex. 3). One other important stylistic feature remains to be mentioned, and that is de Wert's liking for a static kind of harmony in the narrative sections. The deliberately slow harmonic rhythm lends a certain atmosphere of tranquillity to a poem which (to quote Einstein once again) "is more obscene than the coarsest *mascherata*, the most suggestive *canto carnascialesco*, or

[37]Transcription in Einstein, *The Italian Madrigal*, III, p. 190.

[38]A link between Lassus and Willaert may be seen in the seven-part setting by Lassus of *Che fai, alma?* in the *Dialoghi musicali*, but much earlier in date of origin.

[39]*Giaches de Wert: Collected Works*, ed. Carol MacClintock ([Rome], 1966), VII, p.56.

[40]Einstein: *The Italian Madrigal*, II, p. 544.

[41]Discussed in Carol MacClintock, *Giaches de Wert: Life and Works* ([Rome], 1966), p. 110.

Example 3

the most impertinent chanson.''[42]   Guarini's poem is, of course, about love-making, but it is far from being obscene in the contemporary sense. It does not even attempt to paint a picture, let alone fill in the details, and its only reason for existence is to advocate what one might reasonably describe as ''togetherness,'' which is rather more than a four-letter word. And even when the euphemistic *morire* is granted the full force of its physical meaning, the composer, with consummate skill and commendable taste, draws over it a delicate veil of matchless music, adding at one and the same time a feeling of intensity and of modesty.[43]

Thomas Morley's *First Book of Balletts* enjoyed the unusual luxury of three different language-editions: English, Italian, and German. It contains the only genuinely English double-choir dialogue with a secular text, the seven-part *Phillis, I fain would die now*.[44] The anonymous poet's use of the word ''die'' is worlds apart from Guarini's ''morire,'' just as Morley's texture is far removed from that of Andrea Gabrieli or Giaches de Wert. He maintains a clear distinction between the three-part ''Phillis Quier'' and the four-

---

[42]Einstein, *The Italian Madrigal*, II, p. 542.

[43]Nicholas Yonge's apt and sensitive translation, prepared for the Marenzio setting in *Musica Transalpina* (1588), also gives the impression of toning down the poem, although the rendering is in fact carefully literal. See the original version, using Yonge's orthography, in Alfredo Obertello, *Madrigali Italiani in Inghilterra* (Milan, 1949), p. 226, or a modernized version in E. H. Fellowes, *English Madrigal Verse* (revised and enlarged edition by Sternfeld and Greer, Oxford, 1967), p. 323.

[44]E.H. Fellowes, ed., *The English Madrigal School* (London, 192-), IV, p. 85.

part "Amintas Quier." But he avoids the thorny question of counterpoint versus homophony by harmonizing the music for three or four voices, but rhythmicizing it not infrequently as if it were only in two parts (see Ex. 4). This touch of simple rustic charm adds character to the dialogue in the sense that we are never over-awed by complexity, and the total absence of narrative allows a straightforward alternation of direct speech between Phillis and Amintas. Morley's only liberty is to prevent the lady from having the last word, for in the poem it is Phillis who says:

> No, no, dear; do not languish,
> Temper this sadness,
> For time and love with gladness
> Once ere long will provide for this our anguish.[45]

But in the musical setting, the two groups exhange their spirited negative blandishments and proceed immediately to a sonorous seven-part peroration, as if they were simultaneously reassuring each other of their hopes for future bliss.

We come now to the dialogues scored for groups of equal voices—equal in number (the most usual being four plus four), and equal in range of voice-parts. This type of composition can just as easily be used for interchanges in direct speech between two or more persons as for narrative poems in which actual quotations are rare or non-existent. In Giovanni Gabrieli's setting of Tasso's *Dormiva dolcemente la mia Clori*,[46] from the *Dialoghi Musicali* of 1590, the two choirs obey purely musical instructions because the poem itself is not a dialogue but a narrative.[47] It is the poet who speaks, and the only other voice we hear is a disembodied one, possibly one of the cupids, or possibly the young lady talking in her sleep, and to some purpose. The principal subjects, then, are the boy and girl; but they cannot be assigned to one or the other choir because there is no point in so doing.

Giovanni accordingly employs his choirs for spatial alternation and for occasional emphasis or pattern-making. Verbal and musical phrases are passed, now slowly, now rapidly, from one group to the other, and since they share all these motives one cannot associate any particular emotion or character with any one group or choir. Even when the voice reproaches the poet with *"Stolto, che fai?"* as much as to say "Why don't you kiss her, stupid," both groups eventually share in the resounding reproof. There is, of course, some tone-painting, for immediately after the passage sung by the first choir about the poet's leaning gently over the sleeping beauty, the two groups present a kind of half-drop pattern which gives the impression of repeated kisses, after which both choirs ascend one after the other to paradise. Evidently Cloris is in the habit of sleeping very soundly, for the kissing-to-paradise sequence is at once repeated to almost identical music (see Ex. 5).

---

[45]In E. H. Fellowes, *English Madrigal Verse*, p. 152, this final quatrain is assigned to both, in keeping with the musical setting.

[46]Edited by Denis Stevens (Faber Baroque Choral Series, 1970).

[47]Compare Monteverdi's five-voice madrigal in his *Second Book* (1590), where the order of the first two words is reversed.

222

Example 4

Example 5

An exact replica of this type of purely musical dialogue can be found among Hans Leo Hassler's *Neue teutsche Gesang* of 1596.[48] Eight voices are exactly divided into two groups of soprano, alto, tenor, and bass. Once again the protagonists are boy and girl, but since we are in Germany (in Augsburg to be precise) the prevailing ambience has a somewhat military cast, and the anonymous poem begins unhesitantly with *Mein Lieb will mit mir kriegen*. The entire poem is a narrative told in the first person, except for a brief passage in direct speech when the poet invites his bellicose beauty to shoot her poisoned dart at him. Accordingly, the exchanges between first and second choir are usually exact repetitions at the same pitch, and their function is simply to lend excitement to the scene and occasionally to stress a phrase by uniting both choirs in rich eight-part homophony. Hassler achieves amusing results by this method when he unleashes a series of rapid antiphonal fanfares leading up to the firing signal.[49] As the dart strikes home, the two groups exchange groans, and for once they are too shocked even to repeat each other's words. With remorse and humility comes a return to the old pattern, and the ending symbolically joins both choirs in a promise of total subjugation

[48]Edited by Rudolf Schwartz in *Denkmäler der Tonkunst in Bayern*, Jg. V/2 (Vol. 8), p. 243.

[49]Kurt Gudewill refers to these "novel sound effects" in his chapter on German Secular Song in *The New Oxford History of Music* (London, 1968), IV, p. 113.

on the part of the male. One might not call Hassler's technique particularly subtle, but he undoubtedly had his tongue in his cheek, as did the poet, and the dialogue in consequence possesses both personality and spirit.

Among the many dialogues by Lassus in Italian and in French are several of outstanding quality. His seven-part setting of *Che fai, alma?*,[50] the eight-part *O la, O che buon eco!*,[51] and the magnificent ten-part dialogue based on Petrarch's *Passan vostri trionfi*[52] are matched by his sensitive and original settings of poems by Ronsard. *Que dis-tu, que fais-tu, pensive tourterelle?*[53] appeared in 1576, and its text shows that Lassus made use of an early edition of *La Continuations des Amours*. Although at first glance the score seems to present two equal choirs, the upper choir in the modern printed edition is actually the lower of the two as regards overall tessitura. The reason for this is that Lassus gives the poet's questions to this choir, allocating to the higher-sounding group the answers of the turtle-dove.[54] We cannot help but admire the deft strokes of musical characterization that enhance and intensify the differences already inherent in the relative pitch-levels of the two groups, as when the poet asks if the turtle-dove would really have wished to die with its mate, and to this pathetical polyphony comes the reply of *"Oui,"* insistent and thrice-repeated chordally (see Ex. 6). Yet Lassus breaks away from the established dialogue pattern for the poet's closing words (*"O gentilz oyseletz"*), using now both choirs, now one or the other in purely musical dialogue, to add strength and variety to the close.

All the dialogues thus far discussed belong to the sixteenth century. The age of the *seconda prattica* witnessed further change and development in dialogue techniques, not the least important being the growing enthusiasm for solo voices accompanied by appropriate continuo instruments. One result was a more lifelike, more dramatic kind of dialogue, in which a conversation between a boy and a girl would be interpreted by two soloists instead of two choirs as in the previous era. It should not, however, be assumed that the old-fashioned polyphonic dialogue died a natural death in a short space of time, for even with the continuo well established, composers often made use of its ability to support soloists as well as its aptitude for strengthening choral harmonies in one and the same composition. Monteverdi's *Questi vaghi concenti*,[55] for instance, begins as a polyphonic dialogue for two equal choirs, but soloists soon detach themselves from the background with such success that tuttis recur only towards the close. A later

---

[50]*Sämtliche Werke*, ed. Haberl and Sandberger, X, p. 23.

[51]*Ibid.*, X, p. 140.

[52]*Ibid.*, X, p. 53.

[53]Modern edition in Henry Expert, *La Fleur des musiciens de P. Ronsard* (Paris, 1923), p. 81.

[54]Van den Borren singles out for special mention these "tones of other-worldly tenderness" in his article on the French chanson in *The New Oxford History of Music* (1968), IV, p. 25.

[55]This nine-voice dialogue is the last item in his *Fifth Book* (1605).

Example 6

and equally impressive example by the same composer is *Presso un fiume tranquillo,*[56] featuring a shepherd and shepherdess as soloists backed by a five-part chorus, the entire forces being sustained by a suitable assortment of continuo instruments.

A Bohemian composer whose life-span agrees precisely with that of Monteverdi has bequeathed to us, in a publication of 1609, three excellent dialogues in the old style. His name is Christoph Demantius,[57] and he included in his *Convivialium Concentuum Farrago*[58] two dialogues in Latin and one in German. Each one has a certain distinguishing feature. *Huc ades insignis nympharum plantula*[59] calls for two four-part choirs which follow the earlier Venetian custom of contrast in relative tessitura, the reason here being a desire on the part of Demantius to give a deeper color to the bridegroom's part and a lighter color to the bride's. This work, like the other Latin dialogue, is strictly speaking an epithalamium, and both are dedicated to friends about to get married. But Demantius is not always in favor of such realism, for in the German dialogue about the courting of a young man and a young lady, the choirs are absolutely equal in range. *Jungfraw, ich het ein Bit an euch*[60] bears no dedication and the poet is unknown. The exact matching of choirs could give the impression of utter neutrality if not sexlessness, yet the style of the poem and its musical setting helps the listener to differentiate quite easily between the words of the boy and the girl, for his requests tend to be lengthier than her replies (see Ex. 7). They share a musical as well as a poetical rhyme-scheme, and this fact combined with the brevity of the girl's utterances almost place this work in the category of an echo composition.

For a true echo we must turn to the other Latin dialogue of Demantius—*Echo! responsum si vis mihi reddere*[61]—composed for the wedding of a Silesian gentleman, Matthias Schmettau. The poem, very much influenced by the *Metamorphoses* of Ovid, presents what is essentially a narrative whose line-endings are echoes in such a way as to produce a new word and a new meaning. *"Sollicitabo"* is answered by *"dabo,"* for example, and *"clamat"* by *"amat"* (see Ex. 8). And as the poet's enthusiasm warms to his task, there is even an exchange of Greek and Latin: ἔρως, gives rise to the slightly dubious echo *"Heros",* and *"Dira fugeris"* is followed by ἔρις ("strife")—a pun which

---

[56]Based on a poem by Giambattista Marino, and published in Monteverdi's *Sixth Book* (1614).

[57]This was the Latinized form of his name, the original of which is retained by R. Kade in his article on the composer in *Vierteljahrsschrift für Musikwissenschaft,* VI (1890), p. 469.

[58]Modern edition by Kurt Stangl in *Das Erbe deutscher Musik,* Sonderreihe I, beginning after p. [44]. It is an unfortunate feature of this edition that the German strophic songs are printed with only their first verse, the remainder being relegated to a textual appendix. The composer, who wished all the verses to be sung, carefully underlaid them in his original edition with the express intention of helping singers. This is one of several examples of a modern edition failing to achieve the practical advantages of an old one.

[59]*Das Erbe deutscher Music,* Sonderreihe I, second section, p. 116.

[60]*Ibid.,* p. 95.

[61]*Ibid.,* p. 102.

Example 7

Example 8

is missed by the edition in *Das Erbe deutscher Musik* because of the incorrect repeat of the first Greek word.[62]

Each verbal echo carries with it, of course, a repeat of the musical phrase immediately preceding, and it is at least possible that the effect was heightened in performance by placing the second choir at some distance from the first, or even in an adjoining room. The choral writing is vigorous and resourceful, and the texture alternates between homophony and counterpoint as befits the meaning of the words at any given moment. When Demantius wrote his dialogues, the Italians were already engaged in successful experiments ultimately destined to destroy the style that he knew so well, yet from his remote hilltop silver-mining town of Freiberg in what was then the markgravate of Meissen on the borderland of Bohemia, he was able to disregard at least for a few years the inroads of newer musical fashions, and so bring to a glorious and resounding end a long-standing tradition whose detailed ramifications still await the attention of research in more than one discipline.[63]

[62]This error occurs both in the music, p. 113, measure 111, and in the text for No. XXVII, at the end of the volume.

[63]We might name lexicography, musicology, textual criticism, translation, and even performance, which often reveals subtleties of an unusual or unsuspected nature, and capable therefore of contributing to an overall view of the work or genre under observation.

THE INSTRUMENTAL RECITATIVE IN BEETHOVEN'S COMPOSITIONS*

by Jurgen Thym

I

Recitative is primarily a vocal genre, the purpose of which is to imitate the inflections of speech in a musical-declamatory manner. Tempo, rhythm, phrase-structure, harmonic movement, and melodic contours are shaped according to the declamatory gestures and expressive nuances of the text and, thus, recitatives are rather free in contrast to closed musical forms. The structure-establishing components of closed musical forms such as harmonic framework, periodicity, and thematic-motivic elaboration are usually absent or play only a subordinate role in a recitative. The vocal part is all-dominating in the *recitativo semplice* and the *accompagnato*, while the instruments function mainly as accompaniment, providing the harmonic background for the voice. Only in the *recitativo obbligato* do instruments perform a more substantial role through motivic interjections in strict meter.[1]

During the history of the practice, certain formulas for vocal recitative were developed and used over and over again. Such clichés include the conventional opening of a recitative with a first-inversion triad or the downward skip of a fourth in the voice, confirmed by the continuo with the cadence formula V-I as a sort of punctuation. Included in the conventional idiom of the recitative are also certain mannerisms of performance practice, such as the habit of singers to transform the skip of a third down to two repeated tones into a stepwise descending line, thus spicing the vocal part with an appoggiatura. Likewise, the arpeggio accompaniment of the harpsichordist has to be counted among the conventions of the recitative. We find all these characteristics, or at least most of them, in the instrumental recitative. When Beethoven and other composers use recitative style in instrumental compositions, they are usually aiming at an imitation of the highly expressive type of recitative—the *accompagnato*—rather than the continuo-accompanied *recitativo semplice*. The contrast between voice and instruments in the vocal recitative is translated here, of course, into a texture in which a dominating, distinctly melodic part is contrasted with a chordal accompaniment.

Beethoven was not the first to use this hybrid genre. From the beginning of the eighteenth century, one can occasionally find recitative as a phenomenon in purely

*An earlier version of this study was read as a paper at the fall meeting of the Midwest Chapter of the American Musicological Society in Chicago on October 11, 1971. Several friends and colleagues have helped me to improve on the earlier version; I am particularly grateful for the constructive criticism of Dr. Aubrey S. Garlington, Jr., and Dr. Frank E. Kirby.

[1]See Friedrich Heinrich Neumann, "Die Theorie des Rezitativs im 17. und 18. Jahrhundert unter besonderer Berücksichtigung des Musikschrifttums des 18. Jahrhunderts," (Dissertation Göttingen, 1955), pp. 266ff. The first chapter of this study is published as *Die Ästhetik des Rezitativs* (Strasbourg and Baden-Baden, 1962).

instrumental music, disconnected from its original function of imitating the inflections of speech, for instance in the works of J. S. Bach (Chromatic Fantasy), C. P. E. Bach ("Prussian" Sonata No. 1), and J. Haydn (Symphony No. 7 "Le Midi").[2] However, the instrumental recitatives in the works of these composers are rather isolated cases; they do not establish a representative repertoire from which one could deduce generalizations about the function of this device with regard to each individual composer.

With Beethoven, the instrumental recitative becomes a frequently used syntactical formula, particularly in his later works.[3] This device appears, aside from the relatively early piano sonata in D minor (op. 31, no. 2), only in compositions usually subsumed under the so-called third period of Beethoven's career. These works are (in chronological order): the piano sonata in A♭ major (op. 110), the Ninth Symphony, and the string quartets in A minor (op. 132) and C♯ minor (op. 131). Beethoven applied the term "recitative" only to the introductory passages of the finales of both op. 110 and the Ninth Symphony; the beginning of the recapitulation of the first movement of op. 31, no. 2, the transition from the fourth to the fifth movement in op. 132, and the third section of op. 131 also reveal characteristic features of the vocal recitative and may, therefore, be considered instrumental representations of this genre.[4]

Various authors have attached the labels "recitative" or "recitative-like" to several other passages in Beethoven's works. However, close inspection shows that these passages bear the stylistic characteristics of the eighteenth-century fantasy (such as the "free" passages of Beethoven's op. 77 and op. 80), the cadenza (such as the oboe solo in the Fifth Symphony), or they are written-out improvisations (such as the introduction to the finale of the *Hammerklavier* Sonata).[5] Although the instrumental recitative has some stylistic features in common with the fantasy and the cadenza, it is advisable to apply the term "recitative" only to those passages in which the above-mentioned characteristics make the derivation from the vocal model obvious.[6]

---

[2]D. G. Türk acknowledges in 1789 that passages designated as *recitativo* appear now and then in sonatas, concertos, etc. See: Daniel Gottlob Türk, *Klavierschule* (facsimile of the 1789 edition), ed. Erwin R. Jacobi (Kassel, 1962), p. 370.

[3]See M. Bauer, "Formprobleme des späten Beethoven," *ZfMw* IX (1926/27), p. 341.

[4]During a conversation between Beethoven and his friends about the performance of the A minor quartet, the term "recitative" was used in reference to the respective passages of op. 132, apparently without Beethoven objecting. See J. G. Prod'homme, *Les cahiers de conversation de Beethoven* (Paris, 1946), p. 365; and Luigi Magnani, *Beethovens Konversationshefte* (München, 1967), p. 162.

[5]About the terminological difficulties, see Paul Mies, *Das instrumentale Rezitativ: Von seiner Geschichte und seinen Formen* (Bonn, 1968), pp. 7-20.

[6]Beethoven was well-versed in the composition of vocal recitatives. During the years 1802-04, he carefully studied the article on recitative by J. A. P. Schulz in Sulzer's *Enzyklopädie der Schönen Künste* II (Leipzig, 1774). See Richard A. Kramer, "Beethoven and Carl Heinrich Graun," *Beethoven Studies*, ed. by A. Tyson (New York, 1973), pp. 18-44.

II

The various discussions of Beethoven's instrumental recitatives may be grouped in two categories: the hermeneutic and and the structural interpretations. It should be noted, however, that these two analytical approaches are not mutually exclusive but instead overlap in the writings of some authors. The hermeneutic interpretations attempt to translate the recitative passages into verbal concepts; they assume a meaning behind the music and try to describe it in general or specific terms. For W. R. Griepenkerl, a music critic closely associated with Schumann, the recitatives of the Ninth Symphony are the monologues of a sick world, responding to the attempts of Satan to lead it astray.[7] Paul Bekker's interpretation of op. 31, no. 2 reads at times like a gothic novel. The initial first-inversion triad is considered a mystical depth from which a spooky apparition emerges quietly; the recitatives translate into the sentences, "Suddenly at the second return of the beginning, the spell seems to be broken. The theme begins to speak."[8]

The culmination of the hermeneutic Beethoven interpretation is reached in the writings of Arnold Schering, who claimed in the 1930's to have found the true key for the understanding of Beethoven's music. In an attempt to overcome the vague novelization of his predecessors, he deciphered many compositions as musical representations of scenes and situations from the plays, novels, and epic poems of Homer, Shakespeare, Goethe, and Schiller. Thus, the recitatives are no longer hypothetical monologues of fictitious characters but instrumental declamations of actual lines from those plays on which the works are presumably based. The passages in op. 31, no. 2 are explained as being derived from two lines of Shakespeare's *Tempest* in the German translation by Schlegel.[9] According to Schering, the *recitativo* section of op. 110 follows some statements of the heroine of Schiller's *Maria Stuart;*[10] the one in op. 132 is modelled after line from Goethe's *Faust.*[11]

Schering's method, although originally conceived as a means to overcome the vagueness of psychological, biographical, and poetical descriptions of Beethoven's music, failed to gain freedom from the subjectivity and arbitrariness of the hermeneutic interpretations that it tried to replace. Although it is generally considered a pitiful aberration with which an otherwise meritorious musicologist concluded a distinguished

[7]Wolfgang Robert Griepenkerl, *Das Musikfest oder die Beethovener* (Leipzig, 1838), pp. 199-202.

[8]Paul Bekker, *Beethoven* (Berlin and Leipzig, 1911), pp. 118-19. "Da—bei der zweiten Wiederkehr des Anfangs scheint der Bann gebrochen zu sein. Das Thema beginnt zu sprechen." For the full account of the story, the reader is referred to the German original. The English translation of Bekker's book by M. M. Bozman (London and Toronto, n.d.) is considerably abridged.

[9]Arnold Schering, *Beethoven in neuer Deutung* (Leipzig, 1934), p. 82. In the introduction, however, Schering admits that Beethoven did not think much about Schlegel's translations and preferred instead those by J. J. Eschenburg. Actually, neither Eschenburg's nor Schlegel's renditions seem to match the instrumental recitative, and Schering has to add a passage of his own in order to make the text fit the music.

[10]Schering, *Beethoven und die Dichtung* (Berlin, 1936), pp. 532-34.

[11]*Ibid.*, pp. 342-43.

career, the method is nevertheless a logical outgrowth of an aesthetic system which propagated the synthesis of the arts and culminated in the Wagnerian conception of the *Gesamtkunstwerk*. By hypothesizing the combination of literature and music in the works of Beethoven, Schering revealed himself as a faithful disciple of artistic principles of the *neudeutsche Schule*.[12] Schering's stubborn insistence on the validity of his method, however, can hardly conceal the frequent misinterpretation of sources, the one-sided distortion of information, and the profound anachronism that pervade his writings on Beethoven.

III

Although deviating from the realm of scholarly certainty in many respects, the hermeneutic attempts to decipher a meaning behind the recitatives have some points in their favor. The dramatic conception of the introduction to the finale of the Ninth Symphony is a case in point. The instrumental recitatives of the basses are usually understood as passages signifying a rejection of the thematic snatches from previous movements and a final agreement to the *Freudenmelodie*. The programmatic interpretation can be deduced from the words of the baritone solo that later uses some of the same material as the instrumental recitatives ("O Freunde, nicht diese Töne . . ."); the explanation is further supported through Beethoven's sketches.[13]

In these sketches, Beethoven notates the recitatives in conjunction with certain verbal exclamations. However, the sketches are not attempts to find the appropriate text,[14] nor are they documents to support the assumption of an earlier vocal conception of the recitatives.[15] Beethoven indicates that the expressive content of these instrumental recitatives should be understood as mimetic gestures. The recitatives do not declaim actual words but represent gestures—non-verbal means of expression—signifying various degrees of rejection and final consent.[16]

---

[12]Schering could refer to an earlier model in which words had been applied to "clarify" instrumental music. In 1787, the poet Gerstenberg published the Free Fantasy in C minor by C. P. E. Bach (1753), to which he had added vocal parts reciting Hamlet's monologue and Socrates' farewell, respectively. The fantasy with Gerstenberg's texts was reprinted and faithfully discussed in Wagnerian terms by F. Chrysander, "Eine Klavier-Phantasie von Karl Philipp Emanuel Bach mit nachträglich von Gerstenberg eingefügten Gesangsmelodien zu zwei verschiedenen Texten," *Vierteljahresschrift für Musikwissenschaft*, VII (1891), pp. 1-25. A more recent, less biased, account of Gerstenberg's experiment is Eugene Helm's article, "The 'Hamlet' Fantasy and the Literary Element in C. P. E. Bach's Music," *MQ*, LVIII (1972), pp. 277-96.

[13]Gustav Nottebohm, *Zweite Beethoveniana* (Leipzig, 1887), pp. 189-92; also in *Thayer's Life of Beethoven*, rev. and ed. by E. Forbes (Princeton, 1967), pp. 891-94.

[14]*Ibid.*, p. 189. "In den Skizzen . . . hat Beethoven, um die geeigneten Worte zu finden . . ., umständliche Versuche angestellt."

[15]Bekker, *Beethoven*, p. 219. "Die Skizzen verraten die ursprünglich geplanten Texte dieser Bassrezitative."

[16]Antonín Sychra has discussed in the sketches in a similar way. He states: "Beethoven tries here to find an adequate expression in purely instrumental music, i.e., an expression which conceives the rejection of in-

Immediacy of communication has been pointed out by Kerman as one facet of the style of the late Beethoven.[17] One approach for achieving this "striking new directness of emotional appeal" is his partial reliance on vocal models in his instrumental music, i.e., on genres such as the *cavatina, arioso,* and recitative. The recitatives want to communicate something, and the pains Beethoven took in providing the instrumental recitatives with performance prescriptions (one only need study the passage in op. 110) indicate clearly that he was concerned with every possible nuance of musical expression. However, the recitatives aim for an expressiveness, definitely not of the story-telling kind and not based on the declamation of a secret text. They represent a type of expression that can only insufficiently be translated into verbal concepts, because they are a pre-verbal or non-verbal kind of communication—through mimesis and gesture rather than through words.[18]

IV

The search for the expressive element of the instrumental recitative is not without pitfalls, nor is the analytical method that interprets the phenomenon in purely structural terms. Hugo Riemann, who considered the recitative in instrumental music as a more or less inorganic element, tried to make the respective passages fit his dogmatic notions of four- or eight-measure phrases.[19] Hermann Wetzel proceeds in a similar way; he goes one step further by "correcting" Beethoven's notation in op. 110, thus making the recitative passages fit his theories of rhythmic-metric organization.[20] By forcing the recitatives into the straitjackets of four-measure phrases, Riemann and Wetzel fail to recognize a specific characteristic of these passages, i.e., their freedom from the schemes

dividual themes from previous movements in terms of typical intonations of language." ("Beethoven bemühte sich hier darum, einen adäquaten Ausdruck in rein instrumentaler Musik zu erreichen, d.h. einen Ausdruck, der die Ablehnung einzelner Themen aus den vorausgehenden Sätzen mittels Gestaltung der Sprache, ihrer typischen Intonationen erfasst.") "Ludwig van Beethovens Skizzen zur IX. Sinfonie," *Beethoven-Jahrbuch* IV, 1959/60 (Bonn, 1962), p. 101.

[17]Joseph Kerman, *The Beethoven Quartets* (New York, 1967), pp. 191ff.

[18]Kerman, whose enthusiastic discussion of the string quartets has provided many insights into Beethoven's work, has, however, occasionally indulged in arbitrary hermeneutic interpretations. He asserts that op. 132 is a reversal of the Ninth (the theme of the string quartet's finale was at one time to serve as material for an instrumental conclusion of the symphony). Kerman writes: "The last cadence cedes to an annihilation, a sudden bleeding, palpitating cry in recitative for the first violin. *O Freunde, nicht diese Töne! sondern lasst uns Unangenehmere anstimmen . . .*" And he comes to the quick conclusion: "The gesture is a real inversion of the Ninth Symphony." (*The Beethoven Quartets,* p. 262) Kerman succumbs here to the fascination of a fictitious composition, "Doktor Fausti Weheklag" by Thomas Mann's Adrian Leverkühn. Kerman grafts onto the A minor quartet the idea of an inverted Ninth Symphony, which Mann himself got from Adorno.

[19]Hugo Riemann, *L. van Beethovens sämtliche Klaviersonaten* III (Berlin, 1903), p. 391 (op. 31,2) and pp. 439f. (op. 110).

[20]Hermann Wetzel, "Beethovens Sonate op. 110: Eine Erläuterung ihres Baus," *Beethoven-Jahrbuch* II, ed. by Theodor v. Frimmel (München and Leipzig, 1909), pp. 75-154, particularly pp. 123ff.

of periodicity. They do not make the recitative a more organic element, but distort its qualities by eliminating an essential aspect of musical prose.

Most authors mention the recitative sections in Beethoven's music only in passing; they either briefly acknowledge their existence or correctly assign to them structural functions such as introduction or transition.[21] Since instrumental recitatives are considered connecting tissues between weightier sections, they are treated in analyses in a rather perfunctory way; the main thrust of the discussion is usually reserved for the more substantial centers of attraction. Only August Halm, Heinrich Schenker, and Paul Mies have faced up to the structural problems of the instrumental recitative. Halm makes some astute observations on op. 31, no. 2 in relating the recitatives of the recapitulation to the corresponding passages in the exposition of the first movement.[22] Schenker's detailed analysis of op. 110 and the Ninth Symphony have revealed some subtleties with which Beethoven manages to integrate the recitatives into the musical discourse.[23] Mies investigates Beethoven's instrumental recitatives in the context of the whole history of this genre and makes some perceptive remarks regarding the individual structure of each passage;[24] however, his discussion suffers from mere juxtaposition of individual analyses without attempts to conceptualize the insights.

Since the middle of the seventeenth century, the vocal recitative has appeared in conjunction with the aria, to which it stands in sharp contrast. The difference is primarily of dramatic function, revealed in both text and music. The contrast between the musical prose of the recitative and the closed musical form of the aria remains an essential feature wherever Beethoven uses the recitative in an instrumental context. The recall of vocal models is most evident in op. 110, where the *recitativo* section leads to an *arioso dolente (Klagender Gesang).* The recitative-aria contrast manifests itself also in the juxtaposition of instrumental recitatives and the Ode to Joy in the Ninth Symphony. It is also apparent in op. 131, where a recitative prepares for a *molto cantabile,* and in op. 132, where a recitative precedes "a magnificently vocal melody which will dominate" the finale "to an exceptional extent."[25] While all instrumental recitatives of the late Beethoven are embedded in the conventional recitative-aria contrast, this contrast is singularly absent in op. 31, no. 2, a feature which is partly responsible for the genuine uniqueness of this sonata.

Stylistic models can be invoked, nevertheless, for explaining the use of instrumental recitatives in op. 31, no. 2. The relationship of the recitative to other musical genres serves as a justification here, not the conventional recitative-aria contrast. Freedom from

[21]However, the instrumental recitatives are certainly not interruptions, as J. G. Prod'homme asserts in his *Les Sonates pour piano de Beethoven* (Paris, 1937), p. 145.

[22]August Halm, *Von zwei Kulturen der Musik* (München, 1913), pp. 38-78. Analysis later amplified in Halm, *Beethoven* (Berlin, 1927), pp. 306-10.

[23]Heinrich Schenker, *Beethoven: Die letzten Sonaten (Sonate As-dur, op. 110),* ed. Oswald Jonas (Vienna, 1972) and *Beethovens Neunte Symphonie* (Vienna and Leipzig, 1912).

[24]Paul Mies, *Das instrumental Rezitativ,* pp. 73-85.

[25]Kerman, *The Beethoven Quartets,* p. 262f.

the bounds of periodicity, strict tempo, motivic elaboration, and harmonic framework is a musical characteristic which the recitative shares with the free fantasy, the toccata and the cadenza,[26] i.e., genres which are generally considered as manifestations of the *stylus phantasticus*. Although the recitative is usually not discussed under such a label in the writings of eighteenth-century theorists, it has all the elements of the fantastic style. Freedom from the norms of closed musical forms is caused in the recitative by an extramusical factor—the text. The recitative text which—unlike a text for an aria—is free in content and poetic structure, is conducive to a musical style characterized by harmonic surprises, rhythmic and metric irregularities, and a melodic discourse in leaps and bounds.[27] The Piano Sonata op. 31, no. 2 is conceived from an improvisatory impulse; the juxtaposition of contrasting sections (such as the Largo, Allegro, and Adagio measures at the beginning) relates this section to the fantasy. The recitatives as well as the toccata-like passagework that follows do not constitute a stylistic contradiction in such a genre. The Sonata op. 110 is similarly pervaded by genre-characteristics of the fantasy.[28] The introduction to the finale of the Ninth Symphony reveals fantasy-like features in the juxtaposition of contrasting sections; the compositional conception is, indeed, strikingly similar to an earlier work of Beethoven which even carries the generic term "fantasy" in its title, i.e., the Choral Fantasy, op. 80.[29]

V

After pointing out some conventional means of integrating a recitative in a musical structure, we may proceed to the specific structural functions that the instrumental recitatives fulfill in Beethoven's compositions. The modulatory, melodic, and metric freedom of the recitative allows the composer a high degree of flexibility in working with the tonal material, a flexibility that is quite unknown in more strictly organized musical forms. The characteristics of the recitative are directly related to its function. The

---

[26]D. G. Türk (*Klavierschule*, p. 370) remarks on the interrelationship of these genres: "Mehr nach Gefühl als taktmässig müssen, ausser den freyen Fantasien, Kadenzen, Fermaten, etc. unter anderem auch die mit dem Worte *Rezitativo* bezeichneten Stellen vorgetragen werden."

[27]See Peter Schleuning, *Die freie Fantasie: Ein Beitrag zur Erforschung der klassischen Klaviermusik* (Göppingen, 1973), pp. 42ff. and pp. 74ff.

[28]Frank E. Kirby, "A Typology of Beethoven's Piano Sonatas," *Piano Quarterly,* No. 73 (Fall 1970), pp. 12-15, and Egon Voss, "Zu Beethoven's Klaviersonate As-dur, op. 110," *MF,* XXIII (1970), p. 262, suggest the influence of C. P. E. Bach's fantasies on some of Beethoven's sonatas, which Bekker categories as fantasia sonatas (*Beethoven*, Engl. transl., pp. 105-12). The repeated tones in the *recitativo* section of op. 110, usually interpreted as an imitation of *Bebung*, may indicate a generic descent from the clavichord fantasies of C. P. E. Bach. Schering's explanation of the passage as an imitation of the *trillo* of the monody of the early Baroque is perhaps a bit far-fetched (*Beethoven und die Dichtung*, p. 534).

[29]Kirby, "Beethoven and the 'geselliges Lied'," *ML,* XLVII (1966), p. 125, states: "With respect to the earlier Choral Fantasia, the instrumental variations of the theme before the vocal strophic presentation are retained, but the fantasia is replaced by recitative, and furthermore the process of formulating the proper theme is written into the composition itself."

freedom of the composer in dealing with such a material in opera renders possible a quick adaptation to the actions on stage. Beyond this dramatic function, the recitative also fulfills a musical one; arias in different keys, in different meters, and with different tempo indications can easily be connected in a musically logical way by means of the recitative.

Various authors have thought of the role of the recitative in Beethoven's instrumental compositions as one of "transition" between contrasting elements. The term seems somewhat weak, however; I prefer to view the process as one of "mediation," meaning the interrelationship of two contrasting parts by means of a reciprocal flux between them. This concept has been perhaps best expressed by G. W. F. Hegel in his *System der Philosophie:*[30]

> Mediation [*Vermittlung*] is a beginning and a development [from a First object] toward a Second, so that this Second exists only insofar as it was arrived at from the First distinctly different element.

I do not want to claim a general similarity between Hegelian thought and the structure of Beethoven's music, but it is interesting that Hegel's concept of *Vermittlung* so closely fits the specific aspect of Beethoven's compositional procedure under examination.

Beethoven did not conceive of musical form as a positing of phrases linked to each other by connecting tissues of secondary importance, but as a continuously unfolding process achieved mainly by means of developmental procedures. The succession of tonal events is determined by causality and interdependence, thus giving the impression of musical form being spontaneously created as an organic process. The recitative style, due to the flexibility and pliability of the tonal material, is able to mediate between contrasts; it makes that which is distinct enter into a mutual relationship. The recitative is an important device in achieving the dynamic character of musical form; it helps Beethoven to overcome a static juxtaposition of phrases, sections, or movements, and thus to concretize his concept of musical form as a process.[31]

However, the very feature which qualifies the instrumental recitative as a mediating device brings it into opposition with all closed musical forms. Flexibility and pliability of the tonal material stand in sharp contrast to compositions which are more strictly organized. The recitative, even when occurring in a purely instrumental context, is not able to deny its principal difference from the aria, to which it is linked in vocal music. Beethoven's dynamic concept of form demands that the instrumental recitative be made a logical outgrowth from the firmly outlined musical structure and, vice versa, that it be brought back into the structure in a musically logical way. The mediating device itself

---

[30]G. W. Friedrich Hegel, *System der Philosophie (Erster Teil: Die Logik)* in *Sämtliche Werke*, ed. H. Glockner (Stuttgart, 1929), VIII, p. 57. "Denn die Vermittlung ist ein Angangen und ein Fortgegangensein zu einem Zweiten, so dass dieses Zweite nur ist, insofern zu demselben von gegen dasselbe Andern gekommen worden ist."

[31]Kurt von Fischer, *Beziehungen von Form und Motiv in Beethovens Instrumentalwerken*, 2nd ed., (Baden-Baden, 1972), pp. 24f., characterizes the instrumental recitative as being related to developmental motives (*Entwicklungsmotivik*).

needs to be mediated. A discussion of musical examples may illuminate the processes of mediation.

VI

In the Piano Sonata op. 110, an instrumental recitative is part of a transition mediating between the boisterous scherzo and the lamenting *arioso*. The scherzo is predominantly shaped by harmonic and rhythmic means; the *arioso* features a *cantilena* superimposed on the background of a chordal accompaniment. This textural contrast, specifically the contrast between a pointedly instrumental and a pointedly vocal style, is mediated by the transition. For the duration of this section, both styles are reconciled: the soloistic treatment of the melodic element foreshadows the *arioso*, while the chordal measures, establishing the punctuation marks for the *recitativo*, look back to the previous movement. The recitative is itself carefully prepared. The content of the introductory measures is a modulation from B♭ minor via C♭ major to A♭ minor. One can recognize a gradual simplification of the factors shaping the tonal material. In other words, the first measure still has a melodic and rhythmic profile, whereas in the following measures these components are neglected almost entirely in favor of simple cadence formulas. The abstention from completely controlling all aspects of the tonal material—or in other words, the flavor of improvisation as revealed in these measures—prepares for the pliability of the recitative passage. One could even consider the end of the coda of the preceding scherzo as included in the mediating process: a slower tempo is prepared at the end of this movement, and the Picardy third makes the concluding harmony a dominant for the B♭ minor with which the next movement begins.

A mediating function can be recognized also in the recitative of op. 131. Bridge passages link all movements of this string quartet, thus organizing the seven sections as a through-composed unit. The need for fluctuating transitions is an essential aspect of the structural conception of this piece. The third section consists of two parts, a connective *Allegro moderato* and the recitative proper, marked *Adagio;* this section mediates between the preceding *Allegro molto vivace* in D major and the variations with their song-like theme in A major. Besides preparing a new key, the recitative functions as a device that introduces the pointedly vocal melodic style pervading much of the variation movement. The textural properties of the recitative (isolated melody against harmonic background) are prepared in the short connective passage *(Allegro moderato)* through the chordal accents and the unison line, which is divided into its motivic components and distributed to different instruments. As in op. 110, we can include the end of the preceding section in the mediating process. A slower tempo is prepared in the last measures of the second section through a written-out retard. The incomplete D major chord (the fifth is missing) suggests the entry of B minor in the third section. As in op. 110, reducing the degree to which the tonal material is articulated is a means to prepare the improvisatory character of the recitative.

In the A minor quartet, a recitative of the first violin accompanied by tremolos of the other strings mediates between a boisterous *Alla marcia* in A major and the final *Allegro appassionato* in the parallel minor key. The intervention of the recitative serves to smooth the progression between these two sharply contrasting movements. The recitative reminds the listener of previous movements by means of certain motivic allusions;[32] it foreshadows the vocal quality of the theme of the finale. The *recitativo* phrases are introduced twice by chordal accents in which the end of the march movement reverberates. The descending minor second at the end of the recitative becomes part of the accompaniment in the finale. Thus, the recitative is carefully integrated in the musical discourse.

It is somewhat more difficult to pinpoint the function of the recitative in the first movement of op. 31, no. 2. First of all, it can be seen that the recitatives that appear at the beginning of the recapitulation are latently present in the Largo measures at the outset of both exposition and development. The realization of the recitative is postponed, but the potential of its occurrence is structurally embodied in the introductory measures. Beethoven does not merely satisfy a need for variety when he modifies the material of the exposition at the repeat. He avoids a full return of the principal theme of the movement (mm. 21ff., derived from the arpeggiated sixth-chord of the Largo measures), perhaps because he has used it so heavily throughout the exposition and development. In the recapitulation, the introductory sixth-chords act as germ-cells for the recitatives, which substitute for the omitted principal theme. In addition, the recitatives serve Beethoven as connecting ties for parts of the sonata which were still far apart in the exposition; by using recitative passages, he is able to curtail the recapitulation.

The recitatives are carefully mediated. The first phrase is preceded by a passage which renounces harmony and the previously established rhythmic patterns; this unison passage in simple quarter notes prepares for the dominating role of the melodic element in the recitatives. Beethoven also mediates between the recitatives and the rest of the recapitulation by a passage (mm. 159-70) which retains certain improvisatory features; with its chordal accents, arpeggiated triads, and diminished seventh chords, the passage has the character of a toccata or fantasia, i.e., of very freely organized musical forms which—as we have seen—are closely related to the recitative.

In the introduction to the finale of the Ninth Symphony the instrumental recitatives function in connection with thematic allusions to preceding movements as a device mediating between intrumental and vocal sections of the composition. Schenker points out in his analysis that, after three instrumental movements, a vocal section must appear out of place because of the sudden entry of the vocal parts and the novelty of the themes.[33] Beethoven uses the instrumental recitative to smooth out the contrast between instrumental and vocal movements. As a mixed genre, vocal in style but instrumental in representation, the instrumental recitative functions as a strategem to mediate between opposites, to justify the synthesis of symphony and oratorio taking place in this work. The refined techniques of mediation which we encountered in the piano sonatas and the string quartets are not employed in the Ninth Symphony. The orchestral means, characterized by both forcefulness and inertia, necessitate a certain

[32]Kerman, *The Beethoven Quartets,* p. 262.

[33]Schenker, *Beethoven's Neunte Symphonie,* p. 258.

239

simplification of compositional devices. Perhaps for this reason, Beethoven does not mediate between the instrumental recitatives and the thematic snatches from previous movements, but instead merely juxtaposes these passages, thus achieving a symphonic *al fresco* effect whose meaning was to be immediately understood.

VII

The recitative in instrumental disguise has presented an enigma to many a musicologist. While admitting half-heartedly that the usage of the instrumental recitative could be justified, both Riemann and Westrup have doubts about the validity of such a hybrid. For Riemann, the direct imitation of a recitative in instrumental music is an aberration, a "more or less inorganic element."[34] Westrup considered it "a terminological contradiction, since the purpose of the recitative lies in the reproduction of speech inflections."[35] Riemann sees the problem in the fact that the recitative is too alien an element to be satisfactorily integrated in a purely instrumental context; Westrup sees the problem in the text-generated qualities of the recitative which, if rendered by instruments only, would constitute results without cause.

This study has shown that the instrumental genre can very well exist by itself and without reference to pre-existent speech patterns. Meaning does not have to be verbal in order to be communicated; to discuss the instrumental recitative in terms of mimesis and gesture is perhaps a more viable avenue of investigation than the hermeneutic interpretations of the past. This study has also determined the structural function of the instrumental recitative and shown possibilities of integrating the device in the musical discourse without disruptive effect. The instrumental recitative is a compositional tool of considerable structural significance for Beethoven's concept of musical form as a process; it is used primarily in a function of mediation toward the reconciliation of contrasts.

[34]*Riemann Musik Lexikon*, 11th edition by A. Einstein (Berlin, 1929), p. 1502: "Das Instrumentalrezitativ ist daher in einem Instrumentalwerke immer ein mehr oder minder unorganischer Bestandteil."

[35]Jack Allen Westrup, "Rezitativ," *MGG* (1963), XI, col. 963: "Ein sogenanntes Rezitativ für Instrumente ist strenggenommen ein terminologischer Widerspruch, da der Zweck des Rezitativs in der Reproducktion der Sprachbetonungen liegt."

THE GREGORIAN CHANT MELISMAS OF CHRISTMAS MATINS

by Ruth Steiner

How Christmas was celebrated in word and song during the Middle Ages is the subject of this paper. Yet, only one small detail of the liturgy for this day can be discussed here, for in the manuscripts of the Middle Ages the lessons, prayers, and chants for Christmas fill page after page. On Christmas, for example, there was not one Mass, but three. The first of these was celebrated while it was still dark, when the first cock crowed, the second at dawn, and the third at the usual hour. Even in addition to these, in the early hours of the morning, a very long service took place, the canonical hour of Matins. [1]

Matins was divided into three sections, or Nocturnes, and each of them began with the chanting of several psalms and antiphons and continued with the reading of lessons. After each lesson a responsory was sung. The number of these varied from place to place, but usually in a cathedral there were three lessons and responsories in each nocturne, and, in a monastery, four.

Though the lessons and responsories vary from one manuscript to another, and a particular responsory may appear in the first Nocturne in one source, in the third Nocturne in another, certain procedures were common. One of these was, on a few important feasts, to give the final responsory of one or more Nocturnes a special character. This was done musically by adding a melisma, a long melody sung to one syllable, near the end of it. Responsories are rather ornate chants, in any case; yet their melodies are usually not unique, being instead based on a group of well-known musical formulas, so the addition of a melisma would add a good deal of musical interest to one of them.

It is impossible to say when this custom of adding melismas began. Amalarius of Metz (who wrote toward the middle of the 9th century) describes it in terms that suggest it was gaining currency at his time. Nonetheless, one theory concerning these melismas is that the few that appear in the earliest notated sources represent a more wide-spread procedure that was almost entirely suppressed in a reform of chant that took place at some time earlier than that when the manuscripts were written. [2]

It is difficult to evaluate this particular idea, but a consideration of two Christmas responsories to which melismas were sometimes added may shed some light on the

---

[1] At Rome, the office of Matins was doubled; see Giuseppe Löw, "Natale," *Enciclopedia cattolica*, VIII (1952), pp. 1671-72. The relationship of the two Matins services has been studied by Dom Raymond Le Roux, "Aux origines de l'Office Festif: Les antiennes et les psaumes de Matines et de Laudes pour Noël et le 1er janvier," *Etudes grégoriennes*, IV (1961), pp. 65-171.

[2] Dom Louis Brou, "Le joyau des antiphonaires latins," *Archivos Leoneses*, VIII (1954), pp. 31-2.

practice. The responsories will be studied here basically as they were in use at the monastery of St. Gall.

Manuscripts 390 and 391 of the St. Gall Stiftsbibliothek together form an antiphonary that was written around the year 1000. The fourth responsory given there for Christmas, the one that ends the first Nocturne, is *Descendit de celis*. It comes at the end of a page. At the beginning of the next page, one finds the last two words of the chant written three times, each time with a different series of neumes over them — "fabricae mundi" (see Plate I).[3]

Though the neumes of this manuscript show some fascinating things about the rhythm of the melismas, they are not precise enough about intervals to enable the melodies to be transcribed. The melodies have to be found in another source. There is no great difficulty in this, for a 13th-century antiphonary from Worcester has the melismas clearly written in staff notation.[4] At least it has the first two of them; but a problem arises with the third, for the St. Gall neumes for the third melisma cannot be made to match the one in Worcester. One must look in manuscripts that are more closely related to the St. Gall one, and thus in two 12th-century antiphonaries from Klosterneuburg (near Vienna) the third melisma does match, and it is also written in such a way that it can be transcribed.[5]

In the Klosterneuburg sources the melody is provided with a text: "Facture plasmator et conditor." The length of the text is determined by the melody, for each note has been given just one syllable. The phrasing of the text also follows the musical phrasing closely; one finds that notes grouped together in a neume in the St. Gall antiphonary are grouped together in the later sources by being given the various syllables of a single word. Such texts as these are called by several different terms: the manuscripts most often call them "prosae" though "prosulae" might be a better term, since it is generally used to refer only to texts, such as these, that are composed to fit pre-existing melismas.

The Klosterneuburg antiphonaries are not the only sources to give a text for the St. Gall version of the third of the "fabricae" melismas. On p. 7 of St. Gall 390 a 13th-century hand has written another text, "Ausculate omnes ubique fideles," that fits this

[3]Just at this point, the otherwise excellent facsimile edition fails the reader (*Paléographie musicale*, Series 2, Vol. I, p. 46). The third melisma is made partly illegible by shadows that cover the writing. A look at the manuscript itself removes the difficulty. I am indebted to Dr. Eva Irblich of the Stiftsbibliothek St. Gallen for allowing me to consult this manuscript, and for arranging for me to have a good photograph of this page.

[4]Worcester, Cathedral Library, Codex F. 160; facsimile in *Paléographie musicale*, XII.

[5]The Klosterneuburg antiphonaries 1010 and 1013 are referred to in Bruno Stäblein's article "Tropus," *Die Musik in Geschichte und Gegenwart* (henceforth *MGG*), XIII (1966), Example 9 d, after col. 816. This example shows the text for the melisma that is for use on the feast of St. John the Evangelist, but both manuscripts also have a text for the same melisma that is to be used on Christmas. Two other manuscripts that give this melisma in neumes are the 12th-century antiphonaries Bamberg, Staatsbibliothek, Msc. Lit. 23 (f. 19r) and Msc. Lit. 24 (f. 11r).

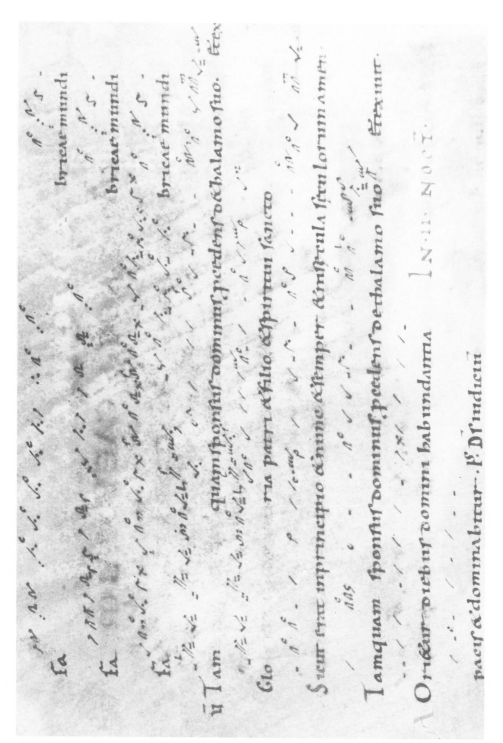

Plate I: St. Gall, Stiftsbibliothek, 390, p. 46, detail.

melisma.[6] A third text for it appears in an 11th-century troper-proser from Germany, Oxford, Bodleian Library, Selden supra 27.[7]

The way the text is presented in this manuscript deserves comment. At the beginning of the section of the manuscript devoted to tropes of the conventional type, several pages are given over to prosulae for various sections of the R. *Descendit* and another Christmas responsory. The first of them, "De celis venit," fits one of the melismas that the St. Gall and Worcester antiphonaries had in common. Next comes a text for the long melisma often found in the verse of this responsory (and concerning which it is not possible to go into detail here). This is followed by a text, "Conditor lucis aeterne deus," for the third melisma of St. Gall; and then comes a text for the *Gloria patri*, which has the same melody as the verse. Then follows the text "Celestis aule rex et glorie," which fits the third melisma of Worcester. It is very unusual to find both of these melismas in a single source—the third melisma of St. Gall and the third melisma of Worcester.[8]

The three melismas of Worcester were widely known and sung, with and without texts, through the middle ages and until the 16th century.[9] Their St. Gall counterparts have not been preserved in nearly so many sources, which suggests that they perhaps enjoyed a more local popularity. Since the difference between the two sets lies in their third melismas, can anything be drawn from a comparison of them?

What stands out about the St. Gall third melisma is its very regular form—a a b b c c. Generally speaking, the more regular a form is, the greater the tendency of many scholars to assign a late date to it; hence, despite the archaic appearance of this melisma

---

[6]The text also appears in St, Gall, Stiftsbibliothek, 380, p. 116. It is published, and another source is referred to, in Léon Gautier, *Histoire de la poésie liturgique au moyen âge, I: Les tropes* (Paris, 1886; reprinted in Ridgewood, N. J.: The Gregg Press Incorporated, 1966), pp. 166-167, fn. XVII. (The manuscript referred to in the second paragraph of fn. XVIII, p. 167, should be Paris, Bibl. nat., nouv. acq. [lat.] 1535, not 1235).

[7]The manuscript may be from Eichstätt, Heidenheim, or Freising-Tegernsee; see H. Husmann, *Tropen- und Sequenzenhandschriften* (Répertoire international des sources musicales, B v ¹; Munich, 1964), pp.163-64.

[8]The texts are as follows:
Oxford, Bodleian Library, Selden supra 27, f. 60r (for the "St. Gall" third melisma):
    Conditor lucis aeterne deus
    fons sapientiae astra creans
    arva regens mari et imperans
    factor matris natus hic de matre
    procedens hodie thalamo patris in gracili nascitur presepio
    angeli psallebant in celis laudes in excelsis domino deo nostro
F. 60v (for the "Worcester" third melisma):
    Celestis aule rex et glorie deus aeternae
    Cui laus ab angelicis ordinibus sonant iugiter
    Volens pro nobis homo fieri hodie natus est ex virgine
    Quem ovantes celi cives terris predicant
    Quem syderis novi splendor annunciat opificem fabrice

[9]See my article "The Responsories and Prosa for St. Stephen's Day at Salisbury," *The Musical Quarterly,* LVI (1970), pp. 162-182; and Wulf Arlt, *Ein Festoffizium des Mittelalters aus Beauvais* (2 vols.; Köln, 1970), Darstellungsband, pp. 110-115.

in the St. Gall antiphonary, it may be a later substitution for an original melisma that has a less regular form.[10] It is possible that this original melisma was the one given in Worcester; it does appear in a quite early source, the 10th-century gradual and antiphonary of Mont-Renaud.[11] The unusual way in which the melody is notated there (in the margin of the page, vertically, written from bottom to top) constitutes part of the abundant evidence that the manuscript was not originally intended to include musical notation. The editor of the facsimile edition of this source believes, however, that the notation was added rather soon after the completion of the text.

Still another version of this third melisma has been preserved. It begins and ends like the third melisma of Worcester, but a little past half way through it has two additional phrases. The earliest sources to contain this melody are of the 10th and 11th centuries, and they come from Aquitaine. In them the melody is given in texted form. There are three texts, and each of them is given in the three manuscripts Paris, Bibliothèque nationale, lat. 1084, 1118, and 1338. (Two of the texts also appear, without musical notation, in n. a. lat. 1871.)[12] The melody is thus written in these sources a total of nine times. Two of the texts, *Fac domine deus* and *Rex regum,*[13] and their music in 1338 are in great part illegible, which is especially to be regretted since 1338 is set up with more space between the lines of text than the other manuscripts, allowing more exactness in the diastematic musical notation. However, the notation of the remaining text, *Facture tue,* in 1338 is not precise enough to permit reliable transcription from it alone (see Plate II).

---

[10]Stäblein refers to it as an "Ersatz-Melisma für das dritte Neuma," *op. cit.* If the reasoning above is valid, then the character of this melisma adds to the evidence that, despite the early date of the St. Gall antiphonary relative to other sources, the liturgy it presents is not that of "la plus pure tradition monastique," but has been subjected to a number of revisions. See Dom René-Jean Hesbert, *Corpus antiphonalium officii,* II: *Manuscripti "Cursus monasticus"* (Rome, 1965), pp. VI-IX.

[11]Facsimile in *Paléographie musicale,* XVI, f. 56v.

[12]For the date and place of origin of these manuscripts, see Husmann, *op. cit.*

[13]This is given in part, with a translation, in Richard L. Crocker, *A History of Musical Style* (New York, 1966), p. 33.

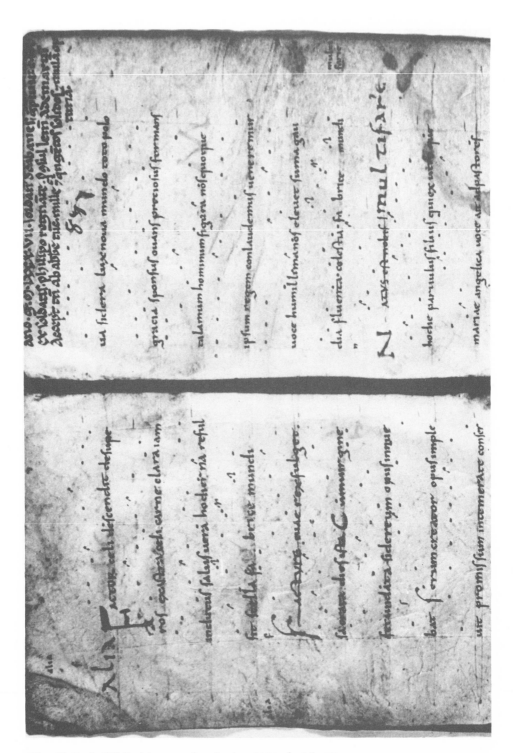

Plate II: Paris, Bibliothèque nationale, lat. 1338, fs. 86v-87r

246

A long search has identified eight manuscripts that have this melody in staff notation or exact diastematic notation.

A. Florence, Curia Arcivescovile, Antiphonary (12th-century antiphonary of Florence)
B. Rome, Biblioteca Vallicelliana, C. 5 (12th-century antiphonary of San Eutizio, near Norcia)
C. Toledo, Biblioteca Capitular, 44.2 (12th-century Aquitanian antiphonary)
D. Amiens, Bibliothèque municipale, MS 112 (13th-century notated summer breviary of Amiens)[14]
E. Lucca, Biblioteca Capitolare, 603 (12th-century antiphonary of Santa Maria di Pontetto, near Lucca)
F. Metz, Bibliothèque municipale, 83 (13th-century antiphonary of Saint Arnould, in Metz)
G. Paris, Bibliothèque nationale, lat 8898 (late 12th-century rituale of Soissons)
H. Verdun, Bibliothèque municipale, MS. 128 (13th-century antiphonary from St. Vanne)[15]

When these manuscripts are compared with each other and with the earlier Aquitanian sources it becomes evident that the melody varied a good deal from place to place. This is particularly true with respect to the end of the sixth and the beginning of

[14]It may seem strange to find a summer breviary on this list. Two of the *fabricae* melismas are given in it for a responsory on the feast of Saint Firmin (Sept. 1), *Honestus vero presbiter* (fs. 270r-270v). The same sort of thing happens in the St. Denis antiphonary Paris, B. n., lat. 17296, where the *fabricae* melismas are appended to the R. *Post passionem* on the feast of St. Denis, as Jacques Handschin pointed out (*New Oxford History of Music*, Vol. II [London, 1955], p. 145). In a 13th-century notated breviary of Marmoutier (Tours, Bibliothèque municipale, 153), one of the shorter *fabricae* melismas is incorporated into the last Matins responsory for Saint Martin (*Martinus abrahe sinu*, f. 183r). Similarly, in the antiphonary of San Eutizio the R. *Iste sanctus digne* has one of the shorter *fabricae* melismas supplied for use in the refrain after the verse (Rome, Bibl. Vallicelliana, C. 5, f. 299r). *Iste sanctus digne* is an adaptation of *Descendit de celis*, so this borrowing is not surprising. In St. Gall 390-391, *Iste sanctus* is the last responsory on the feast of St. Gall (p. 325-*131* of the facsimile edition), and there it is given the melisma referred to earlier as "the St. Gall version of the third melisma."

[15]Of the manuscripts in this list, C and F are known to me only from a brief examination of photographs of them at Solesmes. I am profoundly indebted to Dom Raymond Le Roux who in the most gracious way imaginable made it possible for me to see these photographs, and made many valuable comments and suggestions regarding this study. F was destroyed in World War II; there is a facsimile of one folio in *Paléographie musicale*, III, Pl. 171. D is described in Victor Leroquais, *Les bréviaires manuscrits des bibliothèques publiques de France* (Paris, 1934), I, pp. 12-14. E is referred to in R. Baralli, "Un frammento inedito di 'Discantus'," *Rassegna gregoriana*, XI (1912), col. 5; and in *Paléographie musicale*, IX, Introduction, p. 12*. There is a facsimile of one page in *Paléographie musicale*, II, Pl. 34. I am grateful to Monsignore Giuseppe Casale of the Biblioteca Capitolare Feliniana in Lucca for allowing me to visit his library during August, when it is ordinarily closed, and for calling this manuscript to my attention. The page in G where the melody appears is reproduced in facsimile in Ernst H. Kantorowicz, *Laudes Regiae: A Study in Liturgical Acclamations and Mediaeval Ruler Worship* (Berkeley and Los Angeles, 1946), p. 256. H is briefly described in *Catalogue général des manuscrits des bibliothèques publiques des départements*, V (Paris, 1879), p. 497. There are prosulae for this melody in the manuscripts as follows: A, "Facinora nostra" (see below, fn. 17); B, "Ante secla deus est;" E, "Concepit Maria."

the seventh phrase, where no two sources agree. Musical example 1 shows the various readings of this passage.

Example 1

The transcription that follows as Musical example 2 shows *Facture tue* with the melody that seems to be given for it in lat. 1338.[16]

[16]Professor Daniel J. Sheerin of Catholic University was kind enough to look over this text and suggest some emendations. Lat. 1338 actually has in line 1 *tuae*, line 2 *onus innuebat*, line 3 *Serum*, line 8 *suma*.

Example 2

[1] Fac-tu-re tu-e rex ful-get sa-cra-ta di-es is-ta

[2] Cum uir-gi-ne fe-cun-da-ta si-de-re-um hon-nus in-nu-ba

[3] Re-rum cre-a-tor o-pus im-ple-vit

[4] pro-mis-sum in-te-me-ra-te con-ser-ua

[5] si-de-ra lux no-ua mun-do to-to po-lo gra-ci-a

[6] spon-sus o-uans pre-ci-o-sus for-mans ta-la-mum ho-mi-num fi-gu-ra

[7] nos quo-que ip-sum re-gem con-lau-de-mus ue-ne-re-mur uo-ce hu-mil-li-ma

[8] nos e-le-uet sum-ma gau-di-a flu-en-ta ce-les-ti-a fa - bri-ce mun-di

The close relationship between the longer form of the third melisma given above and the shorter form that appears in the Worcester antiphonary is made particularly clear in two other prosulae given to the longer form. One of them is found in two 11th-century manuscripts from northern Italy: a troper from Novalesa (west of Turin, in the mountains close to the French border), and an Ivrea antiphonary.[17] The other appears in a late 13th-century Dijon breviary.[18] Both of these texts begin with the words "Facinora

[17]Respectively Oxford, Bodleian Library, Douce 222, fs. 4r-4v(see Husmann, *op. cit.*, pp.160-161); and Ivrea, Bibl. cap., CVI (described by Dom René-Jean Hesbert in *Corpus antiphonalium officii, Vol. I: Manuscripti "Cursus Romanus"* [Rome, 1963], pp. XX-XXI; Pl. IV shows f. 8v, where part of the prosula occurs). The prosula on fs. 20v-21r of the Florence antiphonary (A in the list given earlier) is like this one, but not quite the same.

[18]Baltimore, Walters Art Gallery, W. 109, fs. 187r-187v.

nostra," the words of the most popular prosula of the Worcester third melisma; at the point in the melody where the added phrases occur, new words are supplied.

In writing about this triple melisma, Amalarius of Metz tells his readers explicitly that it originated in the responsory *In medio* for the feast of St. John the Evangelist (27 Dec.) and was only later transferred to *Descendit de celis* and Christmas.[19] It is true that in some manuscripts one or another form of the triple melisma is found with this responsory, but it seems unlikely that such a conspicuous musical elaboration could have been invented for a feast that is in comparison to Christmas of so much less importance. It may be appropriate to re-evaluate Amalarius' testimony, especially in view of the two following observations.

First, Amalarius sees himself both as a historian of the liturgy and as an interpreter of it. His interpretations are imaginative—even fanciful—and exhaustive. In discussing the triple melisma and the feast of St. John the Evangelist he seizes upon the fact that in *In medio* the melisma falls on the word "intellectus," and he expatiates on the relevance of this word to the spiritual state of one who sings a melisma.

> In the last responsory, that is the "In medio ecclesiae," contrary to the accustomed manner of the other responsories, a triple *neum* is sung, and its versicle and "gloria" are protracted beyond their usual length by a *neum*. Indeed not without cause has this been done by the men of old. They wished to suggest to us through this some teaching which could, perhaps, have been beyond the minds of the chanters, of whom some part is always changing from the things which pass away to things eternal, and does rejoice rather in things eternal than in things which pass away. For the aforementioned *neum* occurs, among other words, around the word "understanding." So when, o chanter, you come to "understanding," sing the neum, that is, fix your stance in things abiding and permanent. What does this intend? It intends, of course, to teach you that, if ever you come to the "understanding" in which divinity and eternity are beheld, you should pray with the yearning of your mind, tarrying in that "understanding." For if you shall have understood those things, it will delight you to tarry there, in these things which you will joyfully sing, that is you will rejoice without words which pass away.[20]

[19]Stäblein, *MGG,* XIII, cols. 811-812.

[20]In novissimo responsorio, id est "In medio ecclesiae," contra consuetudinem ceterorum responsoriorum, cantatur neuma triplex, et versus eius atque gloria extra morem neumate protelantur. Non enim frustra hoc actum est a prioribus. Voluerunt nobis per hoc aliquam doctrinam insinuare, quae forte poterat excedere mentem cantorum, quorum pars aliqua saepe mutatur a transitoriis ad aeterna, et laetatur potius in aeternis quam in transitoriis. Fit enim neuma memoratum, inter cetera verba, circa verbum intellectus. Quando veneris, cantor, ad intellectum, celebra neuma, id est fige gradum in stantibus et manentibus rebus. Quid hoc vult? Vult nempe te docere, se aliquando veneris ad intellectum in quo conspicitur divinitas et aeternitas, ut desiderio mentis preceris, morans in eo. Si enim intellexeris illa, ibi te delectabit morari, in his quae iubilabis, id est laetaberis sine verbis transitoriis. (J. M. Hanssens, *Amalarii episcopi opera liturgica omnia,* Tomus III [Studi e testi, 140; Vatican City, 1950], p. 54. The translation above is by Prof. Sheerin.)

For Amalarius as interpreter, the word "intellectus" is richer in possibilities than the words associated with the melismas in *Descendit de celis,* "fabricae mundi," which mean, approximately, "of the fabric of creation."[21]

Second, it appears that at least one part of the triple melisma did originate elsewhere in the liturgy of the feast of St. John the Evangelist. The first of the three melismas given in St. Gall is found regularly at the end of the second verse of the offertory *Gloria et honore.* This offertory is assigned in modern chant books to the Common of a Martyr not a Bishop; in the early manuscripts it is assigned to the feasts of a number of individual saints, but it is normally written down in full only the first time it appears in the liturgical year—in the first of the two Masses for the feast of St. John the Evangelist.[22]

What follows is, to be sure, only conjecture; but it seems worthwhile to ask whether Amalarius, knowing of the early connection between one part of the triple melisma and the feast of St. John, and familiar with a contemporary practice of singing the triple melisma on the word "intellectus" in *In medio,* let his imagination be over-stimulated by the link that he saw between the meaning of the word and the character of the music, so that he made a false statement about the origin of the practice.

The second of the responsories for which the St. Gall codex gives a long melisma is *Verbum caro,* the twelfth in the series, and the one that might be expected to close this part of the office of Matins. It does in many sources; in this particular manuscript, however, it is followed by six more responsories, which were perhaps for occasional use as substitutes for responsories in the series or as extra chants ad libitum.

The melisma, on "et veritate," is incorporated into the responsory at the end of p. 48. Its phrases are separated by x's (which seem to have served as indications for articulation), and are roughly in the musical form a a b b c a. (C is short, and there is no x separating it from the final a.)

A melisma which matches these neumes rather well can be found, again, in the Worcester antiphonary, on p. 33 of the facsimile edition. The cue indicates that this melisma is to be sung with the R. *Verbum caro* in second vespers of Christmas, though the responsory itself is given a few pages earlier with the Matins chants.[23] The melisma bears the rubric "prosa," though no text for it is given here. However, textings of this

[21]His interpretation of these words is given *ibid.,* p. 56: Eo neumate monstrant difficultatem magnam inesse in scola cantorum verbis explicare quomodo idem qui natus est hodierna die ex Maria virgine, fabricasset mundum et ornasset, et quomodo ipse sit lux et decus universae fabricae mundi.

[22]Dom René-Jean Hesbert, *Antiphonale missarum sextuplex* (Rome, 1967; originally published 1935), No. 13, pp. 18-19, p. 246. The borrowing of this offertory melisma in the responsory was noted by K. Ott in "Die Buchstabenübertragungen des Kodex von Montpellier," *Die Kirchenmusik: Zugleich Mitteilungen des Diöcesan-Cäcilienvereins Paderborn,* XI (1910), pp. 99-100.

[23]This may explain why this melisma is not included in the list of "melismatic tropes" for Matins responsories in the Worcester antiphonary given in the *Journal of the American Musicological Society,* XVI (1963), pp. 42-44. Dom Louis Brou comments about this melisma that it "n'est guère connu en dehors des mss. de l'école de Saint Gall." (*Op. cit.,* p. 28.) In the gradual and antiphonary of St. Éloi de Noyon this melisma is written upside down in the margin, in a hand other than that of most of the musical notation. (*Paléographie musicale,* XVI, commentary, p. 27, fn. 1.)

melisma have been preserved in other sources, and one of them is widely known. It is "Quem [or quam] aethera;" it is given with the "et veritate" melisma following the R. *Verbum caro* in the Klosterneuburg manuscripts 1010 (f. 23v) and 1013 (f. 31v), in St. Gall 380 (pp. 116-117), and (in a 13th-century hand) earlier in St. Gall 390 (pp. 7-8). The text has been published repeatedly.[24]

There is another text that seems also to have been written for the "et veritate" melisma. It begins "Iubilent superni" and is found in the 11th-century manuscript Cambrai, Bibl. mun.,78 (79) on fs. 50r-50v, after a set of texts for the "fabricae" melismas.[25] In Musical example 3 the melody is transcribed primarily as it appears in the Worcester antiphonary, but with modifications to make it correspond more closely with the neumes of the Cambrai manuscript.

Example 3

Iu-bi-lent su-per-ni ci-ves al-ma quo-que se-ra-phin col-le-gi-a

na-tus est in ter-ris ho-mo chri-stus ex pro-ge-ni-e da-vi-ti-ca

sol-vens ca-te-nas se-vis-si-mi de-cep-to-ris

qua nos te-ne-bat cru-de-li-tas in-fer-na-lis

gau-de-te gen-tes

po-pu-li re-demp-ti ve-ra e-nim no-bis ho-di-e pax de-scen-dit

[24]See Wolfgang Irtenkauf, "Das Seckauer Cantionarium vom Jahre 1345 (Hs. Graz 756)," *Archiv für Musikwissenschaft*, XIII (1956), pp. 122, 138. In addition to the sources referred to above and those Irtenkauf mentions the following can be named: Bamberg, lit. 23, fs.19v-20r, and lit. 24, 11v-12r; Verdun, Bibl. mun., 128, fs. 38v-39r; Metz, Bibl. mun., 83, f. 29v; Rome, Bibl. Vallicelliana, C. 5, f. 29v; and Udine, Arcivescovado, in fol. 25, f. 3r (12th-century antiphonary of Treviso?).

[25]The manuscript is described by Heinrich Husmann, *op. cit.*, pp. 101-102. Still another text for this melody, beginning "Gloria superno genitori," follows "Quem aethera" in Oxford, Bodleian Library, Selden supra 27, f.61r.

There are references to "Quem aethera" as a prose for *Verbum caro* in breviaries and ordinals of the 13th to 16th centuries.[26] The "et veritate" melisma was still known (and perhaps even sung in the liturgy) in the late 17th century. In his study of Gregorian chant, Guillaume Gabriel Nivers published this melisma in full, disapprovingly, as an example of the sort of excess that the chant reforms of the 16th century should have succeeded in eliminating.[27]

This study of melismas for *Descendit de celis* and *Verbum caro* has involved examining how melismas were interpolated into chants originally composed without them, and how texts were provided for them. It has shown some unexpected connections between widely scattered manuscripts. It has offered additional evidence to show that the chants of the office were subject to frequent modifications of various kinds. And it has sought to demonstrate once again the rich imagination and fascinating ways of the medieval mind.

[26]Among them are the following: a Sarum ordinal of *ca.* 1270 (Walter Howard Frere, *The Use of Sarum, II: The Ordinal and Tonal* [Cambridge, 1901], p. 31); an Exeter ordinal of 1337 (*Ordinale Exon.*, I [Henry Bradshaw Society, XXXVII; London, 1909], p. 66); and a printed York breviary of 1526 (*Breviarium ad usum insigis metrop. ecc. Eboracensis* [Paris, 1526], f. diii).

[27]Guillaume Gabriel Nivers, *Dissertation sur le chant grégorien* (Paris, 1683), p. 74.